THE LAST LETTERS
OF THOMAS MORE

THE LAST LETTERS
OF THOMAS MORE

Edited and
with an Introduction by

Alvaro de Silva

WILLIAM B. EERDMANS PUBLISHING COMPANY
GRAND RAPIDS, MICHIGAN / CAMBRIDGE, U.K.

© 2000 Wm. B. Eerdmans Publishing Co.

Wm. B. Eerdmans Publishing Co.
255 Jefferson Ave. S.E., Grand Rapids, Michigan 49503 /
P.O. Box 163, Cambridge CB3 9PU U.K.
www.eerdmans.com

Printed in the United States of America

05 04 03 02 01 00   7 6 5 4 3 2 1

Library of Congress Cataloging-in-Publication Data

More, Thomas, Sir, Saint, 1478-1535.
[Correspondence. Selections]
The last letters of Thomas More /
edited and with an introduction by Alvaro de Silva.
p.   cm.
Includes bibliographical references and index.
ISBN 0-8028-3886-3 (hardcover: alk. paper)
1. More, Thomas, Sir, Saint, 1478-1535 — Correspondence.
2. Great Britain — History — Henry VIII, 1509-1547 — Sources.
3. Christian martyrs — England — Correspondence.
4. Statesmen — Great Britain — Correspondence.
5. Humanists — England — Correspondence.
6. Prisoners' writings, English.
I. De Silva, Alvaro. II. Title.

DA334.M8 A4 2000
942.05'2'092 — dc21
00-023125

The author and publisher are grateful for permission to reprint an excerpt from
The Gulag Archipelago, 1918-1956: An Experiment in Literary Investigation I-II by
Aleksandr I. Solzhenitsyn. Copyright © 1973 by Aleksandr I. Solzhenitsyn. English
language translation copyright © 1973,. 1974 by Harper & Row Publishers, Inc.

Contents

CONTENTS

Acknowledgments

READERS OF MORE'S LETTERS remain indebted to Elizabeth Frances Rogers, editor of *The Correspondence of Sir Thomas More* (Princeton, 1947). I am much obliged to Princeton University Press (which still holds the copyright for the Rogers' edition) for allowing me to use the text for this edition. I should also like to express my gratitude to the scholars who prepared the Yale edition of the *Complete Works of St. Thomas More*. To three of them — Germain Marc'hadour, the late Richard Marius, and Louis Martz — I am particularly grateful for their encouragement and their suggestions on an early draft of the introduction. For their careful reading of these pages, I should also like to thank Sheila Gallagher, John Gueguen, Tracy Shupp, John Waulk, and Johanna Woll. An anonymous reader of the manuscript was responsible for many an improvement, and the anonymity of the job makes it even more deserving of my appreciation. I will always be grateful to Mary Hietbrink, my editor, for her corrections, suggestions, and enthusiasm.

A Note on the Text

THE TEXT OF THE LETTERS is a modernized version of the edition by Elizabeth F. Rogers, *The Correspondence of Sir Thomas More*. This version of the text features footnotes, a glossary, and a commentary. Names and phrases discussed at greater length in the commentary section are bracketed with these symbols: ⌐ ¬.

Good Company

Though the law of every man's conscience be but a private court, yet it is the highest and supreme court for judgment or justice.

HENRY VIII

Howbeit (as help me God), as touching the whole oath, I never withdrew any man from it, nor never advised any to refuse it, nor never put, nor will, any scruple in any man's head, but leave every man to his own conscience. And methinketh in good faith that so were it good reason that every man should leave me to mine.

THOMAS MORE

The two cities, therefore, were created by two loves: the earthly by love of oneself, even to the point of contempt for God; the heavenly by the love of God, even to the point of contempt for oneself. The first glories in itself, the second in the Lord. The first seeks glory from human beings. God, who is the witness of the conscience, is the greatest glory of the other.

AUGUSTINE OF HIPPO

NOTHING IS MORE BEAUTIFUL than innocence, and nothing more dangerous.

On Monday, April 13, 1534, Thomas More appeared before the

1

King's Commissioners at the Archbishop of Canterbury's palace in Lambeth. A few days later he was taken to the Tower of London, and after fourteen months in prison, on July 6, 1535, the former Lord Chancellor of England was beheaded on Tower Hill.

More was the only layman summoned to Lambeth on that spring day in 1534, one clear proof of the man's notable achievement, not only in the public offices he had held but also in the respect and reputation he enjoyed among his fellow citizens of London. The life of Thomas More (1478-1535), with its dramatic culmination in martyrial death, proved consistently intriguing, as evidenced by six or seven "biographies" written in the decades that followed. In less than seventy years there appeared "lives of More" by William Roper, Nicholas Harpsfield, Thomas Stapleton, an anonymous author known as "Ro. Ba.," Cresacre More, and two more that have been lost. This is even more remarkable when one considers that the only other Tudor figure with an immediate biography is Cardinal Wolsey.

Thomas More seems to be even more fascinating in our times, perhaps because, as one of his more recent biographers has rightly said, he was "a magnificent individual whose life summarized an age in a way that few lives have been able to do."[1] The story has been told so many times that the briefest of sketches will suffice here.[2]

More was a hardworking lawyer and judge, diplomat and royal secretary, as well as a married man with parental and family duties. Despite these multiple demands on his time and attention, he devoted all his spare energies to the pursuit of literary excellence. In 1516 his *Utopia* secured for him a permanent place in the literary firmament among the best-known European humanists. The combination of his legal and literary work swiftly elevated him to significant positions in the English royal court. Henry VIII elected More a member of his Privy Council, sent

1. Richard Marius in the introduction to volume 8 of the Yale edition of More's *The Confutation of Tyndale's Answer,* ed. Louis A. Schuster, Richard Marius, James P. Lusardi, and Richard J. Schoeck (New Haven: Yale University Press, 1973), Part III, p. 1272. This volume is part of *The Complete Works of St. Thomas More,* 15 vols. (New Haven: Yale University Press, 1963-1997), which will be cited as *CW* followed by the volume and page.

2. Modern biographies of More are R. W. Chambers, *Thomas More* (London: Jonathan Cape, 1935), E. E. Reynolds, *The Field Is Won: The Life and Death of St. Thomas More* (London: Burns & Oates, 1968), Richard Marius, *Thomas More: A Biography* (New York: Alfred A. Knopf, 1984), and, more recently, Peter Ackroyd, *The Life of Thomas More* (New York: Doubleday, 1998), in which the mind and heart of More — as well as his family, his friends, his city, his church, and his age — come alive in brilliant ways.

him on embassies to continental cities and to the Emperor Charles, appointed him Speaker of Parliament, and finally chose him in 1529 for the highest station and honor in the realm as Lord Chancellor of England, a "great weighty room and office," as More himself would describe it only a few years later in a letter to his sovereign (Letter 4 in this volume).

In 1532 More relinquished the highest honor in England and retired from the world of politics; by 1534 he found himself locked in the Tower of London, a prisoner of the Tudor government. His fourteen months in prison proved to be a blessing in disguise, offering him a chance to put his whole life together, both as a man and as a Christian believer. His friend Erasmus of Rotterdam had portrayed him as *omnium horarum homo*,[3] "a man for all hours." In the Tower he came to his last and finest hour. This book reframes More's correspondence from that last year and a half of his life.

☩   ☩

Prison literature necessarily focuses on the central task in the life of one deprived of liberty and sometimes threatened with the prospect of torture and violent death. This threat gives a special character to letters of historical, political, literary, and religious importance. Given the ominous context in which More found himself, I understand why he has Antony, the character he created for *A Dialogue of Comfort against Tribulation,* describe this earth and earthly life as a prison. Once the Henrician revolution exploded, there was no escape for More, and he well knew it. As he explained to his daughter Margaret in a letter from the Tower, "And this is the least point that any man may with his salvation come to, as far as I can see, and is bounden if he see peril to examine his conscience surely by learning and by good counsel and be sure that his conscience be such as it may stand with his salvation, or else reform it" (Letter 17 in this volume).

More had been pressed to the wall. He faced life's most definitive — because final — moment, the moment that makes a life or breaks it. He knew that the call of conscience, if loyally followed whatsoever its consequences, liberates and fulfills a person, thereby sealing his destiny beyond history into eternity. In this kind of circumstance, in a dramatic way, the moment of freedom signals the moment of truth. Dostoyevsky makes this connection vividly: "Did you forget that man prefers peace, and even

3. *Adagia,* I, iii, 86.

death, to freedom of choice in the knowledge of good and evil? Nothing is more seductive for man than his freedom of conscience, but at the same time nothing is a greater torture." In letter after letter of this moving correspondence, Thomas More appears fighting in "the darkness of our mortality" *(in hac mortalitatis caligine)*.[4] In the advent of Henry VIII he had seen the dawn of a new era full of promise and possibility, a paradise regained. Now he found himself in exile in his own beloved city, his human paradise forever lost.

Alone in the Tower ("for solitude sometimes is best society," as John Milton put it[5]), the once-powerful man dealt with the ultimate concern of even the most obscure human life. These letters record the drama of a man forced to play his last scene long before the final curtain should have fallen. Obeying the voice of conscience, More would die; disobeying it, he would live and be at liberty, at home — but irretrievably lost to himself. He knew that where conscience is concerned, no matter is trivial. And in fact, sooner or later in life, whether in prison or at large in the world, every man and woman will have to face the ultimate issue that confronted the famous humanist and martyr.

It is not only heroic endurance but personal integrity that gives emotional, moral, and spiritual power to literature written by political prisoners. The twentieth century has not been lacking in such testimony. There is a great body of prison literature comprising works of deep emotion and beauty, never more moving than when the author is a guiltless prisoner. The twentieth century has added abundantly to this library with the writing of solitary men and women confined and tortured in the Nazi concentration camps, in the gulags of the Marxist paradise, and in thousands of other obscure jails.

More's "Tower Works" are not only a splendid example of the genre but also represent the height of his literary accomplishments. In spite of the physical and psychological conditions he endured, More did not abandon the craft he had cultivated for many years. Like most Renaissance writers, he wanted to be useful, and so, as helpless prisoner of his conscience, he wrote to strengthen himself, and then others. In the solitude of his room in the Tower, away from his home in Chelsea, cut off from his many friends and the world, More found that writing offered him solace during his ordeal and morally sharpened his own thoughts about the decision that had brought him there.

4. *CW,* vol. 14: *De Tristitia Christi,* p. 241.
5. *Paradise Lost,* IX, 249.

✠   ✠

In the fourteen months of his captivity, among the most critical in the history of England, More wrote *A Dialogue of Comfort against Tribulation,* a masterpiece of consolation literature, and a much shorter book that he never finished, *De tristitia tedio pavore et oratione Christi ante captionem eius* ("The Sadness, Weariness, Fear, and Prayer of Christ before His Capture").[6] The latter is an intimate, powerful commentary, written in the language of the Church, on the Gospel scenes of Jesus in the garden of Gethsemane. The "bitter agony" of Christ had obviously become a constant theme of More's reflection and prayer, and the result is a moving meditation about the ways in which Jesus had himself dealt with his final and decisive hour of suffering and death. The very titles of these last two books unveil More's heart in the hour of his own anguish and perhaps terror. The shadow of imminent and horrifying death looms large on almost every page. Yet, the overall serenity and good humor of both compositions is astounding.

More kept in touch with his family and other friends through letters. While much of this correspondence was lost, each one of the extant letters is a literary gem and key for understanding his heart and mind. The last creation of a long writing career, these final letters deserve close reading, for they shed abundant light on More's personality. Louis Martz has rightly written that they are "of the utmost importance, because they constitute the best account of More's conduct during his interrogations and imprisonment, the best account of his state of mind, and, it is not perhaps too much to say, some of his finest works of art. They are indeed works of art in every sense of that word, for they show the most artful regard for the presence of two or three or more different audiences. More could have no doubt that every letter he wrote might be carefully read by his keepers, perhaps even sent to Cromwell himself, who was, as More well knew, alert to every phrase which might entrap More into a confession or a recantation."[7]

If these letters are works of art, they are also historically important, and equally relevant as religious documents. Indeed, it is not easy to understand why they are not better known and more easily available. William Rastell printed the Tower correspondence in the *English Works* edition of

---

6. Clarence H. Miller translated this volume in the Yale University Series. A reprint of this translation is available (Princeton: Scepter, 1993).

7. Martz, introduction, *CW,* vol. 12, p. lix. See also Martz, *Thomas More: The Search for the Inner Man* (New Haven: Yale University Press, 1990), pp. 55-64.

1557; and Thomas Stapleton, More's first biographer in Latin, gathered some letters and fragments for his *Vita Thomae Mori,* published in Douai in 1588. But otherwise, the whole of More's extant correspondence had a rather obscure existence until the fine edition of Elizabeth Frances Rogers, published in 1947.[8] (It is not right that scholars of the Reformation should be the only ones to read and benefit from these classic documents. They truly deserve a much wider audience.[9])

This edition of More's prison correspondence includes those letters written from early 1534 through July 5 of the following year, the eve of his execution. From his own pen we have four letters to Thomas Cromwell; one to Henry VIII; eight to his daughter Margaret Roper; two letters to theologian Nicholas Wilson and one to another priest, Leder, both his fellow prisoners in the Tower; one in Latin to his dear friend Antonio Bonvisi; a brief note to all his friends; and another letter, the longest and without doubt composed by More himself, although it is addressed "from Margaret Roper to Alice Alington," and according to an old opinion was written jointly by father and daughter.[10] The correspondence also includes two letters from Margaret to her father, one letter to Margaret Roper written by Alice Alington (More's stepdaughter), and another two written by Dame Alice, More's second wife: one of these to Thomas Cromwell and the other to the King. All in all, there are twenty-four letters, a most worthy complement to the two books More wrote in the Tower.

While a prisoner, More wrote on a wide variety of topics, from prayer and penance to the right use of riches and power, from the joys of heaven to psychological depression and suicidal temptations. Often he must have written to carry himself through his own ordeal. Beneath the serenity of his prison writings lies his personal drama. In his last writings More made

8. *The Correspondence of Sir Thomas More* (Princeton: Princeton University Press, 1947). In 1922 Rogers had published a piece entitled "A Calendar of the Correspondence of Sir Thomas More" in the *English Historical Review* (1922): 546-64.

9. There are a couple of English modern editions of More's final letters, unfortunately poorly edited and out of print: *The Last Letters of Blessed Thomas More,* ed. W. E. Campbell (London: Manresa Press, 1924), and *Conscience Decides: More's Prisons Letters and Prayers,* ed. Bede Foord (London: Geoffrey Chapman, 1971). There have been French and Italian editions as well. It was my privilege to translate and edit the letters for the first time into Spanish in the volume entitled *Un hombre solo: Cartas desde la Torre* (Madrid: Rialp, 1988).

10. It could have been planned together by father and daughter, then written by More himself. This would dismiss the notion that the letter is a puzzle, as R. W. Chambers claimed in *The Continuity of English Prose,* p. clxii. See the note to the letter in this volume.

a passionate protest against the moral compromises of those who had sent him to the Tower. Shut up behind thick walls, the unrelenting controversialist could at last leave behind his theological fight, but the old energy remained. More knew that whatever he wrote would be read at least by Cromwell and perhaps by the members of the Royal Council, so he chose very carefully the words to express his indignation; and we should read the letters with this in mind. But More's subtlety does not compromise his clarity, and here at last this Christian man becomes wise as the serpent and simple as the dove. The silence of Thomas More in the Tower has become proverbial.

If he had been *Morus furiosus,* a wrathful apologist of his faith, as a prisoner he could not but be *Morus patiens,* patient and forgiving. Patience, however, need not be passivity, and "to resist" in the midst of hardship and the double threat of torture and death, as More did, is the greatest act of fortitude. This hidden energy adds great power to his final writings. More's personal apologia is now as subtle and refined as it is daring and firm.

From the day he was summoned to Lambeth, More felt his ordeal to be a victory — not final, perhaps, but crucial. That day when he left his home, already in the barge that would take him away, More told his son-in-law, "Son Roper, I thank our Lord the field is won." William Roper would later confess that he did not understand these words. But More was accustomed to paradox, and none of the humiliations and sufferings he had long ago foreseen could diminish in him the realization of his spiritual freedom. "The field is won!" He had to part with everyone and everything he loved in order to secure the victory, but there it was, close at hand.

Even the most casual reading of these letters illuminates his spiritual condition. More is, from beginning to end, from the Island of Utopia to the Tower of London, ever the dedicated Christian humanist. Not to see this is, I think, to misunderstand him and to make him a fanatic, a reactionary, and a humanist writer who completely lost his emotional control and whose voluminous polemical writings should be dismissed not only as boring but as insane. Nothing can be further from the truth.[11] As Rich-

---

11. A critique of this revisionist attempt is offered in an article by Brendan Bradshaw, where he argues for the coherence of Thomas More in this war of words: one million words in defense of his faith against new Protestant doctrines. More became a controversialist because he was a Christian humanist. See "The Controversial Thomas More," *The Journal of Ecclesiastical History* 36 (1985): 535-69. See also the book by Louis Martz already mentioned, *Thomas More: The Search for the Inner Man,* and the work by André Prévost, *Thomas More et la crise de la pensée européenne* (Paris: Mame, 1969).

ard Marius points out, More "died magnificently, but his death was not the headlong rush of a fanatical zealot into oblivion; it was the fearful, considered decision of a man of great self-knowledge, doing what he had to do and wishing almost until the end that he did not have to do it. . . . Perhaps for us the habitual waging of such a hard, inner warfare in Thomas More is lesson enough for our season. For it may be that only those who patiently struggle without victory in such lifelong conflicts within themselves are worthy to be called saints."[12]

✝   ✝

Instead of repeating here what is readily available elsewhere, I would prefer to focus on two themes that have always impressed me while reading these letters: the clarity of More's conscience and his readiness to die for the integrity of his religious faith. Both exhibit in unique fashion the duty of a Christian humanist to witness to the truth.

More believed that Christ entrusted his Church to teach and pass on the truth about God and man. For him, therefore, freedom was found in that obedience to the Church which alone feeds its members with the body of Christ and his eternal truth: "The truth will make you free" (John 8:32). More had no doubt that the passion for freedom must go hand in hand with the passion for truth. In the Tower he used the expression "everlasting liberty."[13] More did not want to lose this inner freedom, the most precious freedom of all.

The word *conscience* is conspicuous throughout the last letters, appearing a total of more than one hundred times, and more than forty times in a single letter (Letter 12 in this volume). Indeed, More's prison epistolary can be read as a lasting monument in praise of conscience. The spirit of modernity has always prided itself on being precisely such a monument, claiming, above all else, the freedom of the individual and his or her conscience, the so-called autonomy of the "I." But More knew of the possibility of a "fabrication of conscience," or what he refers to in another letter as "framing a conscience."

When Søren Kierkegaard praised "conscience alone," he was referring to the most absolute act of courage, that of a human creature conscious of being *alone* with God. In his *Journals* he presented this portrait of the man with a conscience:

12. Marius, *Thomas More*, pp. 519, 520.
13. *CW*, vol. 12, p. 254.

Ideally speaking it may be perfectly true that every man should be given freedom of conscience and freedom of belief, etc.

But what then; where are the men who are spiritually strong enough to be able to use that freedom, who are really capable of standing absolutely alone, alone with God? . . .

. . . In order that it should really and truly be the conscience alone which decides (and not a belch, a slothful idea, a caprice, confused thoughts or a foolish imitation), for that very reason is it necessary to have opposition and constraint. The qualification 'conscience' is so inward that it requires the very finest filters in order to discover it. But if it is found, if it really is conscience, conscience alone, then your regulations be blowed — I should only laugh at them. . . .

The man who can really stand alone in the world, only taking counsel from his conscience — that man is a hero.[14]

More has been praised as a hero of conscience, as a man determined to stand by his own belief against the sovereign king or secular power or against the world. But that is not the real Thomas More. The problem with conscience, More knew, is in how you allow that inner voice to be formed through study and reflection. In the case of the Christian believer, that formation comes through the authority of the Church teaching the truth. Some readers of More are shocked not by his following his conscience but by the fact that, faithful to his inner voice, the humanist author of *Utopia* gave up his life for the spiritual primacy of the Pope in Rome. Immediately the island of Utopia changes (they cannot see the joke) into a concentration camp, and the suspicion grows that More was never and could never have been a liberal-minded person.[15]

The epistolary sheds much light on More himself and on his understanding of *conscience*. In his insistent use of the word, the whole range of meanings becomes present, from the most pedestrian to the sublime, taking the reader, in my view, to the heart of Thomas More and the meaning of his accomplished life and ignominious death.

First of all, *conscience* means his "mind," his "inmost thought," his own "understanding" (and therefore something reasonable, at least for

14. *Journals, 1850-1854*, in *A Kierkegaard Anthology*, ed. Robert Bretall (1946; reprint, Princeton: Princeton University Press, 1973), pp. 428-29.

15. Through the years since his death, Thomas More has been accused of "covetousness" (William Tyndale), of "expediency and thirst for power" (Mandell Creighton), of being a tool of "the blind and enraged fury of priests" (Gilbert Burnet), of "miscalculation and inconsistency" (Sidney Lee), of being a "merciless bigot" (J. Anthony Froude). See R. W. Chambers, *Thomas More*, pp. 352-55.

him) of a particular situation, and thus the building of his own personal conviction about the matter. Second, *conscience* means also his "moral sense," his consciousness of right and wrong, of good and evil. This is how the *Oxford English Dictionary* defines it: "the internal acknowledgment or recognition of the moral quality of one's own motives and actions; the sense of right and wrong as regards things for which one is responsible; the faculty or principle which pronounces upon the moral quality of one's actions or motives, approving the right and condemning the wrong." This definition also refers to the "gradual process of individualizing and personification" that is part of exercising one's conscience. This is the sense in which we understand *conscience,* the sense in which it is used, for instance, in this text from the famous *Oratio de hominis dignitate* by Pico della Mirandola, a layman much admired by the young Thomas More: "Philosophy herself has taught me to rely on my own conscience rather than on the opinions of others, and always to take thought not so much that people may speak no evil of me, as, rather, that I myself may neither say nor do aught that is evil."[16]

However, we should not close the case here, since the etymology of the word should take us further in a deeply interesting way. *Conscience* (from Latin *con-scire, scire cum*) denotes also a "certain knowledge that we have with another." The particle *cum* denotes "a being together, an accompanying" — "it signifies in union, in relation to, in communion, an acting in common, together with." Kierkegaard understood conscience as our "co-knowledge" *(Samviden)* with God — that is, our being alone *with* God; in this sense, the Latin particle becomes formative. Christian doctrine, of course, has always defended an intimate relation between conscience and God. According to Paul Valadier, "Conscience cannot be thought of nor properly lived in the absence of a relation to Another, which is its Absolute."[17] The theme of man as *imago Dei,* the "image of God," has been, following Scripture, the cornerstone of Christian anthropology to the point that when the Christian believer says "conscience," the reference to an "image of God" in humankind is automatic. For theists, the "voice" of conscience is the voice of the Lawmaker, and thus of the Maker, but the Christian takes it a step further — or better, a step closer. In order to be a proper image of God, the Christian looks at himself or herself in Christ as

---

16. *Oratio,* trans. Elizabeth Livermore Forbes, in *The Renaissance Philosophy of Man,* ed. Ernst Cassirer, Paul Oskar Kristeller, and John Herman Randall, Jr. (Chicago, 1948), p. 238n. 22.

17. Paul Valadier, *Eloge de la conscience* (Paris: Seuil, 1994), ch. 6; my translation.

in a mirror and hopes that the reflected image may become more and more Christ's own image, since Christ is believed to be perfect God and perfect man, "like us in all things but sin." In a splendidly accurate expression, John Henry Newman could thus think of conscience as "the aboriginal vicar of Christ." For a Christian, then, *conscience — scire cum —* means the knowledge of Christ, the wisdom of Christ, the knowledge of oneself with Christ and in Christ. This is the extraordinary use that Paul the Apostle makes of the corresponding Greek particle when he refers to the intimate union and even mysterious identity between Christ and his followers.

Therefore the *cum* in *conscience* is one key to understanding the way More valued conscience and how that informed his behavior, both before his arrest and afterward. The Latin particle is also the key to fully understanding two other words intentionally and insistently present in his last writings in the Tower, *comfort (cum + fortitudo)*[18] and *company (cum + panis)*, to which I shall return.

☩   ☩

The letter "from Margaret Roper to Alice Alington" is the longest letter in the collection (Letter 12 in this volume) and one that has been rightly compared to Plato's dialogues. The letter is in itself a dialogue of comfort, a sort of precious miniature of *A Dialogue of Comfort against Tribulation*.[19] A real conversation between father and daughter in the Tower may have been the inspiration for the imaginary dialogue between Antony and Vincent. In the letter, the drama is set by temptation, as it is in the third chapter of Genesis, when Eve tempts Adam, her husband and companion. Margaret, More's beloved daughter and closest of all people to him, tries to persuade her father to take the oath that is demanded of him, arguing that his objections are a mere "scruple of conscience." With admirable literary art, More the writer shows the temptress's joy and reassurance in her father's final decision to have "a respect for his own soul."

This letter shows More at his best as a writer, but also at his best as a man with a conscience fighting for his own spiritual integrity. He uses the story of an honest man called Company as the medium to convey his own predicament. Ever ready to tell a story for fun, More tells this one to his

18. The title *The Dialogue of Comfort against Tribulation* is rendered *A dialogue of cumfort* in John Fowler's edition.
19. Cf. *CW*, vol. 12, p. lxiv.

daughter to entertain as well as enlighten her. This man, Company, alone in a jury of twelve, cannot go along with the conclusion reached by his fellow jurors. Upset because his decision is obstructing their own plans, they tell him that he is not being "good Company," a decent companion who quietly follows what the majority has decided. Company prefers to be true to his own understanding of the case. When they make fun of him, asking him to go along and be "good company with them," he admits that he prefers his own company — that is, he would rather be true to himself even if that leaves him alone. More, relishing a good illustrative story, takes his time to explain to Margaret that this does not make this honest poor man "bad company." On the contrary, by going along with the rest against his own conscience, this fellow would immediately lose himself along with those who did not follow the dictates of their own conscience. Company prefers to remain alone, with himself — not against the others, but simply defending his own self.

Such was the hero so powerfully portrayed by Robert Bolt in his famous play about Thomas More, *A Man for All Seasons*. It was a matter of putting on the stage, as Bolt said, "a Christian Saint as a hero of selfhood." However, the Christian understanding of selfhood flatly denies selfish or obsessive individualism. More did not exhibit an individualism or an autonomy of the "I" that has no room for anything else, even if his behavior could be described casually as that of a stubborn individualist. Before being the "hero of selfhood," More was a "Christian Saint." His religious faith led him to a respect for his own self. His decision, as he explained to his daughter, put him in good company, since it was actually motivated by an intention to remain in such "good company" — that is, in the company of all those who behaved like him throughout history.

Earlier I quoted a text from Kierkegaard in praise of conscience alone. Now I should like to complement it with one closer to us in time and closer to More in the Tower, since its author was a prisoner executed as a traitor by the Nazis in 1945. By then God's voice within man had been lost in the murmur of many other voices. Dietrich Bonhoeffer was familiar with the ways in which his own contemporaries found recourse in a false "conscience" to escape from duty, or to follow convenience, or merely to hide in the crowd. From his cell in a Nazi prison in 1942, Bonhoeffer wrote, "Who stands fast? Only the man whose final standard is not his reason, his principles, his conscience, his freedom, or his virtue, but who is ready to sacrifice all this when he is called to obedient and responsible action in faith and in exclusive allegiance to God — the responsible man, who tries to make his whole life an answer to the question and call of

God." And he had this to say about "the man with a conscience": "Evil approaches him in so many respectable and seductive disguises that his conscience becomes nervous and vacillating, till at last he contents himself with a salved instead of a clear conscience, so that he lies to his own conscience in order to avoid despair; for a man whose only support is his conscience can never realize that a bad conscience may be stronger and more wholesome than a deluded one."[20] More would heartily agree. The choice he made was indeed a matter of his own conscience, part of his human endowment, but he had freely shaped it according to his faith in Christ.

For More, obviously, faith was not yet another role to play by walking in and out of church on Sundays. For him, religion was life, not just one aspect of it. He would have agreed with G. K. Chesterton, who said that "religion is not the church a man goes into but the world he lives in." As More saw it, this was exactly what religion meant, or it meant nothing. More's faith was his whole world and the whole of his life. Here, as I was saying, the etymology of *conscience* is illuminative. For More this meant above all else to know *with* Christ — that is, the knowledge of Christ, the truth of Christ, and the life of Christ. In the oldest Christian tradition, More came to understand that the God who reveals himself in "incarnation" works the salvation of humanity precisely by gathering it in *one* body. He also knew that to preserve such unity alive and unalloyed is impossible unless some sort of community (which necessitates its own authority) has been established to accomplish the task faithfully and unfailingly.

To argue that this is merely a "medieval" conception of Christianity will not do. Certainly for Thomas More, walking in the crepuscular light of the Middle Ages toward the dawn of the modern world, it was still Christianity as the long and uniform community of belief.[21] This idea permeates his understanding of the faith, of the Church, and of society. More's emphasis on "consensus" is well-known and has been studied at length elsewhere,[22] and his criticism of Martin Luther and of the new ecclesiological ideas in general was based on and argued from this foundation. And one may rightly say that this foundation concerns precisely the very existence of the Church as a community, as the company of those who believe, as good fellowship even when there is bad company.

---

20. Bonhoeffer, *Letters and Papers from Prison*, ed. Eberhard Bethge, enlarged ed. (New York: Macmillan, 1971), pp. 4-5.

21. Cf. John Hale, *The Civilization of Europe in the Renaissance* (New York: Atheneum, 1994), p. 112.

22. Cf. Brian Gogan, *The Common Corps of Christendom: Ecclesiological Themes in the Writings of Sir Thomas More* (Leiden: E. J. Brill, 1982).

✠   ✠

More's argument shines in its simplicity. He was telling his daughter Margaret that you cannot change your mind about something just for the sake of going along with the rest of the crowd, either to please them or for mere personal convenience. This fellow Company was not stubborn; in fact, he showed himself reasonably ready to change his mind, but only if a good argument (not mere political expediency) convinced him, only if a better understanding of the case did indeed change his mind. Otherwise, he would not be changing his mind at all, but simply saying what he did not mean. His action would better be described as a betrayal of his own self, as lying to his own mind. The fact that this "honest man" is one against eleven is only an empirical fact, with no bearing on the question of truth.

Yet, there is the real fact that many important and learned men in England took the oath without much ado. Should this not have been a strong indication for More that he was wrong? Throughout his last letters, More speaks with the greatest respect of the opinions and consciences of others, but he also suggests that they should have known or did know better.

More's respect for reason is a trademark of his work, and he took good care in these letters to explain, as much as it was possible in his dangerous situation as prisoner, that his behavior was entirely rational. He liked to remember the meaning of his own name in Greek — *moria*, "a fool" — but being a "fool" for Christ does not mean renouncing reason or dignity. The grace of baptism helped him see from a higher plane and a deeper perspective. He knew that Christian discipleship was also the salvation of his conscience and his dignity as a human being. Niccolò Machiavelli had a very different view of things when he wrote, "And of conscience we should not take account, because where there is, as in us, the fear of hunger and prison, that of hell neither can nor should find room."[23]

More was not immune to fear, but he fought and conquered it. He had learned how to turn his body to stone so that his spirit and his conscience would not yield even when he was threatened with physical torture

---

23. The Italian is as follows: "e della coscienza noi non dobbiamo tenere conto, perche dove é, come é in noi, la paura della fame e delle carcere, non può ne debbe quella dello inferno capere" (*Istorie florentine*, 3, 13, quoted by Sebastian de Grazia in *Machiavelli in Hell* [Princeton: Princeton University Press, 1989]), p. 338.

and a violent death. A man must fight to the death for his conscience to understand its fragility.

The reality of "Company" illuminates More's thought as well as his solitude and loneliness in the last year of his life. Fellowship is behind the name but also the universality of the Church. The man Company is alone and yet not alone, because with him is a whole company of like-minded men and women. More, for example, was aware that all the bishops in England but one had taken the oath and gone along with the new political establishment. But More's fellowship was not shadowed by death; it embraced the living company of men and women, the Church of the saints in heaven. Modernity may have little use for this sense of eternity, or for what Chesterton called "the democracy of the dead," but for More it was undoubtedly a great source of moral strength, consolation, and joy. His Utopians believed that "the dead move about among the living and are witnesses of their words and deeds," and therefore the living "go about their business with more confidence because of reliance on such protection."[24] For him Christ was not a figure of the past worthy of emulation, but a real living presence in the here and now. Indeed, for the prisoner in the Tower, the saints were as alive as (or more so than) the people outside the walls in the city of London.

Thomas More was convinced that "at the death also of every man that so dieth for the faith, God with his heavenly company beholdeth his whole passion and verily looketh on."[25] Thus speaks Antony at the end of *A Dialogue of Comfort against Tribulation*, telling his young nephew Vincent that in the darkness and despair of death for Christ he should never forget that "goodly company" of Christ and the saints. It is a vivid passage:

> Now if it were so, cousin, that ye should be brought through the broad, high street of a great, long city, and that all along the way ye were going, there were on the tone [one] side of the way a rabble of ragged beggars and madmen that would despise you and dispraise you with all the shameful names that they could call you and all the railing words that they could say to you, and that there were then all along the tother side of the same street where you should come by, a goodly company standing in a fair range, a row of wise and worshipful folk allowing and commending you, mo [more] than fifteen times as many as that rabble of ragged beggars and railing madmen are, would you let your way by your will weening that you went unto your shame for the shameful jesting

24. *CW*, vol. 4, p. 225.

25. *A Dialogue of Comfort against Tribulation*, ed. Frank Manley (New Haven: Yale University Press, 1977), p. 295.

and railing of those mad, foolish wretches, or hold on your way with a good cheer and a glad heart, thinking yourself much honored by the laud and approbation of that other honorable sort?[26]

This "glorious company of heaven" Antony imagines as being far bigger and greater than any wretched worldly company. They are in number "mo [more] than an hundred to one," he says, and "of that hundred every one an hundred times more to be regarded and esteemed than of the tother an hundred such whole rabbles."

It is not a coincidence that More wrote about the Eucharist with such feelings of intimacy and urgency in these last years of his life. The word *company* comes from the Latin *cum panis,* that is, "to break bread or to eat with someone," which signifies and builds companionship, friendship, and community. In the Eucharist, the sacramental presence of Christ, More found the most sublime company and companion, the bread of heaven that nourishes eternal life.

Company, comfort, conscience. The three words share the Latin particle that points to the presence of something else, or rather, to someone else, without whom there is no fellowship, no support, no self-knowledge. More thought of the Church as a prolongation of Christ, or rather of the Spirit of Christ, in time and space, the very person indeed whom Christ himself would send to answer all doubts: "Ye must in all these things here believe and obey the Church which is as I say the person whom Christ sendeth you to for the sure solution of all such doubts as to the man in whose mouth he speaketh himself and the Holy Spirit of his Father in heaven."[27]

☩   ☩

Torture followed by beheading was the punishment for refusing to accept the oath demanded by the Tudor revolution, which included the new order of things established by Henry VIII; the new Queen, Anne Boleyn; and the King's new title of "Head of the Church" in England. More knew that to take the oath would mean the loss of his own self, his own spiritual integrity. He had had time to reflect upon the question of the papacy and its universal authority in the Church, and after much thought he had realized its

26. *A Dialogue of Comfort against Tribulation,* ed. Manley, pp. 295-96. In the quotation, *range* means "line"; *allowing,* "praising"; *let your way,* "stop your journey"; *by your will,* "voluntarily"; and *weening,* "thinking."
27. *CW,* vol. 6, p. 166.

absolute importance if the Church was to be one body and remain loyal to its founder. Thomas More, I think, would have agreed wholeheartedly with Pascal when he said, "If one contemplates the Church as unity, then the pope who is her head is also the whole. If one perceives her as plurality, then the pope is only a part. From time to time the Fathers of the Church thought of the Church in one way or the other . . . but they emphasized both; they excluded neither. A plurality that cannot be integrated into unity is chaos; unity unrelated to plurality is tyranny."[28] More based his decision on the universal — that is, catholic — character of the Church founded by Christ. Thus it makes sense, from a historical and theological point of view, to describe, as an English Reformation scholar has done, the new spiritual supremacy of Henry VIII as a sort of "papacy without Catholicism" rather than "Catholicism without the pope."[29] The latter would be the cherished project of many a church historian influenced by the Oxford Movement: the Anglican Church could not merely be "the residue of a Protestant revolt against [the western Catholic Church]."[30]

More could not subscribe to the oath that would change the Church as he knew it because it would severely violate his conscience. More believed that conscience is the voice of God within a human being, the voice of "that judge which cannot be bribed," as St. John Chrysostom, one of his favorite ancient Christian writers, put it.[31] In his First Instruction "addressed to those about to be baptized," Chrysostom went on to explain, "In its role of judge, conscience rises up against us and never ceases to inflict on us unceasing pain, like a public executioner who mangles and strangles us in our minds, and thus shows us the enormity of sin."[32] More knew well that conscience is not to be identified with a feeling of contentment or self-satisfaction, a certain emotional tranquility. The *tranquillitas cordis* is one of the classic signs of moral and human "perfection," but it

28. *Pensées,* 809, as quoted by Hans Urs Von Balthasar in *The Office of Peter and the Structure of the Church,* trans. Andrée Emery (San Francisco: Ignatius Press, 1986), p. 21.

29. Richard Rex makes the point in *Henry VIII and the English Reformation* (New York: St. Martin's Press, 1993), p. 172. Writing on Cromwell's vice-regency, G. R. Elton sees it as representing two things: "Henry's determination to keep his Church and his position in the Church as nearly papal as possible, and Cromwell's desire to organize the whole Church of England under a single control" (*Reform and Renewal: Thomas Cromwell and the Common Weal* [Cambridge: Cambridge University Press, 1973], p. 134).

30. Diarmaid MacCulloch, "Henry VIII and the Reform of the Church," in *The Reign of Henry VIII: Politics, Policy, and Piety* (New York: St. Martin's Press, 1995), p. 161.

31. John Chrysostom, *Baptismal Instructions,* trans. Paul W. Harkins (Westminster, Md.: Newman Press, 1963), p. 34.

32. Chrysostom, *Baptismal Instructions,* I, n. 28, p. 34.

implies *puritas cordis,* the purity of heart. Yet conscience is such that it does not recriminate us when we are deep in the ways of virtue, but neither does it do so when we are deep in the ways of vice. As an ancient voice put it, "Only those who have reached the heights of virtue or the bottom of vice, are not accused by their conscience."[33] We have the sad and tragic power to quiet our conscience and to kill it, and then to swallow it, which leads to even greater corruption and evil.

In More's understanding, the intimate sound of conscience is reinforced by the Word of God coming in all its majesty through Scripture and the living tradition of the Church. The Christian believer shapes conscience according to Christ, since he is accepted as the Way, the Truth, and the Life. Nothing could have been so easy for the ex-Lord Chancellor as to murmur a few words or scribble his own name on the long list of the mighty men of England, a good many of them his own friends and acquaintances, priests and bishops included. But More kept insisting that by doing so he would lose himself. Had he taken the oath, he would have been out in the world, at ease in his home in Chelsea as before. Yet, spiritually — not merely as a Christian but as a human being, in the very core of his existence — he would have had no place to go. In a society where that most basic human right was not respected, the right to have "a respect for his own soul," there remained only one place where he could be truly free — away and alone in prison. He relinquished his physical freedom in order to retain a more fundamental freedom; he lost his head because he wanted to keep it in accord with his conscience. He was convinced that without this primordial liberty — to abide by the truth — other liberties would soon be turned into heavy chains in dark places. More firmly believed that man had been asked — indeed, commanded — from the beginning not to worship falsehood despite its alluring disguises and persistent claims.

"I have of pure necessity for respect unto mine own soul . . ." (Letter 8 in this volume), wrote More to Margaret, and again, "I have myself a respect to mine own soul" (Letter 12). "Honor is the soul's patrimony, and the soul belongs to God alone," proclaims a splendid character created by Calderón de la Barca.[34] Or, as a Shakespearean character would have it, "Every subject's duty is the King's; but every subject's soul is his own."[35] Yet, a contem-

---

33. "Illos solos conscientia sua non arguit, qui vel in virtutum, vel in vitiorum fastigium pervenerunt" (Thalassius, *De caritate ac continentia, necnon de regimine mentis: Centuria* I, 72; PG 91, 1433c).

34. "Al Rey la hacienda y la vida/se ha de dar; pero el honor/es patrimonio del alma,/y el alma sólo es de Dios" (*El alcalde de Zalamea,* Act I, scene 18, l. 875).

35. *Henry V,* Act iv, scene 1, ll. 176-78.

porary of More had no doubts about the motto for his flag. "I love my city more than my own soul," wrote Niccolò Machiavelli to Francesco Vettori.[36] In this brutal assertion, transcendence has been blotted out, and the tragic consequences are better known to us than to Machiavelli.

More must have remembered the passage in *The City of God* (as a young man he had lectured on this classic book) about "the two loves" that generate two cities. There St. Augustine had written, "The two cities, therefore, were created by two loves: the earthly by love of oneself, even to the point of contempt for God; the heavenly by the love of God, even to the point of contempt for oneself. The first glories in itself, the second in the Lord. The first seeks glory from human beings. God, who is the witness of the conscience, is the greatest glory of the other."[37] In this famous passage, Augustine contemplates that city where "the lust to dominate" in princes and nations is what really matters: "dominated by pride, they exalted themselves in their own wisdom," becoming fools. He then contrasts them with those who live and work for "the love of the Lord," the inhabitants of that other city where "there is nothing of human wisdom except the piety by which the true God is rightly worshipped, for it expects to find its reward in the company of the holy ones, not only of human beings, but also of angels, 'so that God may be all in all.'"[38]

Responsibility for his soul kept More a prisoner. This loyal servant of the King was ready to part with every freedom and comfort in life, no matter how precious, rather than sacrifice the freedom of his soul to a capricious sovereign who now desired to be More's Pope as well, a double-headed monster good for neither religion nor politics. This may sound unscholarly, not to mention absurdly papist, but a recent account of the English Reformation makes the same assertion even more bluntly: "The religious changes he [Henry VIII] introduced were often decked out in the rhetoric of 'Reformation,' but they were undertaken chiefly with a view to increasing his power, swelling his coffers, and exacting stricter obedience from his subjects."[39] Indeed, obedience to the temporal sovereign is the "keynote" of the Henrician reformation.[40]

Henry VIII wrote to Pope Clement VII that were he to obey "to the

36. From a letter dated April 16, 1527, in *The Letters of Machiavelli*, ed. Allan Gilbert (New York: Capricorn Books, 1961), n. 225.

37. This translation, by Michael W. Tkacz and Douglas Kries, can be found in *Political Writings* (Hackett: Indianapolis/Cambridge: Hackett, 1994), p. 109.

38. *Political Writings*, p. 109 (*The City of God*, Book XIV, n. 28).

39. Rex, *Henry VIII and the English Reformation*, p. 167.

40. Cf. Rex, *Henry VIII and the English Reformation*, p. 132.

letters of your holiness, in that they do affirm that we know to be otherwise, we should offend God and conscience."[41] He would tell the imperial ambassador Eustace Chapuys that "God and his conscience were on very good terms,"[42] and declare to the English ambassador with the Emperor that "we have now God's word and laws standing with us, with no little advice and deliberation, and in clearing and discharging of our conscience, lawfully ensued and accomplished [the King's great matter, that he had never lawfully married Catherine of Aragon]."[43] Was Henry confusing conscience with desire? The King's "great matter" of his matrimonial status is certainly much more complex than that, but he showed very high regard for his own conscience. Was not precisely that same right to conscience what More was asking for himself?

✠   ✠

"None, apart from the saints, have ever controlled their lives," wrote the French novelist Georges Bernanos. In the end, peace conquered More's heart and made him ready to die with a smile, even with a joke. This bundle of letters from prison records both the anguish of his spiritual struggle and the joyful song of his intimate freedom. For his favorite daughter Margaret, this new freedom could not have been entirely unforeseen. She was probably accustomed to seeing her father as more than just another great man at the royal court. For several years her father had been working as best he could as an apologist. She had been an eager participant in the unsentimental Christian talk at family gatherings; but that kind of talk rings differently within the walls of a prison, in the midst of a dangerous political revolution. Besides, she must have suspected early on that her father's persistence could take him to an ignominious death. The other personages who appear in these letters leave behind the stench of their slavish plight. The swarm of "temporal and spiritual lords," as More called them, those members of the Royal Council charged with administering the oath, had already become the slaves of a tyrant who dictated his own convenience and self-interest in all kinds of temporal and spiritual matters, and who seemed to have his conscience "between his legs," as Juvenal put it.[44]

41. *The Letters of King Henry VIII*, ed. Muriel St. Clare Byrne (1936; reprint, New York: Funk & Wagnalls, 1968), p. 133.

42. *The Letters of King Henry VIII*, p. 123. See *LP*, vol. 6.

43. *The Letters of King Henry VIII*, p. 129.

44. "Between their legs is their conscience," wrote Juvenal at the end of Satire X, the one that More's eldest daughter Margaret quotes in Letter 9 in this volume: *ut sit*

More, without judging or condemning any man, persisted in his free determination. Unsure of where his soul would be taken, he did not want to follow anyone. Not that he distrusted others; far from it. But he alone assumed responsibility for the destiny of his own soul. Shortly before being taken to the Tower, he had written to Thomas Cromwell that "upon that that I should perceive mine own conscience should serve me" (Letter 5 in this volume). And again: "But so purpose I to bear myself in every man's company, while I live, that neither good man nor bad, neither monk, friar nor nun, nor other man or woman in this world shall make me digress from my troth and faith, either toward God, or toward my natural prince, by the grace of Almighty God" (Letter 3). Finally, More was a man alone. Yet, is this not the decisive moment of truth? And does not authentic freedom demand such a response as one would give if it were possible to be alone before God? This was actually the very first lesson the King himself had given More upon coming into his service, "that I should first look unto God and after God unto him" (Letter 5).[45]

✠   ✠

Reading and rereading these last letters of More, I have often recalled the moving correspondence of another martyr of early Christianity. Saint Ignatius of Antioch felt that it was precisely in the very moment he had accepted in his heart to die for Christ that he had become a disciple — only then had he been "initiated into discipleship."[46] Indeed, one must look to early Christian times in order to find something similar in depth and tenderness to the reflections of More in the Tower. "My love has been crucified, and I am not on fire with the love of earthly things," the holy bishop of Antioch wrote, but the words are even more poignant when uttered by a man of the world — father and grandfather, humanist and politician — and an ambitious one at that.

Readiness to die — or, better, the realization that baptism signals death and the beginning of a new life — is the foundation of Christian liv-

---

mens sana in corpore sano ("pray for a healthy mind in a healthy body"); the full quotation can be found in the commentary on Letter 9.

45. Speaking as "one who stands outside the Church," a political prisoner of the twentieth century has written that "the Church is the most important institution in Poland because it teaches all of us that we may bow only before God" (Adam Michnik, *Letters from Prison and Other Essays*, trans. Maya Latynski [Berkeley and Los Angeles: University of California Press, 1985], pp. 164, 94).

46. *Letter to the Ephesians*, 3, 1.

ing, and it was clearly present in Thomas More many years before his actual imprisonment, if not as an accomplished act of fortitude, at least as a
spiritual struggle.[47] When his long agony began, More had known the
horror of imagining the worst that could befall him. This heart of darkness became for him a luminous experience simply because he believed
that Christ himself had been there before. Suddenly the Gospel narratives
of Christ's painful agony became for More not a picture for sentimental
devotion but the very map to guide him in his own hour of fear and trem-
bling. In *De Tristitia Christi*, More wrote that Jesus suffered in order to,
among other things, "offer this unheard of, this marvelous example of
profound anguish as a consolation to those who would be so fearful and
alarmed at the thought of torture that they might otherwise interpret
their fear as a sign of their downfall and thus yield to despair."[48] Some
martyrs have gone eagerly and joyfully to their deaths, without sadness or
fear. But More was concerned not "to deny the triumph of those who do
not rush forth of their own accord but who nevertheless do not hang back
or withdraw once they have been seized, but rather go on in spite of their
fearful anxiety and face the terrible prospect out of love for Christ."[49]

"Once arrived there, I shall be a man," Bishop Ignatius of Antioch
had written, referring to the moment of martyrdom.[50] He was in fact de-
fining the meaning of his whole existence. For the martyred bishop, as
for the English humanist fourteen hundred years later, both his human
and his Christian character were at stake in the supreme act of fortitude.
When More wrote in these prison letters that he had "a respect to mine
own soul," he was not exclusively considering the eternal destiny of what
is called the human soul or spirit. The soul is not something more or
less elusive that begins to exist only at the moment of death. More knew
that if he had taken the oath against his conscience, he would have become, in that very moment, a lost man. For the satisfaction of his King,
he was ready to forgo all things, "except only my soul" (Letter 5 in this
volume).

In his portrayal of More, Robert Bolt has him say, "Finally it is not a
matter of reason but a matter of love." But for More, it was a matter of reason too. His decision to be a martyr, or rather his final acceptance of martyrdom, was a rational decision, and his last letters are a solemn declara-

47. I have explicated this idea in "Martyrdom and Christian Morals," *Communio:
International Catholic Review* 21 (Summer 1994): 286-97.
48. *CW,* vol. 14, p. 237.
49. *CW,* vol. 14, p. 239.
50. *Letter to the Romans,* 6, 3.

tion and proof of that. That was the way More understood what it meant to be truly human. He did not begin as a liberal Renaissance humanist to end up as a sort of rigid Catholic fundamentalist. In prison he realized more clearly than ever that his faith and hope in Christ kept him a whole man, heart and mind.[51] The more he loved Christ, he thought, the more human he would be. Here he had no doubts. More preferred, as he had written to his King, "to depend upon the comfort of the truth and hope of heaven, and not upon the fallible opinion or soon spoken words of light and soon changeable people" (Letter 4).

✠   ✠

"I want to hear the saints converse," wrote Cardinal Newman, seeking men and women he could love and imitate, not pious idealizations that, meant to edify, seldom achieve their lofty purpose. He found this conversation not in hagiography but in the saints' correspondence. "A man's life lies in his letters," Newman wrote. "Biographers varnish; they assign motives; they conjecture feelings; they interpret Lord Burleigh's nods; they palliate or defend."[52] Letters seldom lie. The extant correspondence of Thomas More, no matter how broken and full of gaps, is still the best way to know him. The letters are straightforward, with a pure, unadorned style. "The wording of a letter should resemble a conversation between friends," Erasmus of Rotterdam had written in his manual *On How to Write Letters,* and his friend followed the advice closely.[53] In these final letters we hear More converse with his daughter, a few of his friends, and, beyond them, the future audience they would one day have. In vain we look in these prison letters for signs of more or less spectacular supernatural events. No angelic apparitions, no prophetic revelations, no heavenly voices, no mystical raptures guided More in his long imprisonment. If we found evidence of this, it might disturb us somehow. And it is good for us to see that saints are no different from the rest of humanity.

51. Rodney Stark gave this title to a discussion on early martyrdom: "The Martyrs: Sacrifice as Rational Choice." See his book entitled *The Rise of Christianity: A Sociologist Reconsiders History* (Princeton: Princeton University Press, 1996), ch. 8.

52. John Henry Newman to his sister Jemima (Mrs. John Mozley), in J. H. Newman, *A Packet of Letters,* ed. Joyce Snugg (Oxford: Clarendon Press, 1983), pp. 135-36.

53. *De Conscribendis Epistolis,* in the *Collected Works of Erasmus,* vol. 25, ed. J. K. Sowards (Toronto: University of Toronto Press, 1985), p. 20.

"The clearness of my conscience hath made my heart hop for joy," he wrote to Margaret (Letter 16 in this volume). The joyful serenity of these letters is not to be explained by tricks of literary artifice. It is simply the luminosity of the writer's clear and loyal following of conscience. More persevered through the final storm firmly anchored in human reason — which he never despised — in fidelity to the dictates of his conscience, and in his tender love for Christ and the Church. Here at last, Thomas More the judge did not need to judge and condemn others who had taken a different road in the cruel religious wars of the age. Neither was his respect, loyalty, and love for the King in any way diminished. His love for both his friends and his enemies had only increased in prison. "To consider my most enemies my best friends," he would write there in a moving prayer of petition. He was strong as a tower but not without a gentle heart; through these pages we can still see his tears.

"Can this be real?" the reader may ask in disbelief. As More said, "Time trieth truth," and most readers should be able to judge for themselves, because there is something in this kind of integrity that shatters our human prejudices. While hagiographical anecdotes can make us laugh (not necessarily a bad sign), we may recognize an authentic story because it quiets us. In that silence, we may secretly accept the only honest response to great men and women: to wish to be as good as they. Many of them have passed unnoticed, leaving no record of their heroic integrity. A few are well known to us. Among the Christian saints, few elicit this desire as clearly and strongly as Thomas More.

While he carefully composed these letters, the thought must have come to him that perhaps someday, somewhere, his clear voice would resound and awaken a dormant conscience. *Memento mori*. Remember death; remember More. As he had written many years before, "Many things know we that we seldom think on. And in the things of the soul, the knowledge without the remembrance little profiteth."[54]

Centuries have passed since these letters were written, but they still have the freshness of a letter just received. Now as then, amid the clamor of other voices perhaps more convenient to follow, the voice of true conscience is easily quieted, and even drowned out. In this respect, our world is not different from More's. Thus reading this brief correspondence is good for us. In doing so we keep "good company." We pay a visit to a good man, one who was "allowed on all hands (however erroneous his opinions on religion) to have been the most sincere, candid, and

54. *The Last Things*, in *CW*, vol. 1, p. 138.

truthful of men."[55] The value of the parenthetical remark we can judge for ourselves better than poor Lord Campbell, perhaps as a result of reading this packet of letters. For More himself, his confinement became a providential gift. For readers of these letters, there may be the benefit of the company of an innocent prisoner: "For I assure you it is hard to tell how much good to a man's soul the personal visiting to poor prisoners doth," acknowledges Antony in *A Dialogue of Comfort against Tribulation.*[56]

Discovering, as much as one can in a bundle of letters from the distant past, the thoughts and emotions, the fears and hopes, the anguish and joy of this man, strengthens the human spirit in the never-ending struggle against whatever may still seek to imprison it with chains. The struggle may turn into an agony, and no agony is easy, but Thomas More of London shall ever remind us that indeed "it is a case in which a man may lose his head and yet have none harm, but instead of harm inestimable good at the hand of God."[57]

55. John Campbell, *Lives of the Lord Chancellors and Keepers of the Great Seal of England, from the Earliest Times till the reign of George IV,* 4th ed. (London: John Murray, 1856), vol. 2, p. 38.

56. *CW,* vol. 12, p. 259.

57. Rogers, *The Correspondence of Sir Thomas More,* p. 542.

How can you stand your ground when you are weak and sensitive to pain, when people you love are still alive, when you are unprepared?

What do you need to make you stronger than the interrogator and the whole trap?

From the moment you go to prison you must put your cozy past firmly behind you. At the very threshold, you must say to yourself: "My life is over, a little early to be sure, but there's nothing to be done about it. I shall never return to freedom. I am condemned to die — now or a little later. But later on, in truth, it will be even harder, and so the sooner the better. I no longer have any property whatsoever. For me those I love have died, and for them I have died. From today on, my body is useless and alien to me. Only my spirit and my conscience remain precious and important to me."

Confronted with such a prisoner, the interrogation will tremble.

Only the man who has renounced everything can win that victory.

But how can one turn one's body to stone?

ALEKSANDR I. SOLZHENITSYN
The Gulag Archipelago

THE LAST LETTERS
OF THOMAS MORE
(1534-1535)

To Thomas Cromwell

CHELSEA

1 February 1533/4

A letter written by Sir Thomas More to Master ⌐Thomas Cromwell⌐ (then one of the King's Privy Council) the first day of February in the year of our Lord God 1533, after the computation of the Church of England and in the twenty-fifth year of the reign of King Henry the VIII.

⌐RIGHT WORSHIPFUL,[1] IN MY MOST HEARTY WISE I RECOMMEND ME UNTO YOU⌐.

Sir, ⌐my cousin William Rastell⌐ hath informed me that your Mastership of your goodness shewed him that it hath been reported that I have against ⌐the book of certain articles⌐ (which was late put forth in print by the King's honorable Council) made an answer, and delivered it unto my said cousin to print. And albeit that[2] he for his part truly denied it, yet because he somewhat remained in doubt, whether your Mastership gave him therein full credence or not, he desired[3] me for his farther discharge[4] to declare you the very truth, sir, as help me God neither my said cousin nor any man else, never had any book of mine to print, one or other, since the said book of the King's Council came forth. For of truth the last book that he printed of mine was that book that I made against an unknown heretic which hath sent over a work that walketh in over many men's hands

1. distinguished
2. although, granted that
3. requested
4. acquittal, exoneration

31

named ⌐the Supper of the Lord¬, against the blessed sacrament of the al-
tar. My answer whereunto, albeit that the printer (unaware to me) dated it
Anno 1534, by which it seemeth to be printed ⌐since the Feast of the
Circumcision¬, yet was it of very truth both made and printed and many
of them gone before Christmas. And myself never espied the printer's
oversight in the date, in more than three weeks after. And this was in good
faith the last book that my cousin had of mine. Which being true as of
truth it shall be found, sufficeth for his declaration in this behalf.

As touching mine own self, I shall say thus much farther, that on my
faith I never made any such book nor never thought to do. I read the said
book once over and never more. But I am for once reading very far off
from many things, whereof I would have meetly[5] sure knowledge, ere ever
I would make an answer, though the matter and the book both, concerned
the poorest man in a town, and were of the simplest man's making too.
For of many things which in that book be touched, in some I know not the
law, and in some I know not the fact. And therefore would I never be so
childish nor so play the proud arrogant fool, by whomsoever the book had
been made, and to whomsoever the matter had belonged, as to presume to
make an answer to the book, concerning the matter whereof I never were
sufficiently learned in the laws, nor fully instructed in the facts. And then,
while the matter pertained unto the King's Highness, and the book
professeth openly that it was made by his honorable Council, and by them
put in print with his Grace's license obtained thereunto, I verily trust in
good faith that of your good mind toward me, though I never wrote you
word thereof, yourself will both think and say so much for me, that it were
a thing far unlikely, that an answer should be made thereunto by me. I will
by the grace of Almighty God, as long as it shall please him to lend me life
in this world, in all such places (as I am of my duty to God and the King's
Grace bounden) truly say my mind, and discharge[6] my conscience, as
becometh a poor honest true man, wheresoever I shall be by his Grace
commanded. Yet surely if it should happen any book to come abroad in
the name of his Grace or his honorable Council, if the book to me seemed
such as myself would not have given mine own advice to the making, yet I
know my bounden duty, to bear more honor to my prince, and more reverence to his honorable Council, than that it could become me, for many
causes, to make an answer unto such a book, or to counsel and advise any
man else to do it. And therefore as it is a thing that I never did nor in-

5. suitably
6. clear, exonerate

tended, so I heartily beseech you if you shall happen to perceive[7] any man, either of evil will or of lightness, any such thing report by me,[8] be so good master to me, as help to bring us both together. And then never take me for honest after, but if you find his honesty somewhat impaired in the matter.

Thus am I bold upon your goodness to encumber you with my long rude[10] letter, in the contents whereof, I eftsoons[11] heartily beseech you to be in manner aforesaid good master and friend unto me: whereby you shall bind me ⌜to be your beadsman⌝[12] while I live, as knoweth our Lord, whose especial grace both bodily and ghostly[13] long preserve and keep you.

⌜At Chelsea⌝, in ⌜the Vigil of the Purification of our Blessed Lady⌝ by the hand of

Assuredly all your own,

Thomas More, Knight.

7. observe, know of
8. *by me:* of me
9. *but if:* unless
10. unpolished, inelegant
11. again, a second time
12. one who prays for another. See Notes.
13. spiritually, pertaining to the soul

2

To Thomas Cromwell

CHELSEA

Saturday, February-March 1533/4

*Another letter written by Sir Thomas More to Master Thomas Cromwell
in February or in March in the year of our Lord God 1533, after the computation of the Church of England, and in the twenty-fifth year of the
reign of King Henry the Eighth.*

RIGHT WORSHIPFUL.

After right hearty recommendation, so it is that I am informed, that
there is ⌐a bill put in against me¬ into the higher house before the Lords,
concerning my communication[1] with ⌐the Nun of Canterbury¬, and my
writing unto her. Whereof I not a little marvel, the truth of the matter being such as God and I know it is, and as I have plainly declared unto you
by my former letters, wherein I found you then so good, that I am now
bold eftsoons upon your goodness to desire you to shew me that favor, as
that I might the rather by your good means, have a copy of the bill. Which
seen, if I find any untrue surmise[2] therein, as of likelihood there is, I may
make mine humble suit[3] unto the King's good Grace, and declare the
truth, either to his Grace or by his Grace's commandment, wheresoever
the matter shall require. I am so sure of my truth toward his Grace, that I
cannot mistrust his gracious favor toward me, upon the truth known, nor
the judgment of any honest man. Nor never shall there loss in this matter

1. conversation
2. allegation, suspicion
3. petition

34

grieve me, being myself so innocent as God and I know me, whatsoever should happen me therein, by the grace of Almighty God, who both bodily and ghostly preserve you. At Chelsea, this present Saturday by the hand of

Heartily all your own,

Tho. More, Knight.

To Thomas Cromwell

March? 1534

RIGHT WORSHIPFUL.

After my most hearty recommendation, with like thanks for your goodness in the accepting of my rude long letter, I perceive that of your further goodness and favor toward me, it liked[1] your Mastership to break ⌐with[2] my son Roper⌐ of that, that I had had communication, not only with divers that were of acquaintance with the lewd[3] Nun of Canterbury, but also with herself; and had, over that, by my writing, declaring favor toward her, given her advice and counsel; of which my demeanor,[4] that it liketh you to be content to take the labor and the pain, to hear, by mine own writing, the truth, I very heartily thank you, and reckon myself therein right deeply beholden to you.

It is, I suppose, about eight or nine years ago sith[5] I heard of that huswife[6] first; at which time ⌐the Bishop of Canterbury⌐ that then was, God assoil[7] his soul, sent unto the King's Grace a roll of paper in which were written certain words of hers, that she had, as report was then made, at sundry times spoken in her trances. Whereupon ⌐it pleased the King's Grace to deliver me the roll⌐, commanding me to look thereon and afterward shew him what I thought therein. Whereunto, at another time, when

1. it pleased
2. *to break with:* to disclose
3. ignorant
4. conduct
5. since
6. hussy, worthless woman
7. absolve

his Highness asked me, I told him, that in good faith I found nothing in these words that I could anything regard or esteem, for saving that some part fell in rhyme, and that, God wot,[8] full rude,[9] else for any reason, God wot, that I saw therein, a right simple[10] woman might, in my mind, speak it of her own wit[11] well enough. Howbeit, I said, that because it was constantly reported for a truth that God wrought in her, and that a miracle was shewed upon her, I durst not nor would not, be bold in judging the matter. And the King's Grace, as methought, esteemed the matter as light as it after proved lewd.[12]

From that time till about Christmas was twelvemonth, albeit that continually, there was much talking of her, and of her holiness, yet never heard I any talk rehearsed,[13] either of revelation of hers, or miracle, saving that I had heard some times ⌐in my Lord Cardinal's days⌐, that ⌐she had been both with his Lordship and with the King's Grace⌐, but what she said either to the one or to the other, upon my faith, ⌐I had never heard any one word⌐.

Now, as I was about to tell you, about Christmas was twelvemonth, ⌐Father Risby, Friar Observant, then of Canterbury, lodged one night at mine house⌐; where, after supper, a little before he went to his chamber, he fell in communication with me of the Nun, giving her high commendation of holiness, and that it was wonderful to see and understand the works that God wrought in her; which thing, I answered, that I was very glad to hear it, and thanked God thereof. Then he told me, that she had been with ⌐my Lord Legate⌐ in his life and with the King's Grace, too, and that she had told my Lord Legate ⌐a revelation of hers, of three swords⌐ that God hath put in my Lord Legate's hand, which if he ordered not well, God would lay it sore[14] to his charge. The first, he said, was the ordering of the spiritualty[15] under the Pope, as Legate. The second, the rule that he bare in order of the temporalty[16] under the King, as his Chancellor. And the third, she said, was the meddling[17] he was put in trust with by the

---

8. knows
9. unpolished
10. unlearned, uneducated
11. mind
12. wicked
13. repeated
14. grievously
15. clergy
16. laymen
17. business

King, concerning the great matter of his marriage. And therewithal I said unto him that any revelation of the King's matters I would not hear of: I doubt not but the goodness of God should direct his highness with his grace and wisdom, that the thing should take such end as God should be pleased with, to the King's honor and surety[18] of the realm. When he heard me say these words or the like, he said unto me, that God had specially commanded her to pray for the King. And forthwith he brake again into her revelations, ⌐concerning the Cardinal that his soul was saved by her mediation⌐; and without any other communication went into his chamber. And he and I never talked any more of any such manner of matter, nor since his departing on the morrow, I never saw him after, to my remembrance, ⌐till I saw him at Paul's cross⌐.

⌐After this, about Shrovetide⌐, there came unto me, a little before supper, ⌐Father Rich⌐, Friar Observant of Richmond. And as we fell in talking, I asked him of Father Risby, how he did? and upon that occasion, he asked me whether Father Risby had anything shewed me of the holy Nun of Kent? and I said, yea, and that I was very glad to hear of her virtue. "I would not," quoth he, "tell you again that you have heard of him already, but I have heard and known many great graces that God hath wrought in her, and in other folk, by her, which I would gladly tell you if I thought you had not heard them already." And therewith he asked me, whether Father Risby had told me anything of her being with my Lord Cardinal? and I said, "Yea." "Then he told you," quoth he, "of the three swords." "Yea, verily," quoth I. "Did he tell you," quoth he, "of the revelations that she had concerning the King's Grace?" "Nay, forsooth," quoth I, "nor if he would have done I would not have given him the hearing; nor verily no more I would indeed, for sith she hath been with the King's Grace herself, and told him, methought it a thing needless to tell the matter to me, or any man else." And when Father Rich perceived that I would not hear her revelations concerning the King's Grace he talked on a little of her virtue and let her revelations alone. And therewith my supper was set upon the board where I required[19] him to sit with me, but he would in no wise tarry, but departed to London. After that night I talked with him twice, once in mine own house, another time in his own garden at the Friars, at every time a great space, but not of any revelation touching the King's Grace, but only of other mean folk,[20] I knew not whom; of which

18. safety
19. asked
20. *mean folk:* undistinguished, of low degree

things some were very strange and some were very childish. But albeit that he said that he had seen her lie in her trance in great pains and that he had at other times taken great spiritual comfort in her communication, yet did he never tell me she had told him those tales herself; for if he had I would, for ⌐the tale of Mary Magdalene⌐ which he told me, and for the tale of the host, with which, as I heard, she said she was houseled,[21] ⌐at the King's Mass at Calais⌐; if I had heard it of him as told unto himself by her mouth for a revelation, I would have both liked him and her the worse. But whether ever I heard that same tale of Rich or of Risby or of neither of them both, but of some other man since she was in hold,[22] in good faith, I cannot tell. But I wot well when or wheresoever I heard it, methought it a tale too marvelous to be true, and very likely that she had told some man her dream, which told it out for a revelation. And in effect, I little doubted but that some of these tales that were told of her were untrue; but yet, sith I never heard them reported, as spoken by her own mouth, I thought nevertheless that many of them might be true, and she a very virtuous woman too: as some lies be peradventure written of some that be saints in heaven, ⌐and yet many miracles indeed done by them⌐ for all that.

After this, I being upon a day at ⌐Syon⌐ talking with divers of the Fathers together at the grate, they shewed me that she had been with them, and shewed me divers things that some of them misliked in her, and in this talking, they wished that I had spoken with her and said they would fain[23] see how I should like her. Whereupon, afterward, when I heard that she was there again, I came thither to see her and to speak with her myself. At which communication had, in a little chapel, there were none present but we two. In the beginning whereof I shewed that my coming to her was not of any curious mind, anything to know of such things as folk talked, that it pleased God to reveal and shew unto her, but for the great virtue that I had heard for so many years, every day more and more spoken and reported of her; I therefore had a great mind to see her, and be acquainted with her, that she might have somewhat the more occasion to remember me to God in her devotion and prayers. Whereunto she gave me a very good virtuous answer that as God did of his goodness far better by her than such a poor wretch was worthy, so she feared that many folk yet beside that spake of their own favorable minds many things for her, far

21. received the Eucharist
22. in custody
23. gladly

above the truth, and that of me she had many such things heard, that already she prayed for me and ever would, whereof I heartily thanked her.

I said unto her, "Madam, ⌐one Helen, a maiden dwelling about Tottenham⌐, of whose trances and revelations there hath been much talking, she hath been with me late and shewed me that she was with you, and that after the rehearsal[24] of such visions as she had seen, you shewed her that they were no revelations, but plain illusions of the devil and advised her to cast them out of her mind; and verily she gave therein good credence unto you and thereupon hath left[25] to lean any longer unto such visions of her own. Whereupon she saith, she findeth your words true, for ever since she hath been the less visited with such things as she was wont to be before." To this she answered me, "Forsooth, Sir, there is in this point no praise unto me, but the goodness of God, as it appeareth, hath wrought much meekness in her soul, which hath taken my rude warning so well and not grudged to hear her spirit and her visions reproved." I liked her in good faith better for this answer than for many of those things that I heard reported by her.[26] Afterward she told me, upon that occasion, how great need folk have, that are visited with such visions, to take heed and prove well of what spirit they come of. And in the communication she told me that of late the devil, in likeness of a bird, was fleeing[27] and flickering about her in a chamber, and suffered himself to be taken; and being in hands suddenly changed, in their sight that were present, into such a strange ugly fashioned bird, that they were all afraid, and ⌐threw him out at a window⌐.

For conclusion, we talked no word of the King's Grace or any great personage else, nor, in effect, of any man or woman, but of herself, and myself. But after no long communication had for or ever we met,[28] my time came to go home; ⌐I gave her a double ducat⌐,[29] and prayed her to pray for me and mine, and so departed from her and never spake with her after. Howbeit, of truth I had a great opinion of her, and had her in great estimation as you shall perceive by the letter that I wrote unto her. For afterward, because I had often heard that many right worshipful folks, as well men as women, used to have much communication with her, and many folk are of nature inquisitive and curious, whereby they fall some-

24. relating
25. stopped
26. *by her:* of her
27. flying
28. *or ever:* before
29. a gold coin

time into such talking as better were to forbear, of which thing I nothing thought while I talked with her of charity, therefore I wrote her a letter thereof, which sith it may be peradventure, that she brake[30] or lost, ⌜I shall insert the very copy thereof⌝ in this present letter.

GOOD MADAM, AND MY RIGHT DEARLY BELOVED SISTER IN OUR LORD GOD.

After my most hearty recommendation, I shall beseech you to take my good mind in good worth, and pardon me that I am so homely[31] as, of myself unrequired,[32] and also without necessity, to give counsel to you, of whom for the good inspirations and great revelations that it liketh Almighty God of his goodness to give and shew, as many wise, well learned, and very virtuous folk testify, I myself have need, for the comfort of my soul, to require and ask advice. For surely, good Madam, sith it pleaseth God sometime to suffer such as are far under and of little estimation to give yet fruitful advertisement[33] to others as are ⌜in the light of the Spirit⌝ so far above them, that there were between them no comparison; as he suffered his high prophet ⌜Moses to be in some things advised and counseled by Jethro⌝, I cannot for the love that in our Lord I bear you refrain to put you in remembrance of one thing, which in my poor mind I think highly necessary to be by your wisdom considered, referring the end and order thereof to God and his holy Spirit to direct you.

Good Madam, I doubt not but that you remember that in the beginning of my communication with you, I shewed you that I neither was, nor would be, curious of any knowledge of other men's matters, and least of all of any matter of princes or of the realm, in case it so were that God had, as to many good folks before time he hath any things revealed unto you, such things, I said unto your ladyship, that I was not only not desirous to hear of, but also would not hear of. Now, Madam, I consider well that many folk desire to speak with you, which are not all peradventure of my mind in this point; but some happen to be curious and inquisitive of things that little pertain unto their parts; and some might peradventure happen to talk of such things, as might peradventure after turn to much harm, as I think you have heard how ⌜the late Duke of Buckingham⌝

30. destroyed
31. familiar
32. unasked
33. advice

41

moved[34] with the fame of one that was reported for an holy monk and had such talking with him as after was a great part of his destruction and disheriting[35] of his blood, and great slander and infamy of religion. It sufficeth me, good Madam, to put you in remembrance of such things, as I nothing doubt your wisdom and the spirit of God shall keep you from talking with any persons, ⌈specially with lay persons⌉, of any such manner things[36] as pertain to princes' affairs, or the state of the realm, but only to common[37] and talk with any person high and low, of such manner things as may to the soul be profitable for you to shew and for them to know.

And thus, my good Lady, and dearly beloved sister in our Lord, I make an end of this my needless advertisement unto you, whom the blessed Trinity preserve and increase in grace, and put in your mind to recommend me and mine unto him in your devout prayers. At Chelsea this Tuesday by the hand of

Your hearty loving brother and beadsman,

Thomas More, Kt.

At the receipt of this letter she answered my servant that she heartily thanked me. Soon after this there came to mine house ⌈the proctor of the Charterhouse at Sheen and one brother William⌉ with him, which nothing talked with me but of her and of the great joy that they took in her virtue, but of any of her revelations they had no communication. But at another time brother William came to me, and told me a long tale of her, being ⌈at the house of a knight in Kent⌉, that was sore troubled with temptation to destroy himself; and none other thing we talked of nor should have done of likelihood, though we had tarried together much longer. He took so great pleasure, good man, to tell that tale with all the circumstances at length. When I came again another time to Syon, ⌈on a day in which there was a profession⌉, some of the fathers asked me how I liked the nun? And I answered that, in good faith, I liked her very well in her talking. "Howbeit," quoth I, "she is never the nearer tried by that, for I assure you she were likely to be very bad, if she seemed good, ere I should think her other, till she happed to be proved naught." And in good faith, that is my manner indeed, except I were set to search and examine the

34. *moved with:* was influenced by
35. disinheriting
36. *manner things:* kinds of things
37. converse, communicate

truth upon likelihood of some cloaked evil; for in that case, although I nothing suspected the person myself, yet no less than if I suspected him sore[38], I would as far as my wit[39] would serve me, search to find out the truth as yourself hath done very prudently in this matter; wherein you have done, in my mind, to your great laud and praise, a very meritorious deed in ⌐bringing forth to light such detestable hypocrisy¬, whereby every other wretch may take warning, and be feared to set forth their own devilish dissimuled[40] falsehood, under the manner and color[41] of the wonderful work of God. For verily, this woman so handled herself, with help of the evil spirit that inspired her, that after ⌐her own confession declared at Paul's Cross¬, when I sent word by my servant unto the Proctor of the Charterhouse, that she was undoubtedly proved a false deceiving hypocrite, the good man had had so good opinion of her so long that he could at first scantly believe me therein. Howbeit, it was not he alone that thought her so very good, but many another right good man beside, as little marvel was upon so good report, till she was proved naught.

I remember me further, that in communication between Father Rich and me, I counseled him, that in such strange things as concerned such folk as had come unto her, to whom, as she said, she had told the causes of their coming ere themselves spake thereof; and such good fruit as they said that many men had received by her prayer, he and such other as so reported it, and thought that the knowledge thereof should much pertain to the glory of God, should first cause the things to be well and surely ⌐examined by the ordinaries¬, and such as had authority thereunto; so that it might be surely known whether the things were true or not, and that there were no lies intermingled among them, or else the lies might after hap to away[42] the credence of those things that were true. And when he told me the tale of Mary Magdalene, I said unto him, "Father Rich, that she is a good virtuous woman, in good faith, I hear so many good folk so report her, that I verily think it true; and think it well likely that God worketh some good and great things by her. But yet are, you wot well, ⌐these strange tales no part of our creed¬; and therefore before you see them surely proved, you shall have my poor counsel not to wed yourself so far forth to the credence of them, as to report them very surely for true, lest that if it should hap that they were afterward proved false, it might

38. grievously
39. intelligence
40. dissembled
41. appearance
42. *hap to away:* happen to take away

minish[43] your estimation[44] in your preaching, whereof might grow great loss." To this he thanked me for my counsel, but how he used it after that, I cannot tell.

Thus have I, good Master Cromwell, fully declared you, as far as myself can call to remembrance, all that ever I have done or said in this matter, wherein ⌜I am sure that never one of them all⌝ shall tell you any farther thing or effect; for if any of them, or any man else, report of me as I trust verily no man will, and I wot well truly no man can, any word or deed by me spoken or done, touching any breach of my loyal troth[45] and duty toward my most redoubted sovereign and ⌜natural[46] liege lord⌝, I will come to mine answer, and make it good in such wise as becometh a poor true man to do; that whosoever any such thing shall say, shall therein say untrue. For I neither have in this matter done evil nor said evil, nor so much as any evil thing thought, but only have been glad, and rejoiced of them that were reported for good; which condition I shall nevertheless keep toward all other good folk, for the false cloaked hypocrisy of any of these, no more than I shall esteem ⌜Judas the true apostle, for Judas the false traitor⌝.

But so purpose I to bear myself in every man's company, while I live, that neither good man nor bad, neither monk, friar nor nun, nor other man or woman in this world shall make me digress from my troth[47] and faith,[48] either toward God, or toward my natural prince, by the grace of Almighty God. And as you therein find me true, so I heartily therein pray you to continue toward me your favor and good will, as you shall be sure of my poor daily prayer, for other pleasure can I none do you. And thus the blessed Trinity, both bodily and ghostly, long preserve and prosper you.

I pray you pardon me, that I write not unto you of mine own hand, for verily I am compelled to forbear writing for a while ⌜by reason of this disease of mine⌝, whereof the chief occasion is grown, as it is thought, by the stooping and leaning on my breast, that I have used in writing. And this, eftsoons, I beseech our Lord long to preserve you.

43. diminish
44. reputation
45. truth
46. thoroughly legitimate prince (as opposed to lord by conquest)
47. loyalty
48. fidelity

4

To Henry VIII

CHELSEA

5 March 1534

It may like[1] your Highness to call to your gracious remembrance, that at
such time as of that great weighty room[2] and office of your Chancellor
(with which so far above my merits or qualities able and meet[3] therefor,
your Highness had of your incomparable goodness honored and exalted
me), ye were so good and gracious unto me, as at my poor humble suit ⌐to
discharge and disburden me¬, giving me license with your gracious favor
to bestow the residue of my life in mine age now to come, about the provision for my soul in the service of God, and to be your Grace's beadsman
and pray for you. It pleased your Highness further to say unto me, that for
the service which I before had done you (which it then liked your goodness far above my deserving to commend) that in any suit that I should after have unto your Highness, which either should concern mine honor
(that word it liked your Highness to use unto me) or that should pertain
unto my profit, I should find your Highness good and gracious lord unto
me. So is it now gracious Sovereign, that worldly honor is the thing,
whereof I have resigned both the possession and the desire, in the resignation of your most honorable office; and worldly profit, I trust experience
proveth, and daily more and more shall prove, that ⌐I never was very
greedy¬ thereon.

But now is my most humble suit unto your excellent Highness, partly
to beseech the same, somewhat to tender my poor honesty, but principally

1. It may please
2. position
3. suitable, fit

45

that your accustomed goodness, no sinister[4] information move your noble Grace to have any more distrust of my truth and devotion toward you than I have, or shall during my life give the cause. For in this matter of ⌐the wicked woman of Canterbury⌐ I have unto your trusty Counselor Master Thomas Cromwell, by my writing, as plainly declared the truth as I possibly can, which my declaration, of his duty toward your Grace and his goodness toward me, he hath, I understand, declared unto your Grace. In any part of all which my dealing, whether any other man may peradventure put any doubt or move any scruple of suspicion, that can I neither tell, nor lieth in mine hand to let,[5] but unto myself is it not possible any part of my said demeanor to seem evil, the very clearness of mine own conscience knoweth in all the matter my mind and intent so good.

Wherefore most gracious Sovereign, I neither will, nor well it can become me, with your Highness to reason and argue the matter, but in my most humble manner, prostrate at your gracious feet, I only beseech your Majesty with your own high prudence and your accustomed goodness consider and weigh the matter. And then, if in your so doing, your own virtuous mind shall give you, that notwithstanding the manifold excellent goodness that your gracious Highness hath by so many manner ways used unto me, I be a wretch of such monstruous ingratitude, as could with any of them all, or with any other person living, digress from my bounden duty of allegiance toward your Grace, then desire I no further favor at your gracious hand, than the loss of all that ever I may lose in this world, goods, lands, and liberty and finally my life withal. Whereof the keeping of any part unto myself could never do me pennyworth of pleasure, but only should then my recomfort[6] be, that after my short life and your long, which with continual prosperity to God's pleasure our Lord for his mercy send you, I should once meet with your Grace again in heaven, and there be merry with you, where among mine other pleasures this should yet be one, that your Grace should surely see there then, that (howsoever you take me) I am your true beadsman now and ever have been, and will be till I die, howsoever your pleasure be to do by me.

Howbeit, if in the considering of my cause, your high wisdom and gracious goodness perceive (as I verily trust in God you shall) that I none otherwise have demeaned[7] myself than well may stand with my bounden

4. misleading, malicious
5. prevent
6. comfort, consolation
7. conducted

duty of faithfulness toward your royal Majesty, then in my most humble wise I beseech your most noble Grace that the knowledge of your true gracious persuasion in that behalf may relieve the torment of my present heaviness,[8] conceived of the dread and fear (by that I hear ⌐such grievous bill put by your learned Council into your high Court of Parliament against me¬) lest your Grace might by some sinister information be moved anything to think the contrary, which if your Highness do not (as I trust in God and your great goodness the matter by your own high prudence examined and considered, you will not) then, in my most humble manner, I beseech your Highness further (albeit that in respect of my former request this other thing is very slight) yet sith your Highness hath herebefore of your mere[9] abundant goodness heaped and accumulated upon me (though I was thereto very far unworthy) from time to time both worship[10] and great honor, too, and sith I now have left off all such things, and nothing seek or desire but the life to come, and in the meanwhile pray for your Grace, it may like your Highness of your accustomed benignity somewhat to tender[11] my poor honesty and never suffer, by the mean of such a bill put forth against me, any man to take occasion hereafter against the truth to slander me; which thing should yet by the peril of their own souls do themself more hurt than me, which shall, I trust, settle mine heart, with your gracious favor, to depend upon the comfort of the truth and hope of heaven, and not upon the fallible opinion or soon spoken words of light[12] and soon changeable people.

And thus, most dread[13] and most dear sovereign Lord, I beseech the blessed Trinity preserve your most noble Grace, both in body and soul, and all that are your well willers, and amend all the contrary, among whom if ever I be or ever have been one, then pray I God that he may with mine open shame and destruction declare it. At my poor house in Chelsea, the fifth day of March, by the known rude hand of

Your most humble and most heavy[14] faithful subject and beadsman,

Tho. More, Kg.

8. sadness
9. pure
10. distinction
11. appreciate
12. careless, irresponsible
13. revered
14. sad

$\rightarrow$ 5 $\leftarrow$

To Thomas Cromwell

CHELSEA

5 March 1534

RIGHT WORSHIPFUL.

After my most hearty recommendation, it may please you to understand that I have perceived by the relation[1] of my son Roper (for which I
beseech almighty God reward you) your most charitable labor taken for
me toward the King's gracious Highness, in the procuring at his most gracious hand, the relief and comfort of this woeful heaviness in which mine
heart standeth, neither for the loss of goods, lands, or liberty, nor for any
respect either, of this kind of honesty that standeth in the opinion of people and worldly reputation, all which manner things (I thank our Lord) I
so little esteem for any affection[2] therein toward myself that I can well be
content to jeopard, lose, and forgo them all and my life therewith, without
any further respite than even this same present day, either for the pleasure
of God or of my prince.

But surely, good Master Cromwell, as I by mouth declared unto you,
some part (for all could I neither then say nor now write) it thoroughly
pierceth my poor heart, that the King's Highness (whose gracious favor toward me far above all the things of this world I have evermore desired, and
whereof both for the conscience of mine own true faithful heart and devotion toward him, and for the manifold benefits of his high goodness
continually bestowed upon me, I thought myself always sure), should conceive any such mind or opinion of me, as to think that in my communication ⌐either with the nun or the friars⌐, or in ⌐my letter written unto the

1. account, narrative
2. attachment

48

nun⌐, I had any other manner mind, than might well stand with the duty of a tender loving subject toward his natural prince, or that his Grace should reckon in me any manner of obstinate heart against his pleasure in anything that ever I said or did concerning his great matter of his marriage or concerning the primacy of the Pope. Never would I wish other thing in this world more lief,[3] than that his Highness in these things all three, as perfectly knew my dealing, and as thoroughly saw my mind, as I do myself, or as God doth himself, whose sight pierceth deeper into my heart than mine own.

For, Sir, as for the first matter, that is to wit my letter or communication with the nun (the whole discourse whereof in my former letter I have as plainly declared unto you as I possibly can), so pray I God to withdraw that scruple and doubt of my good mind, out of the King's noble breast and none otherwise, but as I not only thought none harm, but also purposed good, and in that thing most, in which (as I perceive) his Grace conceiveth most grief and suspicion, that is to wit in my letter which I wrote unto her. And therefore Sir, sith I have by my writing declared the truth of my deed, and am ready by mine oath to declare the truth of mine intent, I can devise no further thing by me to be done in that matter, but only beseech almighty God to put into the King's gracious mind, that as God knoweth the thing is indeed, so his noble Grace may take it. Now touching the second point concerning his Grace's great matter of his marriage, to the intent that you may see cause with the better conscience to make suit unto his highness for me, I shall as plainly declare you my demeanor in that matter as I have already declared you in the other, for more plainly can I not.

Sir, upon a time at ⌐my coming from beyond the sea⌐, where I had been in the King's business, I repaired as my duty was unto the King's Grace being at that time ⌐at Hampton Court⌐. At which time suddenly his Highness ⌐walking in the gallery⌐, brake with me[4] of his great matter, and showed me that it was now perceived, that his marriage was not only against the positive laws of the Church and the written law of God, but also in such wise against the law of nature, that ⌐it could in no wise by the Church be dispensable⌐. Now so was it that before my going over the sea, I had heard certain things moved against ⌐the bull of the dispensation⌐ concerning the words of ⌐the Law Levitical and the Law Deuteronomical⌐ to prove the prohibition to be *de iure divino,* but yet perceived I not at that time but that the greater hope of the matter stood in certain faults that

3. more willingly, more dearly
4. *brake with me:* disclosed to me

49

were founden in the bull, whereby ⌜the bull should by the law not be sufficient⌝. And such comfort was there in that point, as far as I perceived a good season,[5] that the Council on the other part were fain[6] to bring forth a brief, by which they pretended those defaults to be supplied, the truth of which brief was by the King's Council suspected, and much diligence was thereafter done for the trial of that point, wherein what was finally founden, either I never knew, or else I not remember.

But I rehearse you this to the intent you shall know that the first time that ever I heard that point moved, that it should be in such high degree against the law of nature, was the time in which, as I began to tell you, the King's Grace showed it me himself, and laid the Bible open before me, and there read me the words that moved his Highness and divers other erudite persons so to think, and asked me further what myself thought thereon. At which time not presuming to look[7] that his Highness should anything take that point for the more proved or unproved for my poor mind in so great a matter, I showed nevertheless as my duty was at his commandment what thing I thought upon the words which I there read. Whereupon his Highness accepting benignly my sudden unadvised answer[8] commanded me to commune[9] further with ⌜Master Foxe, now his Grace's Almoner⌝, and to read ⌜a book with him that then was in making⌝ for that matter. After which book read, and my poor opinion eftsoons declared unto his Highness thereupon, his Highness, like a prudent and a virtuous prince, assembled at another time at Hampton Court a good number of very well learned men; at which time as far as ever I heard there were (as was in so great a matter most likely to be) diverse opinions among them. Howbeit I never heard but that they agreed at that time upon a certain form in which the book should be made, which book was afterward at York Palace in my Lord Cardinal's chamber read in the presence of divers bishops and many learned men. And they all thought that there appeared in the book good and reasonable causes that might well move the King's Highness, being so virtuous a prince, to conceive in his mind a scruple against his marriage, which, while he could not otherwise avoid, he did well and virtuously for the acquieting of his conscience to sue and procure[10] to have his doubt decided by judgment of the Church.

5. *a good season:* for some time
6. willing
7. expect
8. *sudden unadvised answer:* a quick answer not well informed
9. converse
10. cause

⌜After this the suit began⌝, and the Legates sat upon the matter, during all which time I never meddled therein, nor was a man meet to do, for the matter was in hand by an ordinary process of the spiritual[11] law, whereof I could little skill.[12] And yet while the Legates were sitting upon the matter, it pleased the King's Highness to send me in the company of ⌜my Lord of London, now of Durham⌝, in embassiate[13] about ⌜the peace that at our being there was concluded at Cambrai⌝, between his Highness and the Emperor and the French King. And after my coming home his Highness of his only goodness (as far unworthy as I was thereto) made me, as you well know, ⌜his Chancellor of this realm⌝, soon after which time his Grace moved me again yet eftsoons, to look and consider his great matter, and well and indifferently[14] to ponder such things as I should find therein. And if it so were that thereupon it should hap me to see such things as should persuade me to that part, he would gladly use me among other of his councilors in that matter, and nevertheless he graciously declared unto me that he would in no wise that I should other thing do or say therein, than upon that that I should perceive mine own conscience should serve me, and that I should first look unto God and after God unto him, which most gracious words was the first lesson also that ever his Grace gave me at my first coming into his noble service. This motion was to me very comfortable and much I longed, beside anything that myself either had seen or by further search should hap to find for the one part or the other, yet specially to have some conference in the matter with some such of his Grace's learned Council as most for his part had labored and most have found in the matter.

Whereupon his Highness assigned unto me the now most reverend fathers ⌜Archbishops of Canterbury and York⌝ with Master Doctor Foxe, now his Grace's Almoner and Master ⌜Doctor Nicholas⌝ the Italian friar. Whereupon I not only sought and read, and as far forth as my poor wit and learning served me, well weighed and considered every such thing as I could find myself, or read in any other man's labor that I could get, which anything had written therein, but had also diligent conference with his Grace's councilors aforesaid, whose honors and worships I nothing mistrust in this point, but that they both have and will report unto his Highness that they never found obstinate manner or fashion in me, but a mind

11. Church law
12. *I could little skill:* I had little knowledge of
13. embassy
14. impartially

as toward and as conformable[15] as reason could in a matter disputable require.

Whereupon the King's Highness being further advertised[16] both by them and myself of my poor opinion in the matter (wherein to have been able and meet to do him service I would as I then shewed his Highness have been more glad than of all such worldly commodities[17] as I either then had or ever should come to) his Highness, graciously taking in gre[18] my good mind in that behalf, used of his blessed disposition in the prosecuting of his great matter only those (of whom his Grace had good number) whose conscience his Grace perceived well and fully persuaded upon that part. And as well myself as any other to whom his Highness thought the thing to seem otherwise, ⌐he used in his other business¬, abiding (of his abundant goodness) nevertheless gracious lord unto any man, nor never was willing to put any man in ruffle[19] or trouble of his conscience.

After this did I never nothing more therein, nor never any word wrote I therein to the impairing of his Grace's part, neither before nor after, nor any man else by my procurement,[20] but settling my mind in quiet to serve his Grace in other things, I would not so much as look nor wittingly let lie by me any book of the other part, albeit that I gladly read afterward divers books that were made on his part yet, nor never would I read ⌐the book that Master Abell made¬ on the other side, nor other book which were as I heard say made in Latin beyond the sea, nor never give ear to the Pope's proceedings in the matter.

Moreover, whereas I had founden in my study a book that I had before borrowed of ⌐my Lord of Bath¬, which book he had made of the matter at such time as the Legates sat here thereupon, which book had been by me merely gently cast aside, and that I shewed him I would send him home his book again, he told me that in good faith he had long time before discharged his mind of that matter, and having forgotten that copy to remain in my hands, had burned his own copy that he had thereof at home, and because he no more minded[21] to meddle anything in the matter, he desired[22] me to burn the same book too. And upon my faith so did I.

15. disposed to agree
16. informed
17. advantages
18. *in gre:* in good part
19. disturbance
20. causation
21. intended
22. requested

Besides this, divers other ways have I so used myself that if I rehearsed them all, it should well appear that I never have had against his Grace's marriage any manner demeanor[23] whereby his Highness might have any manner cause or occasion of displeasure toward me. For likewise as I am not he which either can, or whom it could become,[24] to take upon him the determination or decision of such a weighty matter, nor boldly to affirm this thing or that therein, whereof diverse points a great way pass my learning, so am I he that among other his Grace's faithful subjects, his Highness being in possession of his marriage ⌜and this noble woman really anointed Queen⌝, neither murmur at it, nor dispute upon it, nor never did nor will, but without any other manner meddling of the matter among his other faithful subjects faithfully pray to God for his Grace and hers both, long to live and well and their noble issue too, in such wise as may be to the pleasure of God, honor and surety to themself, rest, peace, wealth, and profit unto this noble realm.

As touching the third point, the primacy of the Pope, I nothing meddle in the matter. Truth it is, that as I told you, when you desired me to shew you what I thought therein, I was myself sometime not of the mind that the primacy of that see should be begun by the institution of God, until that I read in that matter those things that the King's Highness had written in his most ⌜famous book against the heresies of Martin Luther⌝, at the first reading whereof I moved the King's Highness either to leave out that point, or else to touch it more slenderly[25] for doubt of such things as after might hap to fall in question between his Highness and some pope as between princes and popes divers times have done. Whereunto his Highness answered me that he would in no wise anything minish of that matter, of which thing his Highness shewed me a secret cause whereof I never had anything heard before. But surely after that I had read his Grace's book therein, and so many other things as I have seen in that point by this continuance of these ten years since and more have found in effect the substance of all ⌜the holy doctors⌝ from ⌜Saint Ignatius⌝, disciple to Saint John the Evangelist, unto our own days both Latins and Greeks so consonant and agreeing in that point, and the thing by such general councils so confirmed also, that in good faith I never neither read nor heard anything of such effect on the other side, that ever could lead me to think that my conscience were well discharged, but

23. any kind of behavior
24. befit
25. slightly, with less force

rather in right great peril if I should follow the other side and deny the primacy to be provided by God; which if we did, yet can I nothing (as I shewed you) perceive any commodity[26] that ever could come by that denial, for that primacy is at the leastwise instituted by the corps[27] of Christendom and for a great urgent cause in avoiding of schisms and corroborate[28] by continual succession more than the space of a thousand year at the least, for there are passed almost a thousand years sith the time of ⌐holy Saint Gregory⌐.

⌐And therefore sith all Christendom is one corps⌐, I cannot perceive how any member thereof may without the common assent of the body depart from the common head. And then, if we may not lawfully leave it by ourself, I cannot perceive (but if the thing were a treating[29] in a general council) what the question could avail whether the primacy were instituted by God or ordained by the Church. ⌐As for the general councils⌐ assembled lawfully, I never could perceive but that in the declaration of the truths it is to be believed and to be standen to;[30] the authority thereof ought to be taken for undoubtable, or else were there in nothing no certainty, but through Christendom upon every man's affectionate reason, all things might be brought from day to day to continual ruffle and confusion, from which by the general councils, the spirit of God assisting, every such council well assembled keepeth and ever shall keep ⌐the corps of his Catholic Church⌐.

And verily sith the King's Highness hath (as by the book of his honorable Council appeareth) appealed to the general council from the Pope, in which council I beseech our Lord send his Grace comfortable speed,[31] methinketh in my poor mind it could be no furtherance there unto his Grace's cause if his Highness should in his own realm before, either by laws making, or books putting forth, seem to derogate and deny not only ⌐the primacy of the See apostolic⌐, but also the authority of the general councils too, which I verily trust his Highness intendeth not, for in the next general council it may well happen that this Pope may be deposed and another substituted in his room with whom the King's Highness may be very well content. For albeit that I have for mine own part such opinion of the pope's primacy as I have shewed you, ⌐yet never thought I the Pope

26. advantage
27. body
28. corroborated
29. to be treated
30. obeyed
31. success, outcome

above the general council⌐ nor never have in any book of mine put forth among the King's subjects in our vulgar tongue, advanced greatly the Pope's authority. For albeit that a man may peradventure somewhat find therein that after the common manner of all Christian realms I speak of him as primate, yet never do I stick[32] thereon with reasoning and proving of that point. And in ⌐my book against the Masker⌐, I wrote not I wot well five lines, and yet of no more but only Saint Peter himself, from whose person many take not the primacy, even of those that grant it none of his successors, and yet was that book made, printed, and put forth of very truth before that any of the books of the Council was either printed or spoken of. But whereas I had written thereof at length in ⌐my confutation before⌐, and for the proof thereof had compiled together all that I could find therefor, at such time as I little looked[33] that there should fall between the King's Highness and the Pope such a breach as is fallen since, when I after saw the thing likely to draw towards such displeasure between them, I suppressed it utterly and never put word thereof into my book but put out the remnant without it, which thing well declareth that I never intended anything to meddle in that matter against the King's gracious pleasure, whatsoever mine own opinion were therein.

And thus have I, good Master Cromwell, long troubled your Mastership with a long process[34] of these matters, with which I neither durst nor it could become me to encumber the King's noble Grace, but I beseech you, for our Lord's love, that you be not so weary of my most cumbrous suit but that it may like[35] you at such opportune time or times as your wisdom may find to help that his Highness may by your goodness be fully informed of my true faithful mind, and that in the matter of that wicked woman there never was on my part any other mind[36] than good; nor yet in any other thing else never was there nor never shall there be any further fault found in me, than that I cannot in everything think the same way that some other men of more wisdom and deeper learning do; nor can find in mine heart otherwise to say than as mine own conscience giveth me, which condition hath never grown in anything that ever might touch his gracious pleasure of any obstinate mind or misaffectionate appetite,[37] but of a timorous conscience rising haply for lack of better perceiving, and

32. hesitate
33. expected
34. account
35. please
36. intention
37. disordered

yet not without tender respect unto my most bounden[38] duty toward his noble Grace, whose only favor I so much esteem that I nothing have of mine own in all this world, except only my soul, but that I will with better will forgo it than abide of his Highness one heavy displeasant look. And thus I make an end of my long troublous process, beseeching the blessed Trinity for the great goodness ye shew me, and the great comfort ye do me, both bodily and ghostly to prosper you, and in heaven to reward you. At Chelsea, the fifth day of March by

 Your deeply bounden,

Tho. More. Kg.

38. bound by more than legal obligation

6

To Margaret Roper

TOWER OF LONDON

circa 17 April 1534

Sir Thomas More, upon warning[1] given him, came before the King's
Commissioners at the Archbishop of Canterbury's palace at Lambeth (the
Monday, the thirteenth day of April, in the year of our Lord 1534, and in
the latter end of the twenty-fifth year of the reign of King Henry the
Eighth), where he refused the oath then offered unto him. And thereupon
was he delivered to ⌐the Abbot of Westminster⌐ to be kept as a prisoner,
with whom he remained till Friday following, and then was sent prisoner
to the ⌐Tower of London⌐. And shortly after his coming thither he wrote a
letter and sent unto his eldest daughter Mistress ⌐Margaret Roper⌐, the
copy whereof here followeth.

When I was before ⌐the Lords at Lambeth⌐, I was the first that was called in,
albeit, Master Doctor ⌐the Vicar of Croydon⌐ was come before me, and divers others. After the cause of my sending for, declared unto me (whereof I
somewhat marveled in my mind, considering that they sent for no more
temporal men[2] but me), I desired the sight of the oath, which they shewed
me under the great Seal. Then desired I the sight of the Act of the Succession, which was delivered me in a printed roll. After which read secretly by
myself, and the oath considered with the act, I shewed unto them that my
purpose was not to put any fault either in the act or any man that made it, or
in the oath or any man that sware it, nor to condemn the conscience of any

1. summons
2. laymen

other man. But as for myself in good faith my conscience so moved me in the matter, that though I would not deny to swear to the succession, yet unto the oath that there was offered me I could not swear without the jeoparding of my soul to ⌐perpetual damnation⌐. And that if they doubted whether I did refuse the oath only for the grudge[3] of my conscience, or for any other fantasy,[4] I was ready therein to satisfy them by mine oath. Which if they trusted not, what should they be the better to give me any oath? And if they trusted that I would therein swear true, then trusted I that of their goodness they would not move me to swear the oath that they offered me, perceiving that for to swear it was against my conscience.

Unto this ⌐my Lord Chancellor⌐ said that they all were sorry to hear me say thus, and see me thus refuse the oath. And they said all that on their faith I was the very first that ever refused it; which would cause the King's Highness to conceive great suspicion of me and great indignation toward me. And therewith they shewed me the roll, and let me see the names of the lords and the commons which had sworn, and subscribed their names already. Which notwithstanding when they saw that I refused to swear the same myself, not blaming[5] any other man that had sworn, I was in conclusion commanded to go down into the garden, and thereupon I tarried in the old burned chamber that looketh into the garden and would not go down ⌐because of the heat⌐. In that time saw I ⌐Master Doctor Latimer⌐ come into the garden, and there walked he with divers other doctors and chaplains of ⌐my Lord of Canterbury⌐, and very merry I saw him, for he laughed, and took one or twain about the neck so handsomely, that if they had been women, I would have went[6] he had been waxen wanton.[7] After that came ⌐Master Doctor Wilson⌐ forth from the lords and was with two gentlemen brought by me, and gentlemanly sent straight unto the Tower. What time ⌐my Lord of Rochester⌐ was called in before them, that cannot I tell. But at night I heard that he had been before them, but where he remained that night, and so forth till he was sent hither, I never heard. I heard also that Master Vicar of Croydon, and all the remnant of the priests of London that were sent for, were sworn, and that they had such favor at the Council's hand, that they were not lingered nor made to dance any long attendance to their travail[8] and cost, as suitors

3. murmur of conscience, uneasiness
4. caprice, delusion
5. condemning
6. supposed, thought
7. grown frivolous
8. hardship

were sometimes wont to be, but were sped apace to their great comfort, so far forth that Master Vicar of Croydon, either for gladness or for dryness, or else that it might be seen (⌐quod ille notus erat pontifici¬) went to my Lord's buttery bar,[9] and called for drink, and drank (⌐valde familiariter¬).

When they had played their pageant and were gone out of the palace, then I was called in again. And then was it declared unto me what a number had sworn, even since I went aside, gladly, without any sticking.[10] Wherein I laid no blame in no man, but for mine own self answered as before. Now as well before as then, they somewhat laid unto me for obstinacy, that where as before, sith I refused to swear, I would not declare any special part of that oath that grudged my conscience, and open the cause wherefore. For thereunto I had said to them that I feared lest the King's Highness would as they said take displeasure enough toward me for the only refusal[11] of the oath. And that if I should open and disclose the causes why, I should therewith but further exasperate his Highness, which I would in nowise do, but rather would I abide all the danger and harm that might come toward me, than give his Highness any occasion of further displeasure, than the offering of the oath unto me of pure necessity constrained me. Howbeit when they divers times imputed this to me for stubbornness and obstinacy that I would neither swear the oath, nor yet declare the causes why, I declined thus far toward them that rather than I would be accounted for obstinate, I would upon the King's gracious license or rather his such commandment had, as might be my sufficient warrant that my declaration should not offend his Highness, nor put me in the danger of any of his statutes, I would be content to declare the causes in writing; and over that to give an oath in the beginning, that if I might find those causes by any man in such wise answered, as I might think mine own conscience satisfied, I would after that with all mine heart swear the principal oath too.

To this I was answered that though the King would give me license under his letters patent, yet would it not serve against the statute. Whereto I said, that yet if I had them, I would stand unto the trust of his honor at my peril for the remnant. But yet, it thinketh me, lo, that if I may not declare the causes without peril, then to leave them undeclared is no obstinacy.

⌐My Lord of Canterbury¬ taking hold upon that that I said, that I

---

9. ledge on top of the buttery hatch (pantry), to serve drinks and food
10. hesitation
11. *for the only refusal:* only for the refusal

condemned not the conscience of them that sware, said unto me that it appeared well that I did not take it for a very sure thing and a certain, that I might not lawfully swear it, but rather as a thing uncertain and doubtful. "But then," said my Lord, "you know for a certainty and a thing without doubt, that you be bounden to obey your sovereign lord your King. And therefore are ye bounden to leave off the doubt of your unsure conscience in refusing the oath, and take the sure way in obeying of your prince, and swear it." Now al[12] was it so that in mine own mind methought myself not concluded,[13] yet this argument seemed me suddenly so subtle and namely[14] with such authority coming out of so noble[15] a prelate's mouth, that I could again answer nothing thereto but only that I thought myself I might not well do so, because that in my conscience this was one of the cases in which I was bounden that I should not obey my prince, sith that whatsoever other folk thought in the matter (whose conscience and learning I would not condemn nor take upon me to judge) yet in my conscience the truth seemed on the other side. Wherein I had not informed my conscience neither suddenly nor slightly, but by long leisure and diligent search for the matter. And of truth if that reason may conclude,[16] then have we a ready way to avoid all perplexities. For in whatsoever matters the doctors stand in great doubt, the King's commandment given upon ⌐whither side he list soileth all the doubts⌐.[17]

Then said ⌐my Lord of Westminster⌐ to me, that howsoever the matter seemed unto mine own mind, I had cause to fear that mine own mind was erroneous, when I see the great council of the realm determine of my mind the contrary, and that therefore I ought to change my conscience. To that I answered, that if there were no mo[18] but myself upon my side and the whole Parliament upon the other, I would be sore afraid to lean to mine own mind only against so many. But on the other side, if it so be that in some things for which I refuse the oath, I have (as I think I have) upon my part as great a council and a greater too, I am not then bounden to change my conscience, and confirm[19] it to the council of one realm, against the general council of Christendom. Upon this ⌐Master Secretary⌐

12. although
13. not legally bound
14. especially
15. notable
16. if that reason can legally oblige
17. whichever side he is pleased upon solves all doubts
18. more
19. conform

(as he that tenderly favoreth me), said and sware a great oath, that he had lever[20] that ⌜his own only son⌝ (which is of truth a goodly young gentleman, and shall I trust come to much worship) had lost his head than that I should thus have refused the oath. For surely the King's Highness would now conceive a great suspicion against me, and think that the matter of the nun of Canterbury was all contrived[21] by my drift.[22] To which I said that the contrary was true and well known, and whatsoever should mishap me,[23] it lay not in my power to help it without peril of my soul. Then did my Lord Chancellor repeat before me my refusal unto Master Secretary, as to him that was going unto the King's Grace. And in the rehearsing, his Lordship repeated again that I denied not but was content to swear to the succession. Whereunto I said, that as for that point, I would be content, so that I might see my oath in that point so framed[24] in such a manner as might stand with my conscience.

Then said my Lord: "Marry,[25] Master Secretary, mark that too, that he will not swear that neither, but under some certain manner." "Verily not, my Lord," quoth I, "but that I will see it made in such wise first, as I shall myself see, that I shall neither be forsworn nor swear against my conscience. Surely as to swear to the succession I see no peril, but I thought and think it reason, that to mine own oath I look well myself, and be of counsel also in the fashion, and never intended to swear for a piece,[26] and set my hand to the whole oath. Howbeit (as help me God), as touching the whole oath, I never withdrew any man from it, nor never advised any to refuse it, nor never put, nor will, any scruple in any man's head, ⌜but leave every man to his own conscience⌝. And methinketh in good faith that so were it good reason that every man ⌜should leave me to mine⌝."

20. rather
21. designed
22. scheme
23. befall me
24. composed
25. *Marry:* the name of the Virgin Mary used as a mild oath (OED)
26. part

7

To Margaret Roper

TOWER OF LONDON

April-May? 1534

A letter ⌐written with a coal⌐ by Sir Thomas More to his daughter Mistress Margaret Roper, within a while after he was prisoner in the Tower.

MINE OWN GOOD DAUGHTER.

Our Lord be thanked, I am in good health of body, and ⌐in good quiet of mind⌐: and ⌐of worldly things I no more desire than I have⌐. I beseech him make you all merry in the hope of heaven. And such things as I somewhat longed to talk with you all, concerning the world to come, our Lord put them into your minds, as I trust he doth, and better too, by his Holy Spirit: who bless you and preserve you all. Written with a coal by your tender loving father, who in his poor prayers forgeteth none of you all, nor your babes, nor your nurses, nor your good husbands, nor your good husbands' shrewd[1] wives, nor your father's shrewd wife neither, nor our other friends. And thus fare you heartily well for lack of paper.

Thomas More, Knight.

Our Lord keep me continually true faithful and plain,[2] to the contrary whereof I beseech him heartily never to suffer me live. For as long life (as I have often told thee, Meg) I neither look for, nor long for, but am well con-

1. clever (in More's jesting use)
2. straightforward

tent to go, if God call me hence tomorrow. And I thank our Lord I know no person living that I would had one fillip[3] for my sake, of which mind I am more glad than of all the world beside.

Recommend me to ⌐your shrewd Will¬ and ⌐mine other sons¬, and to ⌐John Harris¬, my friend, and yourself knoweth to whom else, and to ⌐my shrewd wife above all¬, and God preserve you all, and make and keep you his servants all.

3. a flick of the finger released from the thumb

⇥ 8 ⇤

To Margaret Roper

TOWER OF LONDON

May 1534

Within a while after Sir Thomas More was in prison in the Tower, his daughter Mistress Margaret Roper wrote and sent unto him a letter, wherein she seemed somewhat to labor to persuade him to take the oath (though she nothing so thought) to win thereby credence with Master Thomas Cromwell, that she might the rather get liberty to have free resort unto her father (which she only[1] had for the most time of his imprisonment) unto which letter her father wrote an answer, the copy whereof here followeth.

OUR LORD BLESS YOU ALL.

If I had not been, my dearly beloved daughter, at a firm and fast[2] point (I trust in God's great mercy) this good great while before, ⌐your lamentable[3] letter¬ had not little abashed me,[4] surely far above all other things, of which I hear divers times not a few terrible toward me. But surely they all touched me never so near, nor were so grievous unto me, as to see you, my well beloved child, in such vehement piteous manner labor to persuade unto me that thing wherein I have of pure necessity for respect unto mine own soul, so often given you so precise answer before. Wherein as touching the points of your letter, I can make none answer, for

1. alone
2. steadfast
3. pitiable, deplorable
4. confounded me

64

I doubt not but you well remember that the matters which move my conscience (without declaration whereof I can nothing touch the points) I have sundry times shewed you that I will disclose them to no man. And therefore, daughter Margaret, I can in this thing no further, but like as you labor me again to follow your mind, to desire and pray you both again to leave off such labor, and with my former answers to hold yourself content.

A deadly grief unto me, and much more deadly than to hear of mine own death (for the fear thereof, I thank our Lord, the fear of hell, the hope of heaven and the passion of Christ daily more and more assuage), is that I perceive my good son your husband, and you my good daughter, and my good wife, and mine other good children and innocent friends, in great displeasure and danger of great harm thereby. The let[5] whereof, while it lieth not in my hand, I can no further but commit all unto God. ⌜Nam in manu Dei, says the Scripture, cor regis est, et sicut divisiones aquarum quocumque voluerit, impellit illud⌝, whose high goodness I most humbly beseech to incline the noble heart of the King's Highness to the tender favor of you all, and to favor me no better than God and my self know that my faithful heart toward him and my daily prayer for him, do deserve. For surely if his Highness might inwardly see my true mind such as God knoweth it is, it would (I trust) soon assuage his high displeasure. Which while I can in this world never in such wise shew, but that his Grace may be persuaded to believe the contrary of me, I can no further go, but put all in the hands of him, for fear of whose displeasure for the safeguard of my soul stirred by mine own conscience (without insectation[6] or reproach laying to any other man's) I suffer and endure this trouble. Out of which I beseech him to bring me, when his will shall be, into his endless bliss of heaven, and in the meanwhile, give me grace and you both in all our agonies and troubles, devoutly to resort prostrate unto ⌜the remembrance of that bitter agony⌝, which our Saviour suffered before his passion at the Mount. And if we diligently so do, I verily trust we shall find therein great comfort and consolation. And thus, my dear daughter, the blessed spirit of Christ for his tender mercy govern and guide you all, to his pleasure and your weal and comfort both body and soul.

Your tender loving father,

Thomas More, Knight

5. hindrance, obstacle
6. calumniation

9

From Margaret Roper

May? 1534

To this last letter Mistress Margaret Roper wrote an answer and sent it to Sir Thomas More her father, the copy whereof here followeth.

MINE OWN GOOD FATHER.

It is to me no little comfort,[1] sith I cannot talk with you by such means as I would, at the least way to delight myself among in this bitter time of your absence, by such means as I may, by as often writing to you as shall be expedient and by reading again and again your most fruitful and delectable letter, the faithful messenger of your very virtuous and ghostly mind, rid from all corrupt love of worldly things, ⌐and fast knit only in the love of God⌐, and desire of heaven, as becometh a very true worshipper and a faithful servant of God, which I doubt not, good father, holdeth his holy hand over you and shall (as he hath) preserve you both body and soul, ⌐ut sit mens sana in corpore sano⌐, and namely, now when you have abjected[2] all earthly consolations and resigned yourself willingly, gladly and fully for his love to his holy protection.

Father, what think you hath been our comfort since your departing from us? Surely the experience we have had of ⌐your life past and godly[3] conversation⌐, and wholesome counsel, and virtuous example, and a surety not only of the continuance of the same, but also a great increase by

1. strength and consolation
2. rejected, cast off
3. spiritual

the goodness of our Lord to the great rest and gladness of your heart devoid of all earthly dregs, and garnished with the noble vesture of heavenly virtues, a pleasant palace for the Holy Spirit of God to rest in, who defend you (as I doubt not, good father, but of his goodness he will) from all trouble of mind and of body, and give me, your most loving obedient daughter and handmaid, and all us your children and friends, to follow that that we praise in you, and to our only comfort remember and coming together of you,[4] that we may in conclusion meet with you, mine own dear father, in the bliss of heaven to which our most merciful Lord ⌐has bought us with his precious blood⌐.

Your own most loving obedient daughter and beadswoman, Margaret Roper, which desireth above all worldly things to be ⌐in John Wood's stead⌐ to do you some service. But we live in hope that we shall shortly receive you again, I pray God heartily we may, if it be his holy will.

4. *coming together of you:* coming together by means of you

To All His Friends

TOWER OF LONDON

1534

Within a while after Sir Thomas More had been in prison in the Tower, his daughter Mistress Margaret Roper obtained license of the King, that she might resort unto her father in the Tower, which she did. And thereupon he wrote with a coal a letter ⌐to all his friends⌐, whereof the copy followeth.

TO ALL MY LOVING FRIENDS.

For as much as being in prison I cannot tell what need I may have, or what necessity I may hap to stand in, I heartily beseech you all, that if my well-beloved daughter Margaret Roper (which only of all my friends hath by the King's gracious favour license to resort to me) do anything desire of any of you, of such thing as I shall hap to need, that it may like you no less to regard and tender it, than if I moved it unto you and required it of you personally present myself. And I beseech you all to pray for me, and I shall pray for you.

Your faithful lover and poor beadsman,

Thomas More, Knight, prisoner.

Alice Alington to Margaret Roper

17 August 1534

In August in the year of our Lord 1534 and in the twenty-sixth year of the reign of King Henry the Eighth, the Lady ⌐Alice Alington¬ (wife to Sir Giles Alington, Knight, and daughter to Sir Thomas More's second and last wife) wrote a letter to Mistress Margaret Roper, the copy whereof here followeth.

Sister Roper, with all my heart I recommend me unto you, thanking you for all kindness.

The cause of my writing at this time is to show you that ⌐at my coming home¬ within two hours after, my Lord Chancellor did come to take a course at[1] a buck in our park, the which was to my husband a great comfort that it would please him so to do. Then when he had taken his pleasure and killed his deer he went unto ⌐Sir Thomas Barmeston¬ to bed, where I was the next day with him at his desire, the which I could not say nay to, for methought he did bid me heartily, and most specially because I would speak to him for my father.

And when I saw my time,[2] I did desire him as humbly as I could that he would, as I have heard say that he hath been, be still good lord unto my father. And he said it did appear very well when ⌐the matter of the nun¬ was laid to his charge. And as for this other matter, he marveled that my father is so obstinate in his own conceit, as that everybody went forth with

---

1. to hunt
2. *when I saw my time:* when I saw my chance

all ⌐save only the blind³ Bishop⌐ and he. "And in good faith," said my Lord, "I am very glad that I have no learning but in a few of Aesop's fables of the which I shall tell you one. There was a country in the which there were almost none but fools, saving a few which were wise. And they by their wisdom knew, that there should fall a great rain, the which should make them all fools, that should so be fouled or wet therewith. They seeing that, made them caves under the ground till all the rain was past. Then they came forth thinking to make the fools do what they list,⁴ and to rule them as they would. But the fools would none of that, but would have the rule themselves for all their craft. And when the wisemen saw they could not obtain their purpose, they wished that they had been in the rain, and had defoiled⁵ their clothes with them."

When this tale was told my Lord did laugh very merrily. Then I said to him that for all his merry fable I did put no doubts but that he would be good lord unto my father when he saw his time. He said, "I would not have your father so scrupulous of his conscience." And then he told me another fable of a lion, an ass, and a wolf and of their confession. First the lion confessed him⁶ that he had devoured all the beasts that he could come by. His confessor assoiled him because he was a king and also it was his nature so to do. Then came the poor ass and said that he took but one straw out of his master's shoe for hunger, by the means whereof he thought that his master did take cold. His confessor could not assoil this great trespass, but by and by⁷ sent him to the bishop. Then came the wolf and made his confession, and he was straitly⁸ commanded that he should not pass sixpence at a meal. But when this said wolf had used this diet a little while, he waxed very hungry, in so much that on a day when he saw a cow with her calf come by him he said to himself, "I am very hungry and fain would I eat, but that I am bounden by my ghostly father⁹. Notwithstanding that, my conscience shall judge me. And then if it be so, then shall my conscience be thus, that the cow doth seem to me now but worth a groat,¹⁰ and then, if the cow be but worth a groat then is the calf but worth twopence." So did the wolf eat both the cow and the calf. Now,

3. obstinate
4. pleased
5. defiled
6. himself
7. at once
8. strictly
9. spiritual father, confessor
10. silver coin worth fourpence

good sister, hath not my lord told me two pretty[11] fables? In good faith they please me nothing, nor I wist[12] not what to say for I was abashed of this answer. And I see no better suit than to Almighty God, for he is the comforter of all sorrows, and will not fail to send his comfort to his servants when they have most need. Thus fare ye well, mine own good sister.

Written the Monday after Saint Lawrence in haste by Your sister Dame,

Alice Alington.

11. clever, astute
12. knew

➤ 12 ⬅

Margaret Roper to Alice Alington

August 1534

When Mistress Roper had received a letter from her sister Lady Alice Alington, she at her next repair to her father, shewed him the letter. And what communication was thereupon between her father and her, ye shall perceive by an answer here following (as written to the Lady Alington). ⌜But whether this answer were written by Sir Thomas More⌝ in his daughter Roper's name, or by himself it is not certainly known.

When I came next unto my father after, methought it both convenient[1] and necessary, to shew him your letter. Convenient, that he might thereby see your loving labor[2] taken for him. Necessary, that sith he might perceive thereby, that if he stand still in this scruple of his conscience (as it is at the leastwise called by many that are his friends and wise) all his friends that seem most able to do him good either shall finally forsake him, or peradventure not be able indeed to do him any good at all.

And for these causes, at my next being with him after your letter received, when I had a while talked with him, first ⌜of his diseases⌝, both in his breast of old, and his reins[3] now by reason of gravel and stone, and of the cramp also that divers nights gripeth him in his legs, and that I found by his words that they were not much increased, but continued after their manner that they did before, sometime very sore and sometime little grief,

1. appropriate
2. concerned trouble
3. kidneys

72

and that at that time I found him out of pain, and (as one in his case[4] might), meetly well minded,[5] after our ⌐seven psalms and the litany¬ said, to sit and talk and be merry, beginning first with other things of the good comfort of my mother, and the good order[6] of my brother, and all my sisters, disposing themself every day more and more to set little by the world, and draw more and more to God, and that his household, his neighbors, and other good friends abroad, diligently remembered him in their prayers, I added unto this: "I pray God, good Father, that their prayers and ours, and your own therewith, may purchase of God the grace, that you may in this great matter (for which you stand in this trouble and for your trouble all we also that love you) take such a way by time,[7] as standing with the pleasure of God, may content and please the King, whom you have always founden so singularly gracious unto you, that if ye should stiffly refuse[8] to do the thing that were his pleasure, which God not displeased you might do (as many great wise and well learned men say that in this thing you may) it would both be a great blot in your worship[9] in every wise man's opinion and as myself have heard some say (such as yourself have always taken for well learned and good) a peril unto your soul also. But as for that point, Father, will I not be bold to dispute upon, sith I trust in God and your good mind, that ye will look surely thereto. And your learning I know for such, that I wot well you can. But one thing is there which I and other your friends find and perceive abroad, which but if it be shewed you, you may peradventure to your great peril, mistake and hope for less harm (for as for good I wot well in this world of this matter ye look for none) than I sore fear me, shall be likely to fall to you. For I assure you Father, I have received a letter of late from my sister Alington, by which I see well that if ye change not your mind, you are likely to lose all those friends that are able to do you any good. Or if ye lose not their good wills, ye shall at the leastwise lose the effect thereof, for any good that they shall be able to do you."

With this my father smiled upon me and said: "⌐What, mistress Eve¬ (as I called you when you came first), hath my daughter Alington played the serpent with you, and with a letter set you at work to come tempt your father again, and for the favor that you bear him labor to make him swear

4. situation
5. disposed
6. condition
7. *by time:* at once
8. obstinately
9. dignity

against his conscience, and so send him to the devil?" And after that, he looked sadly again, and earnestly said unto me, "Daughter Margaret, we two have talked of this thing ofter than twice or thrice, and that same tale in effect, that you tell me now therein, and the same fear too, have you twice told me before, and I have twice answered you too, that in this matter if it were possible for me to do the thing that might content the King's Grace, and God therewith not offended, there hath no man taken this oath already more gladly than I would do: as he that reckoneth himself more deeply bounden unto the King's Highness for his most singular bounty, many ways shewed and declared, than any of them all beside. But sith standing my conscience, I can in nowise do it, and that for the instruction of my conscience in the matter, I have not slightly looked, but by many years studied and advisedly[10] considered, and never could yet see nor hear that thing, nor I think I never shall, that could induce mine own mind to think otherwise than I do, I have no manner remedy, but ⌜God hath given me to the straight,⌝ that either I must deadly displease him, or abide any worldly harm that he shall for mine other sins, under name of this thing, suffer to fall upon me. Whereof (as I before this have told you too) I have ere I came here, not left unbethought nor unconsidered, the very worst and the uttermost that can by possibility fall. And albeit that I know mine own frailty full well and the natural faintness of mine own heart, yet if I had not trusted that God should give me strength rather to endure all things, than offend him by swearing ungodly[11] against mine own conscience, you may be very sure I would not have come here. And sith I look in this matter but only unto God, it maketh me little matter, though men call it as it pleaseth them and say it is no conscience but a foolish scruple."

At this word I took a good occasion,[12] and said unto him thus: "In good faith, Father, for my part, I neither do, nor it cannot become me, either to mistrust your good mind or your learning. But because you speak of that that some call it but a scruple, I assure you you shall see by my sister's letter, that ⌜one of the greatest estates⌝[13] in this realm and a man learned too, and (as I dare say yourself shall think when you know him, and as you have already right effectually proved him) your tender friend and very special good lord, accounteth your conscience in this matter for a

10. deliberately
11. wickedly
12. *took a good occasion:* took advantage of a good opportunity
13. dignitaries

right simple scruple, and you may be sure he saith it of good mind and layeth no little cause. For he saith that where you say your conscience moveth you to this, all the nobles of this realm and almost all other men too, go boldly forth with the contrary, and stick not thereat, save only yourself ⌐and one other man⌐: whom though he be right good and very well learned too, yet would I ween,[14] few that love you, give you the counsel against all other men to lean to his mind alone."

And with this word I took[15] him your letter, that he might see my words were not feigned, but spoken of his mouth, whom he much loveth and esteemeth highly. Thereupon he read over your letter. And when he came to the end, he began it afresh and read it over again. And in the reading he made no manner haste, but advised[16] it leisurely and pointed[17] every word.

And after that he paused, and then thus he said: "Forsooth, daughter Margaret, I find my daughter Alington such as I have ever found her, and I trust ever shall, as naturally minding me as you that are mine own. Howbeit, her take I verily for mine own too, sith I have married her mother, and brought up her of a child as I have brought up you, in other things and learning both, wherein I thank God she findeth now some fruit,[18] and bringeth her own up very virtuously and well. Whereof God, I thank him, hath sent her good store,[19] our Lord preserve them and send her much joy of them and my good son her gentle husband too, and have mercy on the soul of ⌐mine other good son her first⌐; I am daily beadsman (and so write her) for them all.

"In this matter she hath used herself like herself, wisely and like a very daughter toward me, and in the end of her letter giveth as good counsel as any man that wit hath would wish; God give me grace to follow it and God reward her for it. Now daughter Margaret, as for my Lord, I not only think, but have also found it, that he is undoubtedly my singular[20] good lord. And in mine other business concerning the silly[21] nun, as my cause was good and clear,[22] so was he my good lord therein, and Master

14. think, suppose
15. gave
16. considered
17. emphasized or paused at
18. spiritual fruit
19. supply
20. special, exceptional
21. helpless, naive
22. pure, innocent, blameless

Secretary my good master too. For which I shall never cease to be faithful beadsman for them both and daily do I by my truth,[23] pray for them as I do for myself. And whensoever it should happen (which I trust in God shall never happen) that I be found other than a true man to my prince, let them never favour me neither of them both, nor of truth no more it could become them to do.

"But in this matter, Meg, to tell the truth between thee and me, ⌐my lord's Aesop fables¬ do not greatly move me. But as his wisdom for his pastime told them merrily to mine own daughter, so shall I for my pastime, answer them to thee, Meg, that art mine other daughter. The first fable of the rain that washt away all their wits that stood abroad when it fell, I have heard oft or[24] this: It was a tale so often told among the King's Council by ⌐my Lord Cardinal¬ when his Grace was chancellor, that I cannot lightly forget it. For of truth in times past, when variance[25] began to fall between ⌐the Emperor and the French King¬, in such wise that they were likely, and did indeed, fall together at war, and that there were in the Council here sometime sundry opinions, in which some were of the mind, that they thought it wisdom, that we should sit still and let them alone; but evermore against that way, my Lord used this fable of those wise men, that because they would not be washed with the rain that should make all the people fools, went themself into caves, and hid them under the ground. But when the rain had once made all the remnant fools and that they come out of their caves and would utter their wisdom, the fools agreed together against them, and there all to beat them. And so said his Grace that if we would be so wise that we would sit in peace while the fools fought, they would not fail after to make peace and agree, and fall at length all upon us. I will not dispute upon his Grace's counsel, and I trust we never made war but as reason would.[26] But yet this fable, for his part, did in his days help the King and the realm ⌐to spend many a fair penny¬. But that gear[27] is passed, and ⌐his Grace is gone¬, our Lord assoil his soul.

"And therefore shall I now come to this Aesop's fable, as my Lord full merrily laid it forth for me. If those wisemen, Meg, when the rain was gone at their coming abroad, where they found all men fools, wished themselves fools too, because they could not rule them, then seemeth it, that the foolish rain was so sore a shower, that even through the ground it sank

23. *by my truth:* upon my honor
24. *oft or:* often before
25. disagreement, discord
26. according to reason
27. matter, business

into their caves, and poured down upon their heads, and wet them to the skin, and made them more noddies[28] than them that stood abroad. For if they had had any wit, they might well see, that though they had been fools too, that thing would not have sufficed to make them the rulers over the other fools, no more than the other fools over them: and of so many fools all might not be rulers. Now when they longed so sore to bear a rule among fools, that so they so might, they would be glad to lose their wit and be fools too, the foolish rain had washed them meetly well. Howbeit, to say the truth, before the rain came, if they thought that all the remnant should turn into fools, and then either were so foolish that they would, or so mad to think that they should, so few rule so many fools, and had not so much wit as to consider, that there are none so unruly as they that lack wit and are fools, then were these wise men stark fools before the rain came. Howbeit daughter Roper, whom my Lord taketh here for the wise men and whom he meaneth to be fools, I cannot very well geast,[29] I cannot well read such riddles. For as Davus saith in Terence, *Non sum Œdipus,* I may say you wot well, ⌜*Non sum Œdipus, sed Morus*⌝, which name of mine what it signifieth in Greek, I need not tell you. But I trust my Lord reckoneth me among the fools, and so reckon I myself, ⌜as my name is in Greek⌝. And I find, I thank God, causes not a few, wherefore I so should in very deed.

"But surely among those that long to be rulers, God and mine own conscience clearly knoweth, that no man may ⌜truly number and reckon me⌝. And I ween each other man's conscience can tell himself the same, since it is so well known, that of the King's great goodness, I was one of the greatest rulers in this noble realm and that at mine own great labor by his great goodness discharged. But whomsoever my Lord meaneth for the wise men, and whomsoever his Lordship take for the fools, and whomsoever long for the rule, and whomsoever long for none, I beseech our Lord make us all so wise as that we may, every man here, so wisely rule ourself in this time of tears, this vale of misery, this simple wretched world (⌜in which as Boethius saith⌝, one man to be proud that he beareth rule over other men, is much like as one mouse would be proud to bear a rule over other mice in a barn), God, I say, give us the grace so wisely to rule ourself here, that when we shall hence in haste to meet the great Spouse, we be not taken sleepers and for lack of light in our lamps, shut out of heaven among ⌜the five foolish virgins⌝.

28. fools
29. guess

"⌜The second fable, Marget, seemeth not to be Aesop's⌝. For by that[30] the matter goeth all upon confession, it seemeth to be feigned since[31] Christendom began. For in Greece before Christ's days they used not confession, no more the men then than the beasts now. And Aesop was a Greek, and died long ere Christ was born. But what? who made it, maketh little matter. Nor I envy not that Aesop hath the name. But surely it is somewhat too subtle for me. For whom his Lordship understandeth by the lion and the wolf, which both twain confessed themself of ravin and devouring of all that came to their hands, and the one enlarged his conscience at his pleasure in the construction[32] of his penance, nor whom by the good discreet confessor that enjoined the one a little penance, and the other none at all, and sent the poor ass to the bishop, of all these things can I nothing tell. But by the foolish scrupulous ass, that had so sore[33] a conscience, for the taking of a straw for hunger out of his master's shoe, my Lord's other words of my scruple declare, that his Lordship merrily meant that by me: signifying (as it seemeth by that similitude) that of oversight and folly, my scrupulous conscience taketh for a great perilous thing toward my soul, if I should swear this oath, which thing as his Lordship thinketh, were indeed but a trifle. And I suppose well, Margaret, as you told me right now, that so thinketh many mo beside, as well spiritual as temporal,[34] and that even of those, that for their learning and their virtue myself not a little esteem. And yet albeit that I suppose this to be true, yet believe I not even very surely, that every man so thinketh that so saith. But though they did, Daughter, that would not make much to me, not though I should see ⌜my Lord of Rochester say the same⌝, and swear the oath himself before me too.

"For whereas you told me right now, that such as love me, would not advise me, that against all other men, I should lean unto his mind alone, verily, Daughter, no more I do. For albeit, that of very truth, I have him in that reverent estimation, that I reckon in this realm no one man, in wisdom, learning and long approved virtue together, meet to be matched and compared with him, yet that in this matter I was not led by him, very well and plainly appeareth, both in that I refused the oath before it was offered him, and in that also that his Lordship was content to have sworn of that oath (as I perceived since by you when you moved me to the same) either

30. *by that:* since
31. invented after
32. interpretation
33. troubled
34. clergy and lay people

78

somewhat more, or in some other manner than ever I minded to do. Verily, Daughter, I never intend (God being my good lord) to pin my soul at another man's back, not even the best man that I know this day living; for I know not whither[35] he may hap to carry it. There is no man living, of whom while he liveth, I may make myself sure. Some may do for favor, and some may do for fear, and so might they carry my soul a wrong way. And some might hap to frame himself a conscience and think that while he did it for fear God would forgive it. And some may peradventure think that they will repent, and be shriven thereof, and that so God shall remit it them. And some may be peradventure of that mind, that ⌐if they say one thing and think the while the contrary⌐, God more regardeth their heart than their tongue, and that therefore their oath goeth upon that[36] they think, and not upon that they say, ⌐as a woman reasoned once⌐, I trow,[37] Daughter, you were by. But in good faith, Marget, I can use no such ways in so great a matter: but like as if mine own conscience served me, I would not let to do it, though other men refused, so though other refuse it not, I dare not do it, mine own conscience standing against it. If I had (as I told you) looked but lightly for the matter, I should have cause to fear. But now have I so looked for it and so long, that I purpose at the leastwise to have no less regard unto my soul, than had once a poor honest man of the country that was called Company."

And with this, he told me a tale, I ween I can scant[38] tell it you again, because it hangeth[39] upon some terms and ceremonies of the law. But as far as I can call to mind my father's tale was this, that there is a court belonging of course unto every fair, to do justice in such things as happen within the same. This court hath a pretty fond[40] name, but I cannot happen upon it, but it beginneth with a pie, and the remnant goeth much like the name of a knight that I have known, I wis[41] (and I trow you too, for he hath been at my father's often or[42] this, as such time as you were there), a meetly[43] tall black[44] man, his name was Sir William Pounder. But, tut, let

35. to what place
36. what
37. believe
38. hardly
39. depends
40. foolish
41. think
42. before
43. fairly
44. dark

the name of the court go for this once, or call it if ye will, a court of ⌜pie Sir William Pounder. But this was the matter, lo, that upon a time at such a court holden at Bartholomew fair⌝, there was ⌜an escheator of London⌝ that had arrested a man that was outlawed, and had seized his goods that he had brought into the fair, tolling[45] him out of the fair by a train.[46] The man that was arrested and his goods seized was a northern man, which by his friends made the escheator within the fair to be arrested upon an action, I wot nere what,[47] and so was he brought before the judge of the court of pie Sir William Pounder, and at the last the matter came to a certain ceremony to be tried by a quest of twelve men, a jury as I remember they call it, or else a perjury.

Now had the clothman by friendship of the officers, founden the means to have all the quest almost, made of the northern men, such as had their booths there standing in the fair. Now was it come to the last day in the afternoon, and the twelve men had heard both the parties, and their counsel tell their tales at the bar, and were from the bar had[48] into a place, to talk and common, and agree upon their sentence. Nay let me speak better in my terms yet, I trow the judge giveth the sentence and the quest's tale[49] is called a verdict. They were scant come in together, but the northern men were agreed, and in effect all the other too, to cast[50] our London escheator. They thought they needed no more to prove that he did wrong, than even ⌜the name of his bare office alone⌝. But then was there then, as the devil would, this honest man of another quarter, that was called Company. And because the fellow seemed but a fool and sat still and said nothing, they made no reckoning of him, but said, "We be agreed now, come let us go give our verdict."

Then when the poor fellow saw that they made such haste, and his mind nothing gave him that way that theirs did (if their minds gave them that way that they said), he prayed them to tarry and talk upon the matter and tell him such reason therein, that he might think as they did: and when he so should do, he would be glad to say with them, or else he said they must pardon him. For sith he had a soul of his own to keep as they had, he must say as he thought for his, as they must for theirs. When they heard this, they were half angry with him. "What good fellow," ⌜quoth one of the northern

45. taking
46. by means of a trick, entrapment
47. I know not what
48. taken
49. jury's statement
50. convict

men⌐, 'where wonnes thou?[51] Be not we eleven here and you but one la alone,[52] and all we agreed? Whereto shouldst you stick? What is thy name good fellow?" "Masters," quoth he, "my name is called Company." "Company," quoth they, "now by thy truth good fellow, play then the good companion, come thereon further with us and pass even for good company." "Would God, good masters," quoth the man again, "that there lay no more weight thereby. But now when we shall hence and come before God, and that he shall send you to heaven for doing according to your conscience, and me to the devil for doing against mine, in passing at your request here for good company now, by God, Master Dickonson (that was one of the northern men's name) if I shall then say to all you again: Masters, I went once for good company with you, which is the cause that I go now to hell, play you the good fellows now again with me, as I went then for good company with you, so some of you go now for good company with me. Would ye go, Master Dickonson? Nay nay by our Lady, nor never one of you all. And therefore must ye pardon me from passing as you pass, but if I thought in the matter as you do, I dare not in such a matter pass for good company. For the passage of my poor soul passeth all good company."

And when my father had told me this tale, then said he further thus: "I pray thee now, good Marget, tell me this, Wouldst you wish thy poor father being at the leastwise somewhat learned, less to regard the peril of his soul than did there the honest unlearned man? I meddle not (you wot well) with the conscience of any man that hath sworn, nor I take not upon me to be their judge. But now if they do well, and that their conscience grudge them not, if I with my conscience to the contrary, should for good company pass on with them and swear as they do, when all our souls hereafter shall pass out of this world, and stand in judgment at the bar before the high Judge, if he judge them to heaven and me to the devil, because I did as they did, not thinking as they thought, if I should then say (as the good man Company said): Mine old good lords and friends, naming such a lord and such, yea and some bishops peradventure of such as I love best, I sware because you sware, and went that way that you went, do likewise for me now, let me not go alone; if there be any good fellowship with you, some of you come with me: by my truth, Marget, I may say to thee, in secret counsel, here between us twain (but let it go no further, I beseech thee

---

51. *where wonnes thou:* where are you? what's the matter with you? See Commentary.

52. *one la alone:* Northern vowels matching "lo alone" of the standard English. "La" is an emphatic particle in Middle English.

heartily). I find the friendship of this wretched world so fickle, that for any thing that I could treat[53] or pray, that would for good fellowship go to the devil with me, among them all I ween I should not find one. And then by God, Marget, if you think so too, best it is I suppose that for any respect of them all were they twice as many more as they be, I have myself a respect to mine own soul."

"Surely, Father," quoth I, "without any scruple at all, you may be bold I dare say for to sware that. But Father, they that think you should not refuse to swear the thing, that you see so many so good men and so well learned swear before you, mean not that you should swear to bear them fellowship, nor to pass with them, for good company: But that the credence that you may with reason give to their persons for their aforesaid qualities, should well move you to think the oath such of itself, as every man may well swear without peril of their soul, if their own private conscience to the contrary be not the let: and that ye well ought and have good cause to change your own conscience, in confirming your own conscience to the conscience of so many other, namely being such as you know they be. And sith it is also by a law made by the parliament commanded, they think that you be upon the peril of your soul, bounden to change and reform your conscience, and confirm your own, as I said, to other men's."

"Mary, Marget," quoth my father again, "for the part that you play, you play it not much amiss. But Margaret, first, as for the law of the land, though every man being born and inhabiting therein, is bounden to the keeping in every case upon some temporal pain,[54] and in many cases upon pain of God's displeasure too, yet is there no man bounden to swear that every law is well made, nor bounden upon the pain of God's displeasure, to perform any such point of the law, as were indeed unlawful. Of which manner kind,[55] that there may such hap to be made in any part of Christendom, I suppose no man doubteth, the general council of the whole body of Christendom evermore in that point except: which though it may make some things better than other, and some things may grow to that point, ⌐that by another law they may need to be reformed,⌐ yet to institute anything in such wise, to God's displeasure, as at the making might not lawfully be performed, the spirit of God that governeth his church, never hath it suffered, nor never here after shall, his whole catholic church law-

53. entreat
54. punishment
55. *of which manner kind:* of this particular kind

82

fully gathered together in a general council (as Christ hath made ⌐plain promises in Scripture¬).

"Now if it so hap, that in any particular part of Christendom, there be a law made, that be such as for some part thereof some men think that the law of God cannot bear it, and some other think yes, the thing being in such manner in question, that through divers quarters of Christendom, some that are good men and cunning,[56] both of our own days and before our days, think some one way, and some other of like learning and goodness think the contrary, in this case he that thinketh against the law, neither may swear that law lawfully was made, standing his own conscience to the contrary, nor is bounden upon pain of God's displeasure to change his own conscience therein, for any particular law made anywhere, other than by the general council or by a general faith grown by the working of God universally through all Christian nations: nor other authority than one of these twain (except special revelation and express commandment of God) sith the contrary opinions of good men and well learned, as I put you the case, made the understanding of the Scriptures doubtful, I can see none that lawfully may command and compel any man to change his own opinion, and to translate[57] his own conscience from the one side to the other.

"For an example of some such manner things, I have I trow before this time told you, that whether our Blessed Lady were conceived in original sin or not, was sometime in great question among the great learned men of Christendom. And whether it be yet decided and determined by any general council, I remember not. But this I remember well, that notwithstanding that ⌐the feast of her conception¬ was then celebrated in the Church (at the leastwise in divers provinces) ⌐yet was holy Saint Bernard¬, which as his manifold books made in the laud and praise of our Lady do declare, was of as devout affection toward all things sowning[58] toward her commendation, that he thought might well be verified or suffered, as any man was living, yet (I say) was that holy devout man against that part of her praise, as appeareth well by a pistle[59] of his, wherein he right sore and with great reason argueth there against, and approveth not the institution of that feast neither. Nor he was not of this mind alone, but many other well learned men with him, and right holy men too. Now was there on the

56. learned
57. transfer
58. tending
59. epistle

other side, ⌐the blessed holy bishop, Saint Anselm⌐, and he not alone neither, but many well learned and very virtuous also with him. And they be both twain holy saints in heaven, and many mo that were on either side. Nor neither part was there bounden to change their opinion for the other, ⌐nor for any provincial council either⌐.

"But like as after the determination of a well assembled general council, every man had been bounden to give credence that way, and conform their own conscience to the determination of the council general, and then all they that held the contrary before, were for that holding out of blame, so if before such decision a man had against his own conscience, sworn to maintain and defend the other side, he had not failed to offend God very sore. But Mary, if on the other side a man would in a matter take a way by himself upon his own mind alone, or with some few, or with never so many, against an evident truth appearing by the common faith of Christendom, ⌐this conscience is very damnable⌐, yea, or if it be not even fully so plain and evident, yet if he see but himself with far the fewer part, think the one way, against far the more part of as well learned and as good, as those are that affirm the thing that he thinketh, thinking and affirming the contrary, and that of such folk as he hath no reasonable cause wherefore he should not in that matter suppose, that those which say they think against his mind, affirm the thing that they say, for none other cause but for that they so think indeed, this is of very truth a very good occasion to move him, and yet not to compel him, to conform his mind and conscience unto theirs.

"But Margaret, for what causes I refuse the oath, the thing (as I have often told you) I will never shew you, neither you nor nobody else, except the King's Highness should like to command me. Which if his Grace did, I have ere this told you therein how obediently I have said. But surely, Daughter, I have refused it and do, for mo causes than one. And for what causes so ever I refuse it, this am I sure, that it is well known, that of them that have sworn it, some of the best learned before the oath given them, said and plain affirmed the contrary, of some such things as they have now sworn in the oath, and that upon their truth, and their learning then, and that not in haste nor suddenly, but often and after great diligence done to seek and find out the truth."

"That might be, Father," quoth I, "and yet since they might see more, I will not," quoth he, "dispute, daughter Margaret, against that, nor misjudge any other man's conscience, which lieth in their own heart far out of my sight. But this will I say, that I never heard myself the cause of their change, by any new further thing founden of authority, than as far as I perceive they had looked on, and as I suppose, very well wayed[60] before. Now if the self same things that they saw before, seem some otherwise unto them now, than they did before, I am for their sakes the gladder a great deal. But anything that ever I saw before, yet at this day to me they seem but as they did. And therefore, though they may do otherwise than they might, yet, Daughter, I may not. As for such things as some men would happly say, that I might with reason the less regard their change, for any sample[61] of them to be taken to the change of my conscience, because that the keeping of the prince's pleasure, and the avoiding of his indignation, the fear of the losing of their worldly substance, with regard unto the discomfort of their kindred and their friends, might hap make some men either swear otherwise than they think, or frame their conscience afresh to think otherwise than they thought, any such opinion as this is, will I not conceive of them, I have better hope of their goodness than to think of them so. For if such things should have turned them, the same things had been likely to make me do the same, for in good faith I knew few so faint-hearted as myself. Therefore will I, Margaret, by my will, think no worse of other folk in the thing that I know not, than I find in myself. But as I know well mine only conscience causeth me to refuse the oath, so will I trust in God, that according to their conscience, they have received it and sworn.

"But whereas you think, Marget, that they be so many mo than there are on the other side that think in this thing as I think, surely for your own comfort that you shall not take thought, thinking that your father casteth himself away so like a fool, that he would jeopard the loss of his substance, and peradventure his body, without any cause why he so should for peril of his soul, but rather his soul in peril thereby too, to this shall I say to thee, Marget, that in some of my causes I nothing doubt at all, but that though not in this realm, yet in Christendom about, of those well learned men and virtuous that are yet alive, they be not the fewer part that are of my mind. Besides that, that it were ye wot well possible, that some men in this realm too, think not so clear the contrary, as by the oath received they have sworn to say.

"Now this far forth I say for them that are yet alive. But go we now to them that are dead before, ⌜and that are I trust in heaven⌝, I am sure that it is not the fewer part of them that all the time while they lived, thought in some of the things, the way that I think now. I am also, Margaret, of this

60. to be supplied
61. example

thing sure enough, that of those holy doctors and saints, which to be with God in heaven long ago no Christian man doubteth, whose books yet at this day remain here in men's hands, there thought in some such things, as I think now. I say not that they thought all so, but surely such and so many as will well appear by their writing, that I pray God give me the grace that my soul may follow theirs. And yet I shew you not all, Margaret, that I have for myself in the sure discharge of my conscience. But for the conclusion, daughter Margaret, of all this matter, as I have often told you, I take not upon me neither to define nor dispute in these matters, nor I rebuke not nor impugn any other man's deed, nor I never wrote, nor so much as spake in any company, any word of reproach in anything that the Parliament had passed, nor I meddled not with the conscience of any other man, that either thinketh or saith he thinketh contrary unto mine. But as concerning mine own self, for thy comfort shall I say, daughter, to thee, that mine own conscience in this matter (I damn none other man's) is such as may well stand with mine own salvation, thereof am I, Meg, so sure, as that is, God is in heaven. And therefore as for all the remnant, goods, lands, and life both (if the chance should so fortune) sith this conscience is sure for me, I verily trust in God, he shall rather strength[62] me to bear the loss, than against this conscience to swear and put my soul in peril, sith all the causes I perceive move other men to the contrary, seem not such unto me, as in my conscience make any change."

When he saw me sit with this very sad, as I promise you, sister, my heart was full heavy for the peril of his person, for in faith I fear not his soul, he smiled upon me and said: "How now daughter Marget? What how mother Eve? Where is your mind now? sit not musing with some serpent in your breast, upon some new persuasion, to offer father Adam the apple yet once again?" "In good faith, Father," quoth I, "I can no further go, but am (as I trow Cressida saith in Chaucer) come to ⌈Dulcarnon, even at my wit's end⌉. For sith the sample of so many wise men cannot in this matter move you, I see not what to say more, but if I should look to persuade you with the reason that ⌈Master Harry Patenson⌉ made. For he met one day one of our men, and when he had asked where you were, and heard that you were in the Tower still, he waxed even angry with you and said, 'Why? What aileth[63] him that he will not swear? Wherefore should he stick to swear? I have sworn the oath myself.' And so I can in good faith go now no further neither, after so many wise men whom ye take for no sample, but if

62. strengthen
63. hinders

I should say like Master Harry, Why should you refuse to swear, Father? ⌜for I have sworn myself⌝."

At this he laughed and said, "That word was like Eve too, for she offered Adam no worse fruit than she had eaten herself." "But yet Father," quoth I, "by my truth, I fear me very sore, that this matter will bring you in marvelous heavy trouble. You know well that as I shewed you, Master Secretary sent you word as your very friend, to remember that the Parliament lasteth yet." "Margaret," quoth my father, "I thank him right heartily. But as I shewed you then again, I left not this gear unthought on. And albeit I know well that if they would make a law to do me any harm, that law could never be lawful, but that God shall I trust keep me in that grace, that concerning my duty to my prince, no man shall do me hurt but if he do me wrong (and then as I told you, this is like a riddle, a case in which ⌜a man may leese[64] his head and have no harm⌝), and notwithstanding also that I have good hope, that God shall never suffer so good and wise a prince, in such wise to requite the long service of his true faithful servant; yet sith there is nothing unpossible[65] to fall, I forgat not in this matter ⌜the counsel of Christ in the gospel⌝, that ere I should begin to build this castle for the safeguard of mine own soul, I should sit and reckon what the charge would be. I counted, Marget, full surely many a restless night, while my wife slept, and went that I had slept too, what peril was possible for to fall to me, so far forth that I am sure there can come none above. And in devising, Daughter, thereupon, I had a full heavy heart. But yet (I thank our Lord) for all that, I never thought to change, though the very uttermost should hap me that my fear ran upon."

"No, Father," quoth I, "it is not like[66] to think upon a thing that may be, and to see a thing that shall be, as ye should (our Lord save you) if the chance should so fortune. And then should you peradventure think, that you think not now and yet then peradventure it would be too late." "Too late, daughter," quoth my father, "Margaret? I beseech our Lord, that if ever I make such a change, it may be too late indeed. For well I wot the change cannot be good for my soul, that change I say that should grow but by fear. And therefore I pray God that in this world I never have good of such change. For so much as I take harm here, I shall have at the leastwise the less therefore when I am hence. And if so were that I wist well now, that I should faint and fall, and for fear swear hereafter, yet would I

64. lose
65. impossible
66. alike

wish to take harm by the refusing first, for so should I have the better hope for grace to rise again.

"And albeit, Marget, that I wot well my lewdness[67] has been such: that I know myself well worthy that God should let me slip, yet can I not but trust in his merciful goodness, that as his grace hath strengthed me hitherto, and made me content in my heart, to lose goods, lands and life too, rather than to swear against my conscience, and hath also put in the King toward me that good and gracious mind, that as yet he hath taken fro[68] me nothing but my liberty (wherewith, as help me God, his Grace hath done me so great good by the spiritual profit that I trust I take thereby, that among all his great benefits heaped upon me so thick, I reckon upon my faith ⌐my prisonment even the very chief⌐) I cannot, I say, therefore mistrust the grace of God, but that either he shall conserve and keep the King in that gracious mind still to do me none hurt, or else if his pleasure be, that for mine other sins I shall suffer in such a case in sight as I shall not deserve, his grace shall give me the strength to take it patiently, and peradventure somewhat gladly too, whereby his high goodness shall (by the merits of his bitter passion joined thereunto, and far surmounting in merit for me, all that I can suffer myself) make it serve for ⌐release of my pain in purgatory⌐, and over that for increase of some reward in heaven.

"Mistrust him, Meg, will I not, though I feel me faint, yea, and though I should feel my fear even at point to overthrow me too, yet shall I remember how Saint Peter, with a blast of wind, began to sink for his faint faith, and shall do as he did, ⌐call upon Christ and pray him to help⌐. And then I trust he shall set his holy hand unto me, and in the stormy seas, hold me up from drowning. Yea and ⌐if he suffer me to play Saint Peter further⌐, and to fall full to the ground, and swear and forswear too (which our Lord for his tender passion keep me fro, and let me lose if it so fall and never win thereby): yet after shall I trust that his goodness will cast upon me his tender piteous eye, as he did upon Saint Peter, and make me stand up again and confess the truth of my conscience afresh, and abide the shame and the harm here of mine own fault.

"And finally, Marget, this wot I well, that without my fault he will not let me be lost. I shall therefore with good hope commit myself wholly to him. And if he suffer me for my faults to perish, yet ⌐shall I then serve for a praise of his justice⌐. But in good faith, Meg, I trust that his tender pity shall keep my poor soul safe and make me commend his mercy. And

67. wickedness
68. from

88

therefore mine own good daughter, never trouble thy mind for anything that ever shall hap me in this world. Nothing can come but that that God will. And I make me very sure that whatsoever that be, seem it never so bad in sight, ⌐it shall indeed be the best.⌐ And with this, my good child, I pray you heartily, be you and all your sisters and my sons too comfortable and serviceable to your good mother my wife. And of your good husband's minds I have no manner doubt. Commend me to them all, and to my good daughter Alington, and to all my other friends, sisters, nieces, nephews, and allies,[69] and unto all our servants, man, woman, and child, and all my good neighbors and our acquaintance abroad. And I right heartily pray both you and them, to serve God and be merry and rejoice in him. And if anything hap to me that you would be loath, pray to God for me, but trouble not yourself: as I shall full heartily pray for us all, that we may meet together once in heaven, where we shall make merry for ever, and never have trouble after."

69. relatives by marriage

To Dr. Nicholas Wilson

TOWER OF LONDON

1534

A letter written and sent by Sir T. More to Master Doctor ⌐Nicholas Wilson⌐ (then both prisoners in the Tower of London) in the year of our Lord God 1534, and in the twenty-sixth year of the reign of King Henry the Eighth.

Our Lord be your comfort and whereas I perceive by sundry means that you have promised to swear the oath, I beseech our Lord give you thereof good luck. I never gave any man counsel to the contrary in my days nor never used any ways to put any scruple in other folk's conscience concerning the matter. And whereas I perceive that you would gladly know what I intend to do, you wot well what I told you when we were both abroad, that I would therein neither know your mind nor no man's else nor you nor no man's else should therein know mine, for I would be no part taker[1] with no man nor of truth never I will, but leaving every other man to their own conscience, myself will with good grace follow mine. For against mine own to swear were peril of my damnation and what mine own shall be tomorrow myself cannot be sure and whether I shall have finally the grace to do according to mine own conscience or not hangeth in God's goodness and not in mine, to whom I beseech you heartily remember me in your devout prayers and I shall and daily do remember you in mine, such as they be, and as long as my poor short life shall last, anything that I have, your part shall be therein.

1. *part taker:* partisan

To Dr. Nicholas Wilson

TOWER OF LONDON

1534

Another letter written and sent by Sir Thomas More to Master Doctor Wilson (then both prisoners in the Tower) in the year of our Lord, 1534, and in the twenty-sixth year of the reign of King Henry the Eighth.

MASTER WILSON IN MY RIGHT HEARTY WISE I RECOMMEND ME TO YOU.

And very sorry am I to see you, beside the trouble that you be in by this imprisonment with loss of liberty, goods, revenues of your livelihood and comfort of your friends' company, fallen also into such agony and vexation of mind through doubts falling in your mind, that diversely to and fro toss and trouble your conscience to your great heaviness of heart as I (to no little grief of mine own mind for your sake) perceive. And so much am I for you, good Master Doctor, the more sorry because it lieth not in me to give you such kind of comfort as meseemeth you somewhat desire and look for at mine hand.

For whereas you would somewhat hear of my mind in your doubts, I am a man at this day very little meet therefore. For this you know well, good Master Doctor, that as such time as the matter came in such manner in question as mine opinion was asked therein amongst other and yet you made privy thereunto before me, you remember well that at that time you and I many things talked together thereof. And by all the time after by which I did at the King's gracious commandment both seek out and read and common with all such as I knew made privy to the matter to perceive

91

what I might therein upon both sides and by indifferent[1] weighing of everything as near as my poor wit and learning would serve to see to which side my conscience could incline, and as my own mind should give me so to make his Highness report which way myself should hap to think therein. For other commandment had I never of his Grace in good faith, saving that this knot[2] his Highness added thereto, that I should therein look first unto God and after God unto him, which word was also the first lesson that his Grace gave me what time I came first into his noble service and neither a more indifferent commandment nor a more gracious lesson could there in my mind never King give his counselor or any his other servant.

But as I began to tell you by all this long time, I cannot now tell how many years, of all those that I talked with of the matter and with whom I most conferred[3] those ⌐places of Scripture and of the old holy Doctors¬ that touched either the one side or the other, with the councils and laws on either side, that speak thereof also, the most, as I trow you wot well, was yourself. For with no man communed I so much and so often thereof as with you, both for your substantial learning and for your mature judgment, and for that I well perceived ever in you that no man had or lightly[4] could have, a more faithful respect unto the King's honor and surety both of body and soul than I ever saw that you had.

And yet among many other things which I well liked in you, one specially was that I well perceived in the thing that the King's Grace did put you in trust with, your substantial secret manner. For where I had heard (I wot not now of whom) ⌐that you had written his Highness a book¬ of that matter fro Paris before, yet in all those years of our long acquaintance and often talking and reasoning upon the thing, I never heard you so much as make once any mention of that book. But else (except there were any other things in that book that you peradventure thought not on) I suppose that all that ever came to your mind, that might in the matter make for the one side or the other comprised either in the Scripture or in the old ancient Doctors, I verily think in my mind that you did communicate with me and I likewise with you and at the leastwise I remember well that of those points which you call now newly to your remembrance there was none at that time forgotten.

1. impartial
2. binding condition
3. compared
4. probably

I remember well also by your often[5] conference in the matter that by all the time in which I studied about it, you and I were in every point both twain of one opinion and remember well that the laws and councils and the words of Saint Augustine ⌜*De ciuitate Dei*⌝, and ⌜the epistle of Saint Ambrose⌝ *Ad Paternum* and ⌜the epistle of Saint Basil⌝ translated out of Greek and ⌜the writing of Saint Gregory⌝, you and I read together and over that the places of the Scripture self[6] both ⌜in Leviticus and in the Deuteronomy⌝ and ⌜in the Gospel⌝ and ⌜in Saint Paul's epistles⌝ and over this ⌜in that other place of Saint Augustine that you remember now and beside that other places of his⌝, wherein he properly toucheth the matter expressly with ⌜the words of Saint Jerome⌝ and of ⌜Saint Chrysostom⌝ too, and I cannot now remember of how many more. But I verily think that on your part, and I am very sure that on my part, albeit that it had been peradventure over long to shew and read with you every man's book that I read by myself, whereto the parties peradventure that trusted me therewith gave me no leave to shew their books further as you peradventure used the like manner with me, yet in good faith as it was of reason[7] my part in that case to do, you and I having both one commandment indifferently to consider the matter, everything of Scripture and of the Doctors I faithfully communed with you and as I suppose verily so did you with me too, so that of me, good Master Doctor, though I had all the points as ripe in mind now as I had then and had still all the books about me that I then had, and were as willing to meddle in the matter as any man could be, yet could you now no new thing hear of me more than you have, I ween, heard often before, nor I ween I of you neither.

But now standeth it with me in far other case. For afterward when I had signified unto the King's Highness mine own poor opinion in the matter which his Highness very graciously took in good part and that I saw further progress in the matter wherein to do his Grace service to his pleasure I could not, and anything meddle against his pleasure I would not, I determined utterly with myself to discharge my mind of any farther studying or musing of the matter and thereupon I sent home again such books as I had, saving that some I burned by the consent of the owner that was minded as myself was no more to meddle of the matter, and therefore now good Master Doctor I could not be sufficient and able to reason those points again though I were minded thereto sith many things are out

5. frequent
6. itself
7. *of reason:* with good reason

of my mind which I never purpose to look for again nor though I would were never like to find again while I live. Besides this, all that ever I looked for was, you wot well, concerning two or three questions to be pondered and weighed by the study of Scripture and the interpreters of the same, save for somewhat that hath been touched in the same ⌐by the canon laws of the Church⌐.

But then were there at that time in the matter other things more, divers ⌐faults found in the bull of dispensation⌐, by which the King's Council learned in the spiritual law[8] reckoned the bull vicious, partly for untrue suggestion, partly by reason of unsufficient suggestion. Now concerning those points I never meddled. For I neither understand the doctors of the law nor well can turn[9] their books. And many things have there since in this great matter grown in question wherein I neither am sufficiently learned in the law nor full informed of the fact and therefore I am not he that either murmur or grudge, make assertions, hold opinions or keep dispicions[10] in the matter, but like the King's true, poor, humble subject daily pray for the preservation of his Grace, and the Queen's Grace and their noble issue and of all the realm, without harm doing or intending, I thank our Lord, unto any man living.

Finally as touching the oath, the causes for which I refused it, no man wotteth[11] what they be for they be secret in mine own conscience, some other peradventure, than those that other men would ween, and such as I never disclosed unto any man yet nor never intend to do while I live. Finally as I said unto you, before the oath offered unto us when we met in London at adventure[12] I would be no part taker in the matter but for mine own self follow mine own conscience, for which myself must make answer unto God, and shall leave every other man to his own, so say to you still and I dare say further that no more never intended you neither. Many things every man learned wotteth well there are, in which every man is at liberty without peril of damnation to think which way him list[13] till the one part be determined for necessary to be believed ⌐by a general council⌐, and I am not he that take upon me to define or determine of what kind or nature every thing is that the oath containeth, nor am so bold or presumptuous to blame or dispraise the conscience of other men,

8. church law
9. ponder
10. disputations
11. knows
12. by chance
13. he pleases

their truth nor their learning neither, nor I meddle with no man but of myself, nor of no man's conscience else will I meddle but of mine own. And in mine own conscience, I cry God mercy, I find of mine own life, matters enough to think on.

I have lived, methinketh, a long life and now neither I look nor I long to live much longer. I have since I came in the Tower looked once or twice to have given up my ghost ere this and in good faith mine heart waxed the lighter with hope thereof. Yet forget I not that I have a long reckoning and a great to give account of, but I put my trust in God and in the merits of his bitter passion, and I beseech him give me and keep me the mind to long to be out of this world and to be with him. For I can never but trust that who so long to be with him shall be welcome to him, and on the other side my mind giveth me verily that any that ever shall come to him shall full heartily wish to be with him or ever he shall come at him.[14] And I beseech him heartily to set your heart at such rest and quiet as may be to his pleasure and eternal weal of your soul and so I verily trust that he shortly shall and shall also if it be his pleasure incline the King's noble heart to be gracious and favorable to you and me both, sith we be both twain of true faithful mind unto him, whether we be in this matter of one mind both, or of diverse. ⌜*Sicut diuisiones aquarum, ita cor regis in manu Domini, quocumque voluerit, inclinabit illud*⌝. And if the pleasure of God be on any of us both otherwise to dispose, I need to give you no counsel nor advise.

But for myself I most humbly beseech him to give me the grace in such wise patiently to conform my mind unto his high pleasure therein, that after the troublesome storm of this my tempestuous time his great mercy may conduct me in to the sure haven of the joyful bliss of heaven, and after at his further pleasure (if I have any) all mine enemies too, for there shall we love together well enough and I thank our Lord for my part so do I here too. Be not angry now though I pray not like for you; you be sure enough I would my friends fare no worse than they, nor yet they, so help me God, no worse than myself.

For our Lord's sake, good Master Wilson, pray for me for I pray for you daily and some time when I would be sorry but if I thought you were asleep. Comfort yourself, good Master Doctor, with remembering God's great mercy and the King's accustomed goodness, and by my troth, I think that all his Grace's Council favoreth you in their hearts. I cannot judge in my mind any one of them so evil as to be of the mind that you should do otherwise than well. And for conclusion in God is all. ⌜*Spes non confundit*⌝. I

14. *or ever he shall come at him:* before ever he shall come to him

pray you pardon my scribbling for I cannot always so well endure to write as I might sometime. And I pray you when ye see time convenient at your pleasure send me this rude bill again. ⌜*Quia quanquam nihil inest mali, tamen propter ministrum nolim rescire*⌝.

15

From Margaret Roper

1534

A letter written and sent by Mistress Margaret Roper, to her father Sir Thomas More then shut up in close prison[1] in the Tower, written in the year of our Lord God 1534, and in the twenty-sixth year of the reign of King Henry the Eighth, answering to a letter which her father had sent unto her.

MINE OWN MOST ENTIRELY BELOVED FATHER.

I think myself never able to give you sufficient thanks for the inestimable comfort my poor heart received in the reading of your most loving and godly letter, representing to me the clear shining brightness of your soul, ⌐the pure temple of the Holy Spirit of God¬, which I doubt not shall perpetually rest in you and you in him. Father, if all the world had been given to me, as I be saved it had been a small pleasure, in comparison of the pleasure I conceived of the treasure of your letter, which though it were written with a coal, is worthy in mine opinion to be written in letters of gold.

Father, what moved them to shut you up again, we can nothing hear. But surely I conjecture that when they considered that you were of so temperate mind that you were contended[2] to abide there all your life with such liberty, they thought it were never possible to incline you to their will, except it were by ⌐restraining you from the Church¬, and the company

1. strict confinement
2. contented

97

of my good mother, your dear wife, and us your children and bedsfolk. But Father, this chance[3] was not strange to you. For I shall not forget how you told us when we were with you in the garden, that these things were like enough to chance shortly after. Father, I have many times rehearsed to mine own comfort and divers others, your fashion and words ye had to us when we were last with you: for which I trust by the grace of God to be the better while I live, and when I am departed out of this frail life, which, I pray God, I may pass and end in his true obedient service, after the wholesome counsel and fruitful example of living I have had (good Father) of you, whom I pray God give me grace to follow: which I shall the better through the assistance of your devout prayers, the special stay of my frailty. Father, I am sorry I have no longer leisure at this time to talk with you, the chief comfort of my life; I trust to have occasion to write again shortly. I trust I have your daily prayer and blessing.

Your most loving obedient daughter and beadswoman, Margaret Roper, which daily and hourly is bounden to pray for you, for whom she prayeth in this wise: that our Lord of his infinite mercy give you of his heavenly comfort, and so to assist you with his special grace that ye never in anything decline from his blessed will, but live and die his true obedient servant. Amen.

3. possibility

16

To Margaret Roper

TOWER OF LONDON

1534

A letter written and sent by Sir Thomas More to his daughter Mistress Roper answering her letter here next before.

THE HOLY SPIRIT OF GOD BE WITH YOU.

If I would with my writing, mine own good daughter, declare how much pleasure and comfort, ⌐your daughterly loving letters⌐ were unto me, a peck of coals would not suffice to make me the pens. And other pens have I, good Margaret, none here: and therefore can I write you no long process, nor dare adventure,[1] good daughter, to write often.

⌐The cause of my close keeping⌐ again did of likelihood grow of my negligent and very plain true word which you remember. And verily whereas my mind gave me (as I told you in the garden) that some such things were likely to happen, so doth my mind always give me, that some folk yet ween that I was not so poor as it appeared in the search, and that it may therefore happen, that yet eftsoon ofter than once, some new sudden ⌐searches may hap to be made in every house of ours⌐ as narrowly as is possible. Which thing if ever it so should hap, can make but game[2] to us that know the truth of my poverty, but if they find out my wife's gay[3] girdle and her golden beads.[4] Howbeit I verily believe in good faith that the King's Grace of his benign pity will take nothing from her.

1. venture, risk
2. fun
3. showy
4. rosary beads

I thought and yet think, that it may be that I was shut up again upon some new causeless suspicion, grown peradventure upon some secret sinister information, whereby some folk haply thought that there should be found out against me some other greater things. But I thank our Lord whensoever this conjecture hath fallen in my mind, ⌈the clearness of my conscience hath made my heart hop for joy⌉. For one thing am I very sure of hitherto, and trust in God's mercy to be while I live, that as often I have said unto you, I shall for anything toward my prince never take great harm, but if I take great wrong, in the sight of God, I say, howsoever it shall seem in the sight of men. For to the world, wrong may seem right sometimes by false conjecturing, sometimes by false witnesses, as that good Lord said unto you, which is I dare say my very good lord in his mind, and said it of very good will. Before the world also, my refusing of this oath is accounted an heinous offense, and my religious fear toward God is called obstinacy toward my Prince. But my Lords of the Council before whom I refused it might well perceive by the heaviness of my heart appearing well mo ways than one unto them, that all sturdy stubbornness whereof obstinacy groweth, was very far from my mind. For the clearer proof whereof, sith they seemed to take for one argument of obstinacy in me that refusing of the oath, I would not declare the causes why, I offered with a full heart, that albeit I rather would endure all the pain and peril of the statute than by the declaring of the causes, give any occasion of exasperation unto my most dread Sovereign Lord and Prince, yet rather than his Highness should for not disclosing the causes account me for stubborn and obstinate, I would upon such his gracious license and commandment as should discharge me of his displeasure and peril of any statute, declare those points that letted[5] my poor conscience to receive that oath; and would over that be sworn before, that if I should after the causes disclosed and declared find them so answered as my conscience should think itself satisfied, I would thereupon swear the oath that I there refused. To this, Master Secretary answered me that though the King's Grace gave me such a license, yet it could not discharge me against the statutes, in saying anything that were by them upon heinous pains prohibited. In this good warning he shewed himself my special tender friend.

And now you see well, Margaret, that it is no obstinacy to leave the causes undeclared, while I could not declare them without peril. But now it is accounted great obstinacy that I refuse the oath, whatsoever my

5. prevented

100

causes be, considering that of so many wiser and better men none sticked thereat. And Master Secretary, of a great zeal that he bare unto me, sware there before them a great oath, that for the displeasure that he thought the King's Highness would bear me, and the suspicion that his Grace would conceive of me, which would now think in his mind that all the Nun's business was wrought and devised by me, he had liefer[6] than I should have refused the oath, that his own only son (which is a goodly young gentleman of whom our Lord send him much joy) had had his head stricken off.[7] This word, Margaret, as it was a marvelous declaration of Master Secretary's great good mind and favor toward me, so was it an heavy hearing to me, that the King's Grace my most dread Sovereign Lord, were likely to conceive such high suspicion of me and bear such grievous indignation toward me, for the thing which without the danger and peril of my poor soul lay not in my hand to help, nor doth.

Now have I heard since that some say that this obstinate manner of mine, in still refusing the oath, shall peradventure force and drive the King's Grace to make a further law for me. I cannot let such a law to be made. But I am very sure, that if I died by such a law, I should die for that point innocent afore God. And albeit, good daughter, that I think, our Lord that hath ⌜the hearts of kings in his hand⌝, would never suffer of his high goodness, so gracious a Prince, and so many honorable men, and so many good men as be in Parliament to make such an unlawful law, as that should be if it so mishapped,[8] yet lest I note[9] that point unthought upon, but many times more than one revolved and cast in my mind before my coming hither, both that peril and all other that might put my body in peril of death by the refusing of this oath. In devising[10] whereupon, albeit, mine own good daughter, that I found myself (I cry God mercy) very sensual and my flesh much more shrinking from pain and from death, than methought it the part of a faithful Christian man, in such a case as my conscience gave me, that in the saving of my body should stand the loss of my soul, yet I thank our Lord, that in that conflict, the Spirit had in conclusion the mastery, ⌜and reason with help of faith⌝ finally concluded, that for to be put to death wrongfully for doing well (as I am very sure I do, in refusing to swear against mine own conscience, being such as I am not upon peril of my soul bounden to change whether my death should

6. rather
7. struck with a blow
8. unfortunately happened
9. denote, mean
10. deliberating, meditating

come without law, or by color of a law[11]) it is a case in which a man may lose his head and yet have none harm, but instead of harm inestimable good at the hand of God.

And I thank our Lord, Meg, since I am come hither I set by death every day less than other. For though a man leese[12] of his years in this world, it is more than manifold recompensed by coming the sooner to heaven. And though it be a pain to die while a man is in health, yet see I very few that in sickness die with ease. And finally, very sure am I that whensoever the time shall come that may hap to come, God wot how soon, in which I should lie sick in my death bed by nature, I shall then think that God had done much for me, if he had suffered me to die before by the color of such a law. And therefore my reason sheweth me, Margaret, that it were great folly for me to be sorry to come to that death, ⌐which I would after wish that I had died⌐. Beside that, that a man may hap with less thank of God, and more adventure of his soul to die as violently and as painfully by many other chances as by enemies or thieves. And therefore, mine own good daughter, I assure you (thanks be to God) the thinking of any such albeit it hath grieved me ere this, yet at this day grieveth me nothing. And yet I know well for all this mine own frailty, and that Saint Peter which feared it much less than I, fell in such fear soon after that at the word of a simple[13] girl ⌐he forsook and forsware our Savior⌐. And therefore am I not, Meg, so mad, as to warrant myself to stand. But I shall pray, and I pray thee, mine own good daughter, to pray with me, that it may please God that hath given me this mind, to give me the grace to keep it.

And thus have I, mine own good daughter, disclosed unto you the very secret bottom of my mind, referring the order thereof only to the goodness of God, and that so fully, that I assure you Margaret on my faith, I never have prayed God to bring me hence nor deliver me from death, but referring all thing whole unto his only pleasure, as to him that seeth better what is best for me than myself doth. Nor never longed I since I came hither to set my foot in mine own house, ⌐for any desire of or pleasure of my house⌐, but gladly would I sometimes somewhat talk with my friends, and specially my wife and you that pertain to my charge. But sith God otherwise disposeth,[14] ⌐I commit all wholly to his goodness⌐ and take daily great comfort in that I perceive that you live together so charitably and so

11. *by color of a law:* the semblance or appearance of a law
12. lose
13. ordinary
14. ordains

quietly: I beseech our Lord continue it. And thus, mine own good daughter, putting you finally in remembrance that albeit if the necessity so should require, I thank our Lord in this quiet and comfort is mine heart at this day, and I trust in God's goodness so shall have grace to continue, yet (as I said before) I verily trust that God shall so inspire and govern the King's heart that he shall not suffer his noble heart and courage to requite my true faithful heart and service with such extreme unlawful and uncharitable dealing, only for the displeasure that I cannot think so as other do. But his true subject will I live and die, and truly pray for him will I, both here and in the other world too.

And thus, mine own good daughter, have me recommended to my good bedfellow and all my children, men, women and all, with all your babes and your nurses and all the maids and all the servants, and all our kin, and all our other friends abroad. And I beseech our Lord to save them all and keep them. And I pray you all pray for me, and I shall pray for you all. And take no thought for me whatsoever you shall hap to hear, but be merry in God.

17

To Margaret Roper

TOWER OF LONDON

1534

Another letter written and sent by Sir Thomas More (in the year of our Lord, 1534 and in the twenty-sixth year of King Henry the Eighth) to his daughter Mistress Roper, answering a letter which she wrote and sent unto him.

THE HOLY SPIRIT OF GOD BE WITH YOU.

Your daughterly loving letter, my dearly beloved child, was and is, I faithfully assure you, much more inward comfort unto me than my pen can well express you, for divers things that I marked therein but of all things most especially, for that God of his high goodness giveth you the grace to consider the incomparable difference between the wretched state of this present life and the wealthy state of the life to come, for them that die in God, and to pray God in such a good Christian fashion that it may please him (it doth me good here to rehearse your own words) "of his tender pity so firmly to rest our love in him, with little regard of this world, and so to flee sin and embrace virtue, that we may say with Saint Paul, ⌐*Mihi viuere Christus est et mori luchrum. Et illud, Cupio dissolui et esse cum Christo*⌐." I beseech our Lord, my dearly beloved daughter, that wholesome prayer that he hath put in your mind, it may like him to give your father the grace daily to remember and pray, and yourself as you have written it, even so daily devoutly to kneel and pray it. For surely if God give us that, he giveth us and will give us therewith, all that ever we can well wish. And therefore good Marget, when you pray it, pray for us both: and I shall on my part the like, in such manner as it shall like our Lord to give me, poor

104

wretch, the grace, that likewise as in this wretched world I have been very glad of your company and you of mine, and yet would if it might be (as natural charity bindeth the father and the child) so we may rejoice and enjoy each other's company, with our other kinsfolk, allies, and friends everlastingly in the glorious bliss of heaven; and in the meantime with good counsel and prayer each help other thitherward.

And where you write these words of yourself, "But good Father, I wretch am far, far, farthest of all other from such point of perfection, our Lord send me the grace to amend my life, and continually to have an eye to mine end, without grudge[1] of death, which to them that die in God, is the gate of a wealthy life to which God of his infinite mercy bring us all. Amen. Good Father, strenght my frailty with your devout prayers." The father of heaven mote[2] strenght thy frailty, my good daughter and the frailty of thy frail father too. And let us not doubt but he so will, if we will not be slack in calling upon him therefor. Of my poor prayers, such as they be, ye may be bold to reckon. For Christian charity and natural love and your very daughterly dealing, ⌈*funiculo triplici qui* (vt ait scriptura) *difficile rumpitur*⌉, both bind me and strain me[3] thereto. And of yours I put[4] as little doubt.

That you fear your own frailty, Marget, nothing misliketh[5] me. God give us both twain the grace to despair of our own self, and whole to depend and hang upon the hope and strength of God. The blessed apostle Saint Paul found such lack of strength in himself, that in his own temptation he was fain thrice to call and cry out unto God, to take that temptation from him. And yet sped[6] he not of his prayer, in the manner that he required. For God of his high wisdom, seeing that it was (as himself saith), necessary for him to keep him from pride that else he might peradventure have fallen in, would not at his thrice praying, by and by take it from him, but suffered him to be panged[7] in the pain and fear thereof, giving him yet at the last this comfort against his fear of falling, ⌈*Sufficit tibi gratia mea*⌉. By which words, it well seemeth, that the temptation was so strong (whatsoever kind of temptation it was) that he was very feared of falling, through the feebleness of resisting that he began to feel in himself. Wherefore for his comfort God answered, *Sufficit*

1. complaining
2. must
3. bind tightly
4. have
5. displeases
6. obtained
7. anguished

tibi gratia mea, putting him in surety, that were he of himself never so feeble and faint, nor never so likely to fall, yet the grace of God was sufficient to keep him up and make him stand. And our Lord said further, ⌐*Virtus in infirmitate perficitur*⌐. The more weak that man is, the more is the strength of God in his safeguard declared. And so Saint Paul saith, ⌐*Omnia possum in eo qui me confortat.*⌐

Surely, Meg, a fainter heart than thy frail father hath, canst you not have. And yet I verily trust in the great mercy of God, that he shall of his goodness so stay[8] me with his holy hand, that he shall not finally suffer me to fall wretchedly from his favor. And the like trust, dear daughter, in his high goodness I verily conceive of you. And so much the more, in that there is neither of us both,[9] but that if we call his benefits to mind and give him oft thanks for them, we may find tokens many, to give us good hope for all our manifold offenses toward him, that his great mercy, when we will heartily call therefore, shall not be withdrawn from us. And verily, my dear daughter, in this is my great comfort, that albeit, I am of nature so shrinking from pain, that I am almost afeard of a fillip,[10] yet in all the agonies that I have had, whereof before my coming hither (as I have shewed you ere this) I have had neither small nor few, with heavy fearful heart, forecasting all such perils and painful deaths, as by any manner of possibility might after fall unto me, and in such thought lain long restless and waking, ⌐while my wife had weened I had slept⌐, yet in any such fear and heavy pensiveness, I thank the mighty mercy of God I never in my mind intended to consent, that I would for the enduring of the uttermost do any such thing as I should in mine own conscience (for with other men's I am not a man meet to take upon me to meddle) think to be to myself, such as should damnably cast me in the displeasure of God. And this is the lest[11] point that any man may with his salvation come to, as far as I can see, and is bounden if he see peril to examine his conscience surely by learning and by good counsel and be sure that his conscience be such as it may stand with his salvation, or else reform it. And if the matter be such, as both the parties may stand with salvation, then on whither side his conscience fall, he is safe enough before God. But that mine own may stand with my own salvation, thereof I thank our Lord I am very sure. I beseech our Lord bring all parts[12] to his bliss.

8. sustain
9. neither of us has reason to complain
10. a flick of the finger released from the thumb
11. least
12. parties, sides in disputes

To Margaret Roper

It is now, my good daughter, late. And therefore thus I commend you to the holy Trinity, to guide you, comfort you and direct you with his Holy Spirit, and all yours and my wife with all my children and all our other friends.

Thomas More, Knight.

18

Lady More to Henry VIII

Around Christmas 1534

In lamentable wise, beseech your most noble Grace your most humble subjects and continual beadsfolk, the poor miserable wife and children of your true, poor, heavy subject and beadsman, Sir Thomas More Knight, that whereas the same Sir Thomas being your Grace's prisoner in your Tower of London by the space of eight months and above, in great continual sickness of body and heaviness of heart, during all which space notwithstanding that the same Sir Thomas More had by refusing of the oath forfeited unto your most noble Grace all his goods and cattles[1] and the profit of all his lands, annuities and fees that as well himself as your said beadswoman his wife should live by, yet your most gracious Highness of your most blessed disposition suffered your said beadswoman, his poor wife, to retain and keep still his movable goods and the revenues of his lands to keep her said husband and her poor household with.

So it is now, most gracious Sovereign, that now late by reason of a ⌜new act or twain made in this last passed prorogation of your Parliament⌝, not only the said former forfeiture is confirmed, but also the inheritance of all such lands and tenements as the same Sir Thomas had of your most bountiful gift, amounting to the yearly value sixty pounds is forfeited also. And thus (except your merciful favor be shewed) your said poor beadswoman his wife, which brought fair substance to him, which is ⌜all spent in your Grace's service⌝, is likely to be utterly undone and his poor son, one of your said humble suppliants, standing charged and bounden for the payment of great sums of money due by the said Sir

1. chattels

108

Thomas unto your Grace, standeth in danger to be cast away and undone in this world also. But over all this the said Sir Thomas himself, after his long true service to his power diligently done to your Grace, is likely to be in his age and continual sickness, for lack of comfort and good keeping, to be shortly destroyed, to the woeful heaviness and deadly discomfort of all your said sorrowful suppliants.

In consideration of the premises, for that his offense is grown not of any malice or obstinate mind, but of such a long continued and deep rooted scruple, as passeth his power to avoid[2] and put away, it may like your most noble Majesty of your most abundant grace to remit and pardon your most grievous displeasure to the said Sir Thomas and to have tender pity and compassion upon his long distress and great heaviness, and for the tender mercy of God to deliver him out of prison and suffer him quietly to live the remnant of his life with your said poor beadswoman his wife and other of your poor suppliants his children, with only such intertainment of living[3] as it shall like your most noble Majesty of your gracious alms[4] and pity to appoint him. And this in the way of mercy and pity, and all your said poor beadsfolk shall daily during their lives pray to God for the preservation of your most Royal state.

---

2. refute
3. *intertainment of living:* livelihood
4. charity

19

To Master Leder

TOWER OF LONDON

Saturday, 16 January 1534/5

A letter written by Sir Thomas More to one ⌐Master Leder¬ a virtuous priest the sixteenth day of January in the year of our Lord 1534 after the computation of the church of England, and in the twenty-sixth year of the reign of King Henry the Eighth.

The tale that is reported, albeit I cannot but thank you though you would it were true, yet I thank God it is a very vanity.[1] I trust in the great goodness of God, that he shall never suffer it to be true. If my mind had been obstinate indeed I would not let[2] for any rebuke or worldly shame plainly to confess the truth. For I purpose not to depend upon the fame of the world. But I thank our Lord that the thing that I do is not for obstinacy but for the salvation of my soul, because I cannot induce mine own mind otherwise to think than I do concerning the oath.

As for other men's consciences I will not judge of, nor I never advised any man neither to swear nor to refuse, but as for mine own self if ever I should mishap[3] to receive the oath (which I trust our Lord shall never suffer me), ye may reckon sure that it were expressed and extorted by duress and hard handling. For as for all the goods of this world, I thank our Lord I set not much more by than I do by dust. And I trust both that they will use no violent forcible ways, and also that if they would, God would of his grace and the rather a great deal through good folks' prayers give me

1. idle tale
2. refrain

strength to stand. ⌐*Fidelis Deus,* saith St. Paul, *qui non patitur vos tentari supra id quod potestis ferre, sed dat cum tentatione prouentum vt possitis sustinere*⌐. For this I am very sure, that if ever I should swear it, I should swear deadly against mine own conscience. For I am very sure in my mind that I shall never be able to change mine own conscience to the contrary; as for other men's, I will not meddle of.

It hath been shewed me that I am reckoned wilful and obstinate because that since my coming hither I have not written unto the King's Highness and by mine own writing made some suit unto his Grace. But in good faith, I do not forbear it of any obstinacy, but rather of a lowly mind and a reverent, because that I see nothing that I could write but that I fear me sore that his Grace were likely rather to take displeasure with me for it than otherwise, while his Grace believeth me not that my conscience is the cause but rather obstinate wilfulness. But surely that my let is but my conscience, that knoweth God to whose order[4] I commit the whole matter. ⌐*In cuius manu corda regum sunt*⌐. I beseech our Lord that all may prove as true faithful subjects to the King that have sworn, as I am in my mind very sure that they be, which have refused to swear.

In haste, the Saturday, the 16th day of January, by the hand of your beadsman,

Thomas More, Knight and prisoner.

3. have the misfortune
4. providence

20

To Margaret Roper

TOWER OF LONDON

2 or 3 May 1535

A letter written and sent by Sir Thomas More to his daughter Mistress Roper, written the second or third day of May, in the year of our Lord 1535 and in the twenty-seventh year of the reign of King Henry the Eighth.

OUR LORD BLESS YOU.
MY DEARLY BELOVED DAUGHTER.

I doubt not but by the reason of the Councilors resorting hither, in this time in which (our Lord be their comfort) ⌐these fathers of the Charterhouse⌐ and ⌐Master Reynolds⌐ of Sion be now judged to death for treason (whose matters and causes I know not) may hap to put you in trouble and fear of mind concerning me being here prisoner, specially for that it is not unlikely but that you have heard that I was brought also before the Council here myself. I have thought it necessary to advertise you of the very truth, to the end that you neither conceive more hope than the matter giveth, lest upon other turn it might aggrieve your heaviness, nor more grief and fear than the matter giveth, on the other side. Wherefore shortly you shall understand that on Friday the last day of April in the afternoon, ⌐Master Lieutenant⌐ came in here unto me, and shewed me that Master Secretary would speak with me. Whereupon I shifted my gown, and went out with Master Lieutenant into the gallery to him. Where I met many, some known and some unknown in the way. And in conclusion coming into the chamber where his Mastership sat with ⌐Master Attorney⌐, ⌐Master Solicitor⌐, ⌐Master Bedill⌐ and ⌐Master

Doctor Tregonwell⌐. ⌐I was offered to sit with them, which in no wise I would.⌐

Whereupon Master Secretary shewed unto me, that he doubted not, but that I had by such friends as hither had resorted to me seen the new statutes made at the last sitting of the Parliament. Whereunto I answered: "Yes, verily. Howbeit for as much as being there, I have no conversation with any people, I thought it little need for me to bestow much time upon them, and therefore I redelivered the book shortly and the effect of the statutes I never marked[1] nor studied to put in remembrance." Then he asked me whether I had not read the first statute of them, of the King being ⌐Head of the Church⌐. Whereunto I answered, "Yes." Then his Mastership declared unto me, that sith it was now by act of Parliament ordained that his Highness and his heirs be, and ever of right have been, and perpetually should be, Supreme Head in earth of the Church of England under Christ, the King's pleasure was that those of his Council there assembled should demand mine opinion, and what my mind was therein. Whereunto I answered that in good faith I had well trusted that the King's Highness would never have commanded any such question to be demanded of me, considering that I ever from the beginning well and truly from time to time declared my mind unto his Highness, and since that time I had, I said, unto your Mastership Master Secretary also, both by mouth and by writing. And now I have in good faith discharged my mind of all such matters, and neither will dispute King's titles nor Pope's, but the King's true faithful subject I am and will be, and daily I pray for him and for all his, and for you all that are of his honorable Council, and for all the realm, and otherwise than thus I never intend to meddle.

Whereunto Master Secretary answered that he thought this manner answer should not satisfy nor content the King's Highness, but that his Grace would exact a more full answer. And his Mastership added thereunto, that the King's Highness was a prince not of rigour but of mercy and pity, and though that he had found obstinacy at some time in any of his subjects, yet when he should find them at another time conformable and submit themself, his Grace would shew mercy. And that concerning myself, his Highness would be glad to see me take such confirmable ways, as I might be abroad in the world again among other men as I have been before.

Whereunto I shortly (after the inward affection of my mind) an-

1. considered

swered for a very truth, that I would never meddle in the world again, to have the world given me. And to the remnant of the matter, I answered in effect as before, shewing that I had fully determined with myself, neither to study nor meddle with any matter of this world, but that my whole study should be upon the passion of Christ and mine own passage out of this world.

Upon this I was commanded to go forth for a while, and after called in again. At which time Master Secretary said unto me that though I was prisoner and condemned to perpetual prison, yet I was not thereby discharged of mine obedience and allegiance unto the King's Highness. And thereupon demanded me whether that I thought that the King's Grace might exact of me such things as are contained in the statutes and upon like pains[2] as he might of other men. Whereto I answered that I would not say the contrary. Whereto he said that likewise as the King's Highness would be gracious to them that he found conformable, so his Grace would follow the course of his laws toward such as he shall find obstinate. And his Mastership said further that my demeanor in that matter was of a thing that of likelihood made now other men so stiff[3] therein as they be.

Whereto I answered, that I give no man occasion to hold any point one or other, nor never gave any man advice or counsel therein one way or other. And for conclusion I could no further go, whatsoever pain should come thereof. "I am," quoth I, "the King's true faithful subject and daily beadsman and pray for his Highness and all his and all the realm. I do nobody harm, I say none harm, I think none harm, but wish everybody good. And if this be not enough to keep a man alive, in good faith, I long not to live. And I am dying already, and have since I came here, been divers times in the case[4] that I thought to die within one hour, and I thank our Lord I was never sorry for it, but rather sorry when I saw the pang past. And therefore my poor body is at the King's pleasure, would God my death might do him good."

After this Master Secretary said: "Well, ye find no fault in that statute, find you any in any of the other statutes after?" Whereto I answered, "Sir, whatsoever thing should seem to me other than good, in any of the other statutes or in that statute either, I would not declare what fault I found, nor speak thereof." Whereunto finally his mastership said full gently that of any thing that I had spoken, there should none advantage

2. punishments
3. obstinate, stubborn
4. physical condition

be taken, and whether he said further that there be none to be taken, I am not well remembered. But he said that report should be made unto the King's Highness, and his gracious pleasure known.

Whereupon I was delivered again to Master Lieutenant, which was then called in, and so was I by Master Lieutenant brought again into my chamber, and here am I yet in such case as I was, neither better nor worse. That that shall follow lieth in the hand of God, whom I beseech to put in the King's Grace's mind that thing that may be to his high pleasure, and in mine, to mind only the weal of my soul, with little regard of my body.

And you with all yours, and my wife and all my children and all our other friends both bodily and ghostly heartily well to fare. And I pray you and all them, pray for me, and take no thought whatsoever shall happen me. For I verily trust in the goodness of God, seem it never so evil to this world, it shall indeed in another world be for the best.

Your loving father,

Thomas More, Knight.

→ 21 ←

Lady More to Thomas Cromwell

May 1535

RIGHT HONORABLE, AND MY ESPECIAL GUD MASTER SECRETARY.

In my most humble wise I recommend me unto your good Mastership, knowleging[1] myself to be most deeply bound to your good Mastership, for your manifold gudness and loving favor, both before this time, and yet daily, now also shewed towards my poor husband and me. I pray Almighty God continue your goodness so still, for thereupon hangeth the greatest part of my poor husband's comfort and mine.

The cause of my writing, at this time, is to certify your especial gud Mastership of my great and extreme necessity; which, on and besides the charge of mine own house, do pay weekly 15 shillings for the board-wages of my poor husband, and his servant; for the maintaining whereof, I have been compelled, of very necessity, ⌜to sell part of mine apparel⌝, for lack of other substance to make money of. Wherefore my most humble petition and suit to your Mastership, at this time, is to desire your Mastership's favorable advice and counsel, whether I may be so bold to attend upon the King's most gracious Highness. I trust there is no doubt in the cause of my impediment; for the young man, being a ploughman, had been diseased with the ague by the space of 3 years before he departed. And besides this, it is now five weeks sith he departed, and no other person diseased in the house sith that time; wherefore I most humbly beseech your especial gud Mastership (as my only trust is, and else know not what to do, but utterly in this world to be undone) for the love of God to consider the premises;

1. acknowledging

116

and thereupon, of your most subundant[2] gudness, to shew your most favorable help to the comforting of my poor husband and me, in this our great heaviness, ⌐extreme age⌐, and necessity. And thus we, and all ours, shall daily, during our lives, pray to God for the prosperous success of your right honorable dignity.

By your poor continual Oratrix,[3]

Dame Alice More.

To the Right Honorable, and her
especial good Master, Master Secretary.

2. abundant
3. petitioner, supplicant

✣ 22 ✣

To Margaret Roper

TOWER OF LONDON

3 June 1535

Another letter written and sent by Sir Thomas More to his daughter Mistress Roper, written in the year of our Lord 1535, and in the twenty-seventh year of the reign of King Henry the Eighth.

OUR LORD BLESS YOU AND ALL YOURS.

For as much, dearly beloved daughter, as it is likely that you either have heard or shortly shall hear that the Council was here this day, and that I was before them, I have thought it necessary to send you word how the matter standeth. And verily to be short I perceive little difference between this time and the last, for as far as I can see the whole purpose is either to drive me to say precisely the one way, or else precisely the other.

⌐Here sat my Lord of Canterbury, my Lord Chancellor, my Lord of Suffolk, my Lord of Wiltshire and Master Secretary.⌐ And after my coming, Master Secretary made rehearsal[1] in what wise he had reported unto the King's Highness, what had been said by his Grace's Council to me, and what had been answered by me to them at mine other being before them last. Which thing his Mastership rehearsed in good faith very well, as I knowledged[2] and confessed and heartily thanked him therefore. Whereupon he added thereunto that the King's Highness was nothing content nor satisfied with mine answer, but thought that by my demeanor I had

1. gave an account
2. acknowledged

been occasion of much grudge[3] and harm in the realm, and that I had an obstinate mind and an evil toward him and that my duty was, being his subject; and so he had sent them now in his name upon my allegiance to command me to make a plain and terminate[4] answer whether I thought the statute lawful or not and that I should either acknowledge and confess it lawful that his Highness should be Supreme Head of the Church of England or else to utter plainly my malignity.

Whereto I answered that I had no malignity and therefore I could none utter. And as to the matter I could none other answer make than I had before made, which answer his Mastership had there rehearsed. Very heavy I was that the King's Highness should have any such opinion of me. Howbeit if there were one that had informed his Highness many evil things of me that were untrue, to which his Highness for the time gave credence, I would be very sorry that he should have that opinion of me the space of one day. Howbeit if I were sure that other should come on the morrow by whom his Grace should know the truth of mine innocency, I should in the meanwhile comfort myself with the consideration of that. And in like wise now though it be great heaviness to me that his Highness have such opinion of me for the while, yet have I no remedy to help it, but only to comfort myself with this consideration that I know very well that the time shall come, when God shall declare my truth toward his Grace before him and all the world. And whereas it might happly seem to be but small cause of comfort because I might take harm here first in the meanwhile, I thanked God that my case was such in this matter through the clearness of mine own conscience that though I might have pain I could not have harm, for a man may in such case lose his head and have no harm. For I was very sure that I had no corrupt affection,[5] but that I had alway fro the beginning truly used myself to looking first upon God and next upon the King, according to the lesson that his Highness taught me at my first coming to his noble service, the most virtuous lesson that ever prince taught his servant; whose Highness to have of me such opinion is my great heaviness, but I have no mean[6] as I said to help it but only comfort myself in the meantime with the hope of that joyful day in which my truth towards him shall well be known. And in this matter further I could not go nor other answer thereto I could not make.

3. ill will, resentment, bad influence
4. definitive
5. evil disposition
6. means

To this it was said by my Lord Chancellor and Master Secretary both that the King might by his laws compel me to make a plain answer thereto, either the one way or the other.

Whereunto I answered I would not dispute the King's authority, what his Highness might do in such case, but I said that verily under correction[7] it seemed to me somewhat hard. For if it so were that my conscience gave me against the statutes (wherein how my mind giveth me I make no declaration), then I nothing doing nor nothing saying against the statute, it were a very hard thing to compel me to say either precisely with it against my conscience to the loss of my soul, or precisely against it to the destruction of my body.

To this Master Secretary said that I had ere this when I was Chancellor examined heretics and thieves and other malefactors and gave me a great praise above my deserving in that behalf. And he said that I then, as he thought and at the leastwise Bishops did use to examine heretics, whether they believed the Pope to be the head of the Church and used to compel them to make a precise answer thereto. And why should not then the King sith it is a law made here that his Grace is Head of the Church here compel men to answer precisely to the law here as they did then concerning the Pope.

I answered and said that I protested[8] that I intended not to defend my part or stand in contention, but I said there was a difference between those two cases because that at that time, as well here as elsewhere through the corps of Christendom, the Pope's power was recognized for an undoubted thing which seemeth not like a thing agreed in this realm and the contrary taken for truth in other realms; whereunto Master Secretary answered that they were as well burned for the denying of that, as they be beheaded for denying of this, and therefore as good reason to compel them to make precise answer to the one as to the other.

Whereto I answered that sith in this case a man is not by a law of one realm so bound in his conscience, where there is a law of the whole corps of Christendom to the contrary in matter touching belief, as he is by a law of the whole corps though there hap to be made in some place a law local to the contrary, the reasonableness or the unreasonableness in binding a man to precise answer, standeth not in the respect or difference between heading or burning, but because of the difference in charge of conscience, the difference standeth between heading and hell.

7. *under correction:* subject to correction
8. as a formal asseveration

Much was there answered unto this both by Master Secretary and my Lord Chancellor over long to rehearse. And in conclusion they offered me an oath by which I should be sworn to make true answer to such things as should be asked me on the King's behalf, concerning the King's own person.

Whereto I answered that verily I never purposed to swear any book oath[9] more while I lived. Then they said that was very obstinate if I would refuse that, for every man doth it ⌐in the Star Chamber¬ and everywhere. I said that was true but I had not so little foresight but that I might well conjecture what should be part of my interrogatory,[10] and as good it was to refuse it at the first as afterward.

Whereto my Lord Chancellor answered that he thought I guessed truth, for I should see them; and so they were shewed me and they were but twain. The first whether I had seen the statute. The other whether I believed that it were a lawful made statute or not. Whereupon I refused the oath and said further by mouth, that the first I had before confessed, and to the second I would make none answer.

Which was the end of the communication and I was thereupon sent away. In the communication before it was said that it was marveled that I stack[11] so much in my conscience while at the uttermost I was not sure therein. Whereto I said that I was very sure that mine own conscience, so informed as it is by such diligence as I have so long taken therein, may stand with mine own salvation. I meddle not with the conscience of them that think otherwise, every man ⌐*suo domino stat et cadit*¬. I am no man's judge. It was also said unto me that if I had as lief[12] be out of the world as in it, as I had there said, why did I not speak even out plain against the statute. It appeared well I was not content to die though I said so. Whereto I answered as the truth is, that I have not been a man of such holy living as I might be bold to offer myself to death, lest God for my presumption might suffer me to fall, and therefore I put not myself forward but draw back. Howbeit if God draw me to it himself, then trust I in his great mercy, that he shall not fail to give me grace and strength.

In conclusion Master Secretary said that he liked me this day much worse than he did the last time, for then he said he pitied me much and now he thought that I meant not well; but God and I know both that I mean well and so I pray God do by me.

9. oath sworn on the Bible
10. interrogation, questioning
11. persisted, was fixed
12. if I would as willingly

I pray you be you and my other friends of good cheer whatsoever fall of me,[13] and take no thought for me but pray for me as I do and shall do for you and all them.

Your tender loving father,

Thomas More Kg.

13. may happen to me

23

To Antonio Bonvisi

TOWER OF LONDON

1535

Sir Thomas More, a little before he was arraigned and condemned (in the year of our Lord 1535, and in the twenty-seventh year of the reign of King Henry the Eighth), being shut up so close in prison in the Tower that he had no pen nor ink, wrote with a coal an epistle in Latin to Master ⌐Anthony Bonvisi⌐ *(merchant of Lucca and then dwelling in London), his old and dear friend, and sent it unto him, the copy whereof here followeth.*

AMICORUM AMICISSIME, ET MERITO MIHI CHARISSIME, SALUE.
Quoniam mihi presagit animus (fortasse falso, sed presagit tamen) haud diu mihi superfuturam ad te scribendi facultatem, decreui dum licet, hoc saltem epistolio significare, quantum in hoc fortunae meae deliquio, amicitiae tuae iucunditate reficiar.

Nam ante quidem, vir ornatissime, tametsi mirifice certe, semper amore isto in me tuo delectatus sum, tamen recordanti mihi, annos iam prope quadraginta perpetuum Bonuisae domus, non hospitem sed alumnum fuisse me, nec amicum interim vlla rependenda gratia, sed sterilem tantum amatorem praestitisse, verecundia mea profecto fecerat, vt syncera illa suauitas, quam alioqui ex amicitiae vestrae cogitatione deglutiebam, paululum quiddam pudore quodam rustico, tanquam neglectae vicissitudinis subacesseret. Verum enimuero nunc hac ego me cogitatione consolor, quod bene vicissim mihi merendi de te nunquam se praebebat occasio. Ea siquidem amplitudo fortunae tuae fuit, vt commodandi tibi nullus mihi relinqueretur locus. Conscius igitur mihi, non officii neclectu vicem non rependisse me, sed quia deficiebat occasio;

quum iam te conspiciam, etiam sublata rependendi spe, sic in me amando et demerendo persistere, immo adeo progredi potius, et cursu quodam indefesso procurrere, vt pauci sic amicos fortunatos ambiunt, quomodo tu prostratum, abiectum, afflictum, et addictum carceri Morum tuum diligis, amas, foues, et obseruas; cum pristini pudoris mei qualiquali me amaritie abluo, tum in huius admirabilis amicitiae tuae suauitate conquiesco. Et nescio quo pacto tam fidelis amicitiae prosperitas videtur mihi cum hoc improspero classis meae naufragio propemodum paria facere (certe tollatur indignatio non amati mihi minus quam metuendi Principis) — quod ad reliqua pertinet, propemodum plus quam paria, quippe cum illa sint inter fortunae mala numeranda omnia.

At amicitiae tam constantis possessionem, quam tam aduersus fortunae casus non eripuit, sed ferruminauit fortius, amens profecto fuerim, inter caduca fortunae bona si numerem. Sublimius, haud dubie, bonum est, atque augustius, peculiari quadam Dei benignitate proueniens, amicitiae tam fidelis et reflante fortuna constantis raro concessa foelicitas. Ego certe non aliter accipio atque interpretor, quam eximia Dei miseratione curatum, vt inter tenues amiculos meos, tu vir talis, amicus tantus, iam longo ante tempore parareris, qui magnam istius molestiae partem, quam mihi ruentis in me fortunae moles inuexit, tua consolatione lenires ac releuares. Ego igitur, mi Antoni, mortalium mihi omnium charissime (quod solum possum) Deum Optimum Maxi. qui te mihi prouidit, obnixe deprecor, vt quando tibi talem debitorem dedit, qui nunquam soluendo sit futurus et facturus, beneficentiam istam quam mihi quotidie tam effusus impendis, ipse tibi dignetur pro sua benignitate rependere; tum vt nos ab hoc erumnoso et procelloso seculo in suam requiem pro sua miseratione perducat, vbi non erit opus epistolis, vbi non distinebit nos paries, vbi non arcebit a colloquio ianitor; sed cum Deo Patre ingenito, et vnigenito eius Filio, Domino et Redemptore nostro, Iesu Christo, atque vtriusque Spiritu, ab vtroque procedente Paracleto, gaudio perfruamur eterno. Cuius interea gaudii desiderio faxit Omnipotens Deus, vt tibi, mi Antoni, mihique, atque vtinam mortalibus, vndecunque omnibus, omnes huius orbis opes, vniuersa mundi gloria, nec non istius quoque dulcedo vitae vilescat. Amicorum omnium fidissime mihique dilectissime et (quod predicare iam olim soleo) oculi mei pupilla, vale. Familiam tuam totam, herili in me affectui simillimam, Christus seruet incolumem.

T. Morus: frustra fecero si adiiciam Tuus; nam hoc iam nescire non potes, quum tot beneficiis emeris. Nec ego nunc talis sum, vt referat cuius sim.

To Antonio Bonvisi

The translation into English of the Latin epistle next before:

GOOD MASTER BONVISI, OF ALL FRIENDS MOST FRIENDLIEST, AND TO ME WORTHILY DEARLIEST BELOVED, I HEARTILY GREET YOU.

Sith my mind doth give me (and yet may chance falsely but yet so it doth), that I shall not have long liberty to write unto you, I determined therefore while I may, to declare unto you by this little epistle of mine, how much I am comforted with the sweetness of your friendship, in this decay of my fortune.

For afore (right worshipful Sir) although I always delighted marvelously in this your love towards me, yet when I consider in my mind, that I have been now almost this forty years, not a guest, but a continual nursling in master Bonvisi house, and in the mean season[1] have not shewed myself in requiting you again, a friend, but a barrain lover only my shamefastness[2] verily made, that that sincere sweetness, which otherwise I received of the revolving of your friendship somewhat waxed sourish, by reason of a certain rustical[3] shame as neglecting of my duty toward you. But now I comfort myself with this, that I never had the occasion to do you pleasure. For such was always your great wealth, that there was nothing left, in which I might be unto you beneficial. I therefore (knowing that I have not been unthankful to you by omitting my duty toward you, but for lack of occasion and opportunity, and seeing moreover all hope of recompense taken away, you so to persevere in love toward me, binding me more and more to you, yea rather so to run forward still, and as it were with a certain indefatigable course to go forth, that few men so fawn upon their fortunate friends, as you favor, love, foster and honor me, now overthrown, abjected, afflicted, and condemned to prison) cleanse myself both from this bitterness (such as it is) of mine old shamefastness, and also repose myself in the sweetness of this marvelous friendship of yours.

And this faithful prosperity of this amity and friendship of yours towards me (I wot not how) seemeth in a manner to counterpoise this unfortunate shipwreck of mine, and saving the indignation of my Prince, of me no less loved than feared, else as concerning all other things, doth almost more than counterpoise. For all those are to be accounted amongst the

1. *in the mean season:* meanwhile
2. ashamedness
3. lacking in social graces or polish

mischances of fortune. But if I should reckon the possession of so constant friendship (which no storms of adversity hath taken away, but rather hath fortified and strengthed) amongst the brittle gifts of fortune, then were I mad. For the felicity of so faithful and constant friendship in the storms of fortune (which is seldom seen) is doubtless a high and a noble gift proceeding of a certain singular benignity of God. And indeed as concerning myself, I cannot otherwise take it nor reckon it, but that it was ordained by the great mercy of God, that you Master Bonvisi amongst my poor friends, such a man as you are and so great a friend, should be long afore provided, that should by your consolation, assuage and relieve a great part of these troubles and griefs of mine, which the hugeness[4] of fortune hath hastely brought upon me. I therefore, my dear friend and of all mortal men to me most dearest, do (which now only I am able to do) earnestly pray to Almighty God, which hath provided you for me, that sith he hath given you such a debtor as shall never be able to pay you, that it may please him of his benignity, to requite this bountifulness of yours, which you every day thus plenteously pour upon me. And that for his mercy's sake he will bring us from this wretched and stormy world, into his rest, where shall need no letters, where no wall shall dissever[5] us, where no porter shall keep us from talking together, but that we may have the fruition of the eternal joy with God the Father, and with his only begotten Son our Redeemer Jesu Christ, with the holy spirit of them both, the Holy Ghost proceeding from them both. And in the mean season, Almighty God grant both you and me good Master Bonvisi and all mortal men everywhere, to set at naught all the riches of this world, with all the glory of it, and the pleasure of this life also, for the love and desire of that joy. Thus of all friends most trusty, and to me most dearly beloved, and as I was wont to call you the apple of mine eye, right heartily fare ye well. And Jesus Christ keep safe and sound and in good health, all your family, which be of like affection toward me as their master is.

Thomas More: I should in vain put to it, Yours, for thereof can you not be ignorant, since you have bought it with so many benefits. Nor now I am not such a one that it forceth[6] whose I am.

---

4. huge burden, enormity
5. separate
6. matters

24

To Margaret Roper

TOWER OF LONDON

5 July 1535

Sir Thomas More was beheaded at the Tower hill in London on Tuesday the sixth day of July in the year of our Lord 1535, and in the twenty-seventh year of the reign of King Henry the Eighth. And on the day next before, being Monday and the fifth day of July, he wrote with a coal a letter to his daughter Mistress Roper, ⌐and sent it to her¬ (which was the last thing that ever he wrote). The copy whereof here followeth.

Our Lord bless you good daughter and your good husband and your little boy and all yours and all my children and all my godchildren and all our friends. Recommend me when you may to my good daughter ⌐Cecily¬, whom I beseech our Lord to comfort, and I send her my blessing and to all her children and pray her to pray for me. ⌐I send her an handkercher¬[1] and God comfort my good son her husband. My good daughter ⌐Daunce¬ hath the picture in parchment that you delivered me from ⌐my Lady Conyers¬, her name is on the back side. Shew her that I heartily pray her that you may send it in my name to her again for a token from me to pray for me.

I like special well ⌐Dorothy Colly¬, I pray you be good unto her. I would wit whether this be she that you wrote me of. If not, I pray you be good to the other as you may in her affliction, and to my good daughter ⌐Joan Aleyn¬ to give her I pray you some kind answer, for she sued[2] hither to me this day to pray you be good to her.

1. handkerchief
2. pleaded

127

I cumber[3] you, good Margaret, much, but I would be sorry, if it should be any longer than tomorrow, for it is ⌜Saint Thomas' Even and the Vtas[4] of Saint Peter⌝ and therefore tomorrow long I to go to God, it were a day very meet and convenient for me. I never liked your manner toward me better than ⌜when you kissed me last⌝ for I love when daughterly love and dear charity hath not leisure to look to worldly courtesy.

Fare well my dear child and pray for me, and I shall for you and all your friends that we may merrily meet in heaven. I thank you for your great cost.[5]

I send now unto my good daughter ⌜Clement⌝ her ⌜algorism stone⌝ and I send her and my good son and all hers God's blessing and mine.

I pray you at time convenient recommend me to my good son ⌜John More⌝. I liked well his natural fashion.[6] Our Lord bless him and his good wife my loving daughter, to whom I pray him be good, as he hath great cause, and that ⌜if the land of mine come to his hand⌝, he break not my will concerning his sister Daunce. And our Lord bless ⌜Thomas and Austin⌝ and all that they shall have.

3. trouble, distress
4. octave
5. expenditure of time and labor
6. behavior

A DISTICH OF SIR THOMAS MORE
WRITTEN THREE YEARS BEFORE HE DIED

Qui memor es Mori, longae tibi tempora vitae
Sint, et ad aeternam peruia porta, mori.

You who remember More, may your life be long
and your death an open gate to eternal life.

Commentary

For complete bibliographical information
on the works cited here in shortened form, see the Bibliography.

LETTER 1: TO THOMAS CROMWELL

Thomas Cromwell Thomas Cromwell (c. 1485-1540), son of a blacksmith of Putney, followed a military career as an adventurer and soldier fighting for the French in Italy, where he also worked as an accountant. Subsequently he was a business consultant in the Netherlands, and upon his return to England, he got involved in the legal and commercial professions. Eventually he obtained a job with Cardinal Wolsey, and under his protection Cromwell soon transformed himself into an indispensable royal administrator. After Wolsey's fall from power, Cromwell became the faithful minister of Henry VIII. His career would henceforth depend upon his success in satisfying the King's goals and desires, with which he seemed to have completely identified. "I would do it," he wrote years later, on June 12, 1540, while a prisoner in the Tower, "if it had been or were in my power to make your Majesty so pusant [puissant] as all the world should be compelled to obey you" (Merriman, vol. 2, letter n. 348, p. 265). Eustace Chapuys, the imperial ambassador, usually a good observer of character, saw Cromwell rising "above every one, except it be the lady [Anne Boleyn], and the world says he has more credit with his master than ever the cardinal had. The cardinal shared his influence with the Duke of Suffolk and several others. Now there is not a person who does anything except Cromwell. The Chancellor is only his tool; and although he has, so far, refused to take the Great Seal himself, people say he will be persuaded to catch at it before long." Cromwell was a married man, father of a son and two daughters, and according to Chapuys, "a person of good cheer, gracious words and generous

131

in actions; his equipage and his palace are magnificent" (Williams, vol. 5, p. 00). But, despite all his success, Cromwell eventually alienated the King by negotiating the marriage with Anne of Cleves in 1539. As a consequence, he was accused and convicted of high treason in 1540. Desperately, on June 30, he wrote to the King, "I crye for mercye mercye mercye" (Merriman, vol. 2, letter n. 349, p. 273). He was executed a month later, on July 29.

"Not for Englishmen the superb follies of Spain's self-martyrdom to a fanatic ideal," wrote A. G. Dickens. "In retrospect," he continued, "Cromwell stands out as the leader of an invasion of our public affairs by laymen and the lay spirit. He and his like show a vivid consciousness of the shortcomings of ecclesiastical administration and jurisdiction; behind the thin facade of courteous reverence, they entertained a strong resentment against the professional esprit de corps, the easily-won wealth, the hauteur and fundamental worldliness of their prelatic associates. No fair-minded observer would deny that much hypocrisy marked this lay invasion. It was accompanied by too much greed and self-interest" (pp. 177-78). See also G. R. Elton, *Reform and Renewal: Thomas Cromwell and the Common Weal*. Long before, Hilaire Belloc saw in Cromwell "the true creator of the English Reformation." We are still wanting a scholarly biography of Thomas Cromwell.

right worshipful . . . unto you These and similar expressions are the usual way of beginning the salutation in the official correspondence of the period.

my cousin William Rastell William Rastell (1508-1565), More's nephew, son of John Rastell and Elizabeth More, one of Thomas More's sisters, has been rightly called "probably the best English printer of his day" (A. W. Reed). Rastell followed his father's profession; at age twenty-one, he set up his own press and issued his first book. By the time this letter was written, Rastell had published a number of works by his uncle, among them *The Supplication of Souls,* a second edition of *A Dialogue Concerning Heresies* (the first was published by John Rastell), *The Confutation of Tyndale's Answer, The Apology,* the *Letter against Frith, The Debellation of Salem and Bizance,* and *The Answer to a Poisoned Book,* which is the book referred to in the letter. In January 1534, the young publisher experienced how dangerous his profession had become with the new order of things, and he promptly dropped it to dedicate his efforts to the study of law.

Rastell married Winifred Clement, daughter of John Clement and Margaret Giggs. The couple left England in 1549, and returned when Mary came to power in 1553. To Rastell we owe the publication of More's *English Works* in 1557. (He had rescued the letters and manuscripts from the Tower after More was executed.) The headings of the letters (which are reproduced here) come from Rastell's remarkable edition. He is said to have written an excellent life of Thomas More, most of which has been lost, a deplorable loss if one considers the talents apparent in the so-called *Rastell Fragments*.

A new persecution of Roman Catholics with the advent of Queen Elizabeth again forced Rastell into exile, and he died in Louvain in 1565. Cf. A. W. Reed, pp. 72-93; and Reed's article "William Rastell and More's English Works," reprinted in *Essential Articles for the Study of Thomas More,* pp. 436-46.

the book of certain articles The book's complete title is *Articles devised by the Whole Consent of the King's Council to inform his loving subjects,* and is usually known as *The Book of Nine Articles.* It was printed at the end of 1533, and it is not much more than a pamphlet of government propaganda to justify the King's marital behavior. One of the articles accuses Pope Clement VII (pope from November 1523 to September 1534) of heresy, simony, and illegitimate birth. (This last condition was true indeed.) These accusations were spurred by the Pope's refusal to sanction the King's divorce from Catherine of Aragon.

the Supper of the Lord *The Souper of the Lorde . . . wheryn incidently M. More's letter against Johan Frythe is confuted* was published anonymously on April 5, 1533; it had been written by George Joy or Joye (c. 1490-1553), who, years before, having been charged with heresy, took refuge first in Strasburg and then in Antwerp. In this city he met William Tyndale and John Frith (*DNB,* vol. 10, pp. 1107-9). More thought the book was so impious that its author did not dare to sign it, and immediately responded with *The Answer to the first part of the poisoned book which a nameless heretic hath named the Supper of the Lord.* More finished the book around December 12, 1533, and gave authorization for it to be sold at the same time as his *Letter against Frith,* which William Rastell had printed a year ago but had not sold to avoid giving more publicity to the "new" unorthodox ideas. *The Answer* was to be More's last contribution to the theological wars of his time. In his long letter against John Frith, More defended the Catholic teaching on the Eucharist (see *CW,* vol. 7, pp. 233-38). On George Joye, see *The Complete Works,* vol. 11, pp. 237-39, and R. Pineas, "George Joye's Controversy with Thomas More," *Moreana* 38 (1973): 27-36.

since the Feast of the Circumcision The octave of Christmas, January 1. Many copies of More's book (*The Answer*) were sold before Christmas, but the date of publication was inadvertently printed as 1534. More had to explain and apologize for the printer's error in order to explain that this book could not have been written against "the book of certain articles." A. W. Reed comments, "I believe that Rastell rather perversely dated the New Year from Christmas or 1st January, because it had a bearing on the important question of whether the Papal Brief conveying the dispensation for the marriage of Henry VIII to Katherine was a forgery or not. Since the Papal Briefs dated the New Year from the Feast of the Incarnation, i.e. Christmas Day, the friends of Katherine claimed that the dispensation was good" (p. 81). The judgment on Rastell's *perversity* aside, the canonical dispensation did not depend upon this matter of dating.

to be your beadsman A beadsman or beadswoman is a person who prays for another. The beads, usually some small pellets or bones or bits of glass, are an ancient device for counting vocal prayers, and are also used by Hindus, Buddhists, and Moslems.

At Chelsea The house that More built by the Thames, about ten miles west of London. From 1505 to 1523, More had lived in a large house called "the old Barge" on Bucklersbury Street. In 1524 More moved his family to the new house. This same year or the following, the King paid a visit to More, which he enjoyed so much that he returned from time to time: "And for the pleasure he [Henry VIII] took in his company, would his grace suddenly sometimes come home to his house at Chelsea, to be merry with him; whither on a time, unlooked for, he came to dinner [to him]; and after dinner, in a fair garden of his, walked with him by the space of an hour, holding his arm about his neck" (Roper, pp. 20-21).

the Vigil of the Purification of our Blessed Lady The feast of the Purification of Mary, February 2 (Candlemas day), is now celebrated as the feast of the Presentation of the Lord. See Luke 2:22-38.

LETTER 2: TO THOMAS CROMWELL

a bill put in against me The bill of attainder was introduced into the House of Lords on February 21, 1534. More's name appeared along with that of Bishop John Fisher in a bill accusing Elizabeth Barton and some of her followers of high treason. More must have written this letter to Cromwell immediately afterwards, and then, on March 5, written another letter to the King (Letter 4).

the Nun of Canterbury There is no reliable biography of Elizabeth Barton (c. 1506-1534), the Nun of Canterbury or the Holy Maid of Kent, as she was also called. She was a servant in the household of one Thomas Cobb, in the parish of Aldington, a land agent for William Warham, the Archbishop of Canterbury. In 1525, around Easter, the young woman fell sick, and it was on occasion of this sickness that a certain reputation for "divination and foretelling" began to spread about her in the vicinity. Apparently, there were a number of instances of clairvoyance, and a prediction over a sick child in the same house. The child died, but Elizabeth was cured in an allegedly miraculous manner. The ecclesiastical authorities proceeded to study the case with the result that soon afterwards the young maid entered the Order of St. Benedict as a novice and was professed a nun in 1528. As her visions continued to recur, her fame spread over the country, and the young woman began to speak her mind on the King's marital situation and other matters relating to the spread of heresy and new "evangelical" ideas.

Up to this point, she had not been treated much differently than those who had made similar pronouncements throughout the history of the Church. However, in July 1533, there was a change. Suddenly there were official orders to take her out of the convent. The exact cause is unknown, although it is possible that Henry VIII himself ordered it as a reaction to the news of his recent excommunication, which was given in Rome at the beginning of July. The Nun was arrested again in November and brought to the Tower of London. Subsequent information about her is doubtful or biased. The "confession" of the woman may have been a moment of weakness rather than the revelation of a fraud by the monks and other priests of her company. She was accused of speaking against both the King's divorce from Catherine of Aragon and his marriage to Anne Boleyn (they had secretly married in January of 1533), thus influencing the public opinion against the King. However, even if the accusations were true, they did not constitute legal treason, and therefore a bill of attainder from Parliament was needed. The document, prepared by Cromwell, accused Barton as well as Edward Bocking, the appointed confessor of the Nun; John Richard Dering, another Benedictine priest; Richard Master, parish priest of Elizabeth Barton in Aldington; Henry Gold, a priest; and two Franciscan friars, Hugh Rich and Richard Risby. Cromwell had written that they all "shall be attainted of high treason and suffer death" (*LP*, vol. 7, p. 70). A second list mentioned Bishop Fisher and one of his chaplains but not More, although Henry already wanted him to be included. The bill was introduced, and the Nun of Kent and her adherents were sentenced to death. She was executed on April 20, 1534, in Tyburn, along with Edward Bocking, John Richard Dering, Richard Risby, Hugh Rich, and Henry Gold. (Richard Master was not executed.) The same day, John Husee wrote to Lord Lisle: "And the saying is that this day the Nun of Kent, with two Friars Observant, two monks and one secular priest, were drawn from the Tower to Tyburn, and there hanged and headed. God, if it be his pleasure, have mercy on their souls. Also this day the most part of this City are sworn to the king and his legitimate issue by the Queen's Grace now had and hereafter to come, and so shall all the realm over be sworn in like manner. The bishops of Durham, Winchester, and York, are now sent for, to what intent God knoweth" (*The Lisle Letters*, vol. 2, 130). The execution was a way to frighten others into acquiescing to the oath of succession. "The execution of the Holy Maid and her companions was one of the many ways in which judicious use of judicial terror (albeit falling short of tyranny) was employed to secure compliance with the English Reformation" (Richard Rex, "The Execution of the Holy Maid of Kent," *Historical Research* 64 [1991]: 220).

Although there is a book about the Nun — Allan Neame's *The Holy Maid of Kent* — we still lack a scholarly, unbiased study. The text of a sermon against the Nun, which may have been the actual official proclamation against her at St. Paul's and later in Canterbury, was edited by L. E. Whatmore. Cf. also Bridgett, *The Life of Blessed John Fisher*, chap. 11, "The Holy Maid of Kent"; Knowles, vol. 3, chap. 15, "Elizabeth Barton"; and Marius, *Thomas More*, pp. 446-53.

LETTER 3: TO THOMAS CROMWELL

with my son Roper His son-in-law, William Roper (c. 1496-1578), the husband of Margaret, More's eldest daughter. The Ropers were an old and wealthy family. William's father, John Roper, was a member of Lincoln's Inn like the Mores — Sir Thomas and his father, Judge John More — with whom he sat on several commissions in Kent. William Roper was destined to have a rather successful public career under Henry VIII, Edward VI, Queen Mary, and Queen Elizabeth, holding the office of protonotary for more than fifty years and sitting several times as member of Parliament. In the first enthusiasm for the new evangelical doctrines arriving from the Continent, Roper had embraced Lutheran ideas (this was at the time of his marriage to Margaret), but he later returned to the Catholic faith.

It was Roper who asked Nicholas Harpsfield to write a biography of Thomas More, and in order to help him, he put down his own recollections. These constitute the most intimate memoir of More, *The Life of Sir Thomas More, Knight*, which has rightly been considered a literary masterpiece. In his own full-fledged biography, Harpsfield wrote this dedication to Roper: "He was your worthy Father in law: what say I? your father in law? nay, rather your very father indeed; and though a temporal man, yet your very spiritual father" (p. 5). There are several editions of Roper's *Life:* by Elsie Vaughan Hitchcock (London, 1935), James Mason Cline (New York, 1950), Richard S. Sylvester and Davis P. Harding (New Haven, 1962), and E. E. Reynolds (London, 1963). See also the introduction to Hitchcock's edition (pp. xxix-xlvii).

the Bishop of Canterbury Richard Master, then the parson or priest of Aldington, Elizabeth Barton's parish, prepared an official report on the young woman for his immediate ecclesiastical superior, William Warham, Archbishop of Canterbury. As far as the evidence goes, Warham did not dislike her. Thomas Goldwell, prior of Christ's Church in Canterbury, explained in a letter to Cromwell that the Nun was many times with the archbishop and the latter "gave much credence unto her words in such things as she knew, and surmised to know, that she did shew unto him. She said also that if Almighty God did suffer his grace to reign king, yet he should not be so accepted in the reputation of God, as she said it was shewed unto her by revelation" (Wright, p. 20).

it pleased the King's Grace to deliver me the roll This document could be the report of the ecclesiastical tribunal in charge of the investigation of the young woman's visions and voices, raptures and ecstasies. Her miraculous cure had been related to the popular devotion around the chapel of our Lady at Court-at-Street. In her trances, as Thomas Cranmer recollected years later, "[was] there heard a voice speaking within her belly as it had been in a tun [large cask]" (*LP,* vol. 6, 1546). Oftentimes the voice spoke in not very elegant rhyme, as More told the King. What the Lord Chancellor had read in those papers most likely consisted of words encouraging the basic acts and emphases of traditional Christian piety: regular attendance of Church, confession, warnings of the last things to come, the joys of heaven and the pains of hell, prayers to the saints, and so forth. The official sermon accuses her of heresy but without any convincing argument.

in my Lord Cardinal's days Thomas Wolsey (c. 1475-1530), the Cardinal Archbishop of York and Lord Chancellor of England. After completing his studies at Oxford, Wolsey entered into the service of Henry VII, and later continued serving the King's son and successor to the throne. Wolsey became bishop of Lincoln in 1514, was named cardinal the following year, and papal legate in 1518. As chancellor, this ambitious prelate dominated secular and ecclesiastical life in England, but his failure in the matter of Henry's divorce cost him the King's favor and the Great Seal, emblematic of his high office in the realm. In the spring of 1530, the cardinal undertook, for the first time in his life, a visit to his own archbishopric. However, he was detained by Henry's agents and forced to return to London; he died on his way to the city in the abbey of Leicester on November 29, 1530. Thomas More succeeded him as Chancellor of England. The cardinal's secretary, George Cavendish, wrote a glorified account of Wolsey entitled *The Life and Death of Cardinal Wolsey by George Cavendish,* which can be found in *Two Early Tudor Lives.* See also A. F. Pollard, *Wolsey,* and, more recently, P. Gwyn, *The King's Cardinal.*

she had been both with his Lordship and with the King's Grace On October 1, 1528, Warham wrote to Cardinal Wolsey to inform him that Elizabeth Barton, now a Benedictine nun or novice, wished to speak with him and with the King. According to the prelate, she was a "very well disposed and virtuous woman." Without being duplicitous, the archbishop gave the clear impression that he was merely introducing the visionary young woman to the two most powerful men in England. "What she hath to say," wrote Warham, "or whether it be good or ill, I do not know; but she hath desired me to write unto your Grace and to desire the same (as I do), that she may come into your Grace's presence. Whom, when your Grace have heard, ye may order as shall please the same. For I assure your Grace she hath made very importunate suit to me to be a mean to your Grace that she may speak with you" (quoted in Neame, p. 109).

I had never heard any one word It it is impossible to know what influence, if any, Elizabeth Barton had on Wolsey. (Cavendish, Wolsey's biographer, never mentions the Nun.) But she visited him more than once. And she rebuked the powerful prelate and apparently showed him his coming fall from power. The official "Sermon against the Nun" gives her a large and influential role: "And that said cardinal was as well minded and bent to go forth in the King's Grace's said cause of matrimony and divorce as any man living (according to the law of God and the law of nature) till he was perverted by this nun — and induced to believe that if he proceeded in the same God would sore strike him" (Whatmore, p. 467).

This is the first item in the report sent to Secretary Cromwell: "First, of an angel that appeared and bade the nun: Go unto the King, that infidel prince of England, and say that I command him to amend his life, and that he leave three things which he loveth and purposeth upon; that is, that he take none of the Pope's right and patrimony from him; the second, that he destroy all these new folks of opinion and the works of their new learning; the third, that, if he married and took Anne to wife, the vengeance of God should plague him, and (as she saith) she shewed this unto the king, etc" (Wright, p. 14; the version in *LP,* vol. 6, 1466, has been summarized).

Father Risby . . . at mine house Richard Risby (1490-1534) had studied at Oxford University and then entered the Franciscan Order in 1513. At the time More is referring to, he was the warden of the community of Friars Observant at Canterbury. Soon after making the Nun's acquaintance, Father Risby became one of her adherents, acting as confessor for people who went to listen to her. Under the Nun's inspiration, this priest, with other companions, gave himself to all kinds of penance and extreme forms of mortification. Risby was arrested in November 1533, appeared in the court of the Star Chamber, in Westminster, with Elizabeth Barton and the rest of the prisoners, and was executed along with them on April 20, 1534, at Tyburn.

my Lord Legate Cardinal Thomas Wolsey. A *Legatus a latere* (*legate* meaning "from or at one's side") is a cardinal representing the Roman Pontiff as his alter ego for a particular purpose. In 1518 Pope Leo X (1513-1521) nominated four papal legates to announce a peace plan for Christian princes and a crusade against the Turks; Lorenzo Campeggio (or Campeggi) was to go to England, but Henry VIII objected and then set as one of the conditions that Wolsey be made a legate with equal powers. Campeggio was later the Cardinal Protector of England and returned as legate for the King's "great matter" in 1528.

a revelation . . . of three swords This oracle for Cardinal Wolsey appears also in the list compiled for Cromwell: "*Item,* that she was charged to go unto the cardinal when he was most in his prosperity, and shew him of three swords that he had in his hand: one of the spiritualty, another of the temporalty, and the other of the king's marriage; a long matter" (Wright, p. 15).

concerning the Cardinal that his soul was saved by her mediation That is, by her intercession. According to Doctor Edward Bocking, the Nun's spiritual director, who was already gathering material for a "great book" about her revelations, Elizabeth Barton thought that Cardinal Wolsey had died prematurely. Thus the report sent to Cromwell reads, "*Item,* it is written in the great book (which I shewed you right now) as a revelation of hers, that my lord cardinal came to his death before God would have had him by the space of fifteen years." Therefore no sentence was pronounced on his soul at the time of his death. *"Item,* another season after the angel commanded her to go unto the said cardinal, and shew him of his fall, and that he had not done as she had commanded him by the will of God, etc." According to this report to Cromwell, the Nun saw "the disputations of the devils" for the prelate's soul and told "how she was three times lift up and could not see him neither in heaven, hell, nor purgatory; and at the last, where she saw him, and how by her penance he was brought unto heaven; and what souls she saw fly through purgatory" (Wright, pp. 15, 16; and *LP,* vol. 6, 1466).

till I saw him at Paul's cross More didn't see him again until November 23, 1533, in the churchyard of St. Paul's Cathedral in London, the site of the most famous pulpit in England, where the Nun of Canterbury and her followers publicly "confessed" their crimes. According to Whatmore, the reading of the "Sermon against the Holy Maid of Kent and Her Adherents" was part of the ceremony, and it may have been repeated in other settings.

After this, about Shrovetide The days before Ash Wednesday: the last Sunday before Lent, Shrove Monday, and Shrove Tuesday, when Christians would be shriven — that is, absolved after confessing their sins to a priest. That year Mardi Gras (Shrove Tuesday) was February 25th.

Father Rich Hugh Rich was the Warden of the Friars Observant of Richmond, and another enthusiastic follower of the Nun of Kent. His visit to Thomas More is just one instance of the friar's zeal in spreading the word about Elizabeth Barton and her "divine" mission in England. Father Rich visited bishops, religious houses, important London families, members of the nobility, and even personages at the royal court. He was arrested with the other followers of the Nun, and included with them in the act of attainder, and executed on April 20, 1534. See Rex, "The Execution of the Holy Maid of Kent," pp. 216-20.

the tale of Mary Magdalene Elizabeth Barton admitted to having had a series of visions and conversations with St. Mary Magdalene at the end of 1532. Here More seems to be referring to one of the stories that were told about the Nun, the affair of the Golden Letter. According to the official sermon preached against Barton at St. Paul's, it was Mary Magdalene herself who would have written in heaven a message in the Nun's name and then, conveniently disguised as her servant, delivered it to a certain widow in London. The letter declared "that if she did minish any part of certain gold hidden by her husband while he was alive, and bestowed it not entirely in the ornaments of the church, she should do it to her husband's utter damnation and hers both" (Whatmore, p. 470; Wright, p. 18, n. 29). The story gets its name from the two words in gold that appeared at the head of the letter: JHESUS and MARIA. The story is reminiscent of the story of Ananias and his wife Sapphira told in Acts 5:1-11. One of Cromwell's annotations reads, "To know whether Sir Hawkehurst, who wrote the letter of Mary Magdalen, shall be put in the Act" (*LP*, vol. 7, 70). Apparently this man was only the possessor of a "copy" of the strange document.

at the King's Mass at Calais More thinks that what Elizabeth Barton had dreamed and later told her audience had been repeated by others as part of her revelations. According to the letter sent to Cromwell, the abridged "tale of the host" goes like this: "When the king's highness was over at Calais, she saw the host taken from the priest with the blessed blood, and that angels brought it her for to receive, saying, etc. Two sheets would scant write this story" (Wright, p. 15; *LP*, vol. 6, 1466). The same story is referred to in a letter of Thomas Goldwell to Cromwell (*LP*, vol. 6, 20). Another item in the same list refers to "the vision that she had, if the king should have married at Calais, of the great shame that the Queen should have had, etc." (*LP*, vol. 6, 17). Anne Boleyn was, as a matter of fact, with the court at Calais.

and yet many miracles indeed done by them More accepted miracles as part of the universal order of divine providence. The inhabitants of his Utopia were actually impressed by the miracles that the Europeans proudly related of Christ. They admitted that "in their country, too, miracles often occur" (*CW*, vol. 4, p. 225). More dealt with this topic at length in a number of chapters of his *Dialogue Concerning Heresies* (*CW*, vol. 6, First Book, chaps. 4 to 17).

Syon Syon Abbey was the only house of the Order of Saint Bridget in England. Despite the rigors of its rule, the abbey had attracted and continued to attract many vocations from important English families. The monastery enjoyed great prestige as an institution where authentic religious and intellectual life was cultivated, due largely to the work of Richard Reynolds and Richard Whytford, a Bridgettine of Syon, a friend of More and Erasmus, and translator of the *Imitation of Christ*. When the Henrician persecution exploded, this religious community remained solidly united against the King's divorce. David Knowles has described this religious family as "an orthodox Port Royal, a key position in the religious life of the country," and "something unique in Tudor England" (p. 215). Perhaps this will make it easier to understand the efforts by the Royal Commission to force the prestigious monks to surrender to the new Tudor order.

one Helen, a maiden dwelling about Tottenham This visionary woman, living north of London, not far from the city, seems to have been psychically disturbed or unbalanced. In *A Dialogue of Comfort against Tribulation,* Antony gives his nephew Vincent some guidance on how to help those who may be deceived by "illusions of the devil" which they take for divine revelations. There More followed the guide of the French medieval theologian Jean Gerson, who had written a treatise on the matter, *De probatione spirituum*: "Many other tokens are there in that work of Master Gerson spoken of, to consider by, whether the person never having revelations of God, nor illusions from the devil, do either for winning of money or worldly favour feign his revelations himself, and delude the people withal" (*CW*, vol. 12, pp. 133-34).

threw him out at a window The scene describes what the modern spirit could easily take for a case of collective hallucination; for More, Elizabeth Barton was simply admitting in all humility the dangerous edge that religious visionaries walk. On the Nun's temptations and encounters with the devil, see Neame, *The Holy Maid of Kent*, pp. 148-53, and *LP*, vol. 6, 1466, 585-86.

I gave her a double ducat The ducat was a Venetian gold coin.

I shall insert the very copy thereof This is letter n. 192 in the Princeton edition of Elizabeth F. Rogers (1947).

in the light of the Spirit For the scriptural foundation of the gifts of the Spirit, see 1 Cor. 12:1-11 and 14:1-40, where St. Paul says that "the particular way in which the Spirit is given to each person is for a good purpose." Paul acknowledged that "to aspire to spiritual gifts" was something good, but also asked his brethren in the faith to "concentrate on those which will grow to benefit the community." More's advice to Elizabeth Barton is again wholly Pauline and humanistic in that he reminds her, above all things, "to pray not only with the spirit but with the mind as well" (1 Cor. 14:15).

Moses . . . counseled by Jethro Jethro, a priest of Midian, was Moses' father-in-law. The well-known story is told in chapter 18 of the book of Exodus.

the late Duke of Buckingham Edward Stafford (1478-1521), Duke of Buckingham, was the leading nobleman in England. Immensely popular, he was reckless and arrogant, and ever a dangerous contender for the throne if Henry VIII died without a male heir. More here refers to conversations the duke had with Nicholas Hopkins, a monk of the Carthusian priory at Henton. The monk said that he had been told by divine revelation that one day Buckingham would "have all." The treasonous conversation was exposed by the duke's surveyor, and then by interrogation of both his chancellor and his confessor. Stafford was executed in May of 1521. This fatal incident darkly underscored the dangerous political climate long before the actual Tudor revolution. Scarisbrick offers this comment in his superb biography of Henry VIII: "What he [Buckingham] had said and done were manifest treason. What he was said to have said and done were manifest treason and would have cost anyone his life in early Tudor England. Indeed, if he had done, or been said to have done, no more than to note that there was no heir to the throne, and state that there never would be, he would have been in jeopardy; for, as early as 1521, the King's failure to beget an heir was probably already a sufficient cause of anxiety to make it dangerous for such as he to remark the fact" (p. 122). See also Barbara J. Harris, *Edward Stafford,* chap. 8.

specially with lay persons Either directly or through the work of her priest friends (especially Hugh Rich, who had the longest list of people he had talked to), the Nun's revelations concerning Henry and his kingdom reached a fair number of important lay persons, among others, the Queen herself, Lady Mary, the Countess of Salisbury (Lady Margaret Pole), Lord and Lady Husee, the Marchioness of Exeter, Lady Dareby, Mr. White, Mr. Dabney, Mr. Percy, Mr. Nele and his wife, merchants of London, and others (*LP,* vol. 6, 1468). Eustace Chapuys informed the emperor, Charles V, that Queen Catherine had always refused to see the Nun (*LP,* vol. 6, 1419). Gertrude Courtenay, the Marchioness of Exeter, had a connection with the Nun that was especially dangerous, since her husband was the King's first cousin and a possible heir to the throne. Lady Exeter, who was devoted to the Queen, once disguised herself in a religious habit and rode sixty miles to see and consult with the Nun, then in Canterbury. Later, she invited Elizabeth Barton to come to her house in Surrey. Subsequently she implored Henry for mercy, and the King pardoned her. Afterward she sent a note to Cromwell, "trusting he [the King] will remember that it is much less marvel that I, being a woman, shall thus be deluded by such pestilent hypocrites, seeing so many wise persons have been equally abused" (*LP,* vol. 6, 1465).

the proctor . . . at Sheen and one Brother William The Proctor or Procurator was Henry Man, then thirty-three years old, and his companion was most likely one William Howe, the Sacristan at the Charterhouse, probably appointed to accompany him whenever they had business in the city. Women were strictly forbidden in the cloister, but the religious knew of the "Holy Maid of Kent" through visits and talks with Hugh Rich and Henry Gold. Henry Man wrote a letter full of exaggerated spiritual enthusiasm to Edward Bocking, asking to be accepted as his "spiritual son." Later he embraced the new Henrician order of things and was made Prior of Witham in Somerset. Cf. Neame, *The Holy Maid of Kent,* pp. 226-30, 300-301.

at the house of a knight in Kent From the list sent to Cromwell: "*Item* xxiii: Of a certain gentleman dwelling about Canterbury, that had long times been tempted to drown himself by the sprite of a woman that he had kept by his wife's days, which is damned, etc., a long matter and a strange" (Wright, p. 18). This afflicted knight might have been Sir James Hales.

on a day in which there was a profession A "profession" is the act of entering a religious order by declaring certain promises or vows; it follows a period of initiation and probation.

bringing forth to light such detestable hypocrisy Under orders from Cromwell, Thomas Cranmer, then Archbishop of Canterbury, commanded Philippa John, the prioress of St. Sepulchre, to meet with him "and bring with you your Nun which was sometime at Court-at-Street." The interrogation took place in August 1533, and soon afterward Elizabeth Barton was in the custody of Cromwell. A few months later, the young woman and the priests associated with her were taken to Lambeth to be interrogated by a commission of three Privy Councilors: Thomas Cromwell, Thomas Cranmer, and Hugh Latimer. From this moment on it is possible to follow the events more closely. Christopher Hales, the Attorney General, made the arrests. The Nun was said to have confessed that "she had never in her whole life any revelation from God, but that they were of her own feigning, wherein she used much craft to make and devise them consonant and agreeable to the minds of them who were resorting to her" (see *LP*, vol. 6, 1546). In November she was charged with treason and heresy.

her own confession declared at Paul's Cross On Sunday, November 23, 1533, the "Sermon against the Holy Maid of Kent and Her Adherents" was read by Doctor John Capon, alias Salcot (although it was probably written by another person, one Nicholas Heath), proclaiming the treasonous crimes of all the prisoners in the affair of the Nun. Each one of them confessed in public. The Nun's confession reads as follows: "I, Dame Elizabeth Barton, do confess that I, most miserable and wretched person, have been the original of all this mischief, and by my falsehood have grievously deceived all these persons here and many more, whereby I have most grievously offended Almighty God and my most noble sovereign, the King's Grace" (*LP*, vol. 6, 1468; Neame, p. 270). Afterward, they were all taken back barefoot to the Tower. According to the imperial ambassador, there may have been a plan to take the Nun on tour "through all the towns in the kingdom to make a similar representation, in order to efface the general impression of the Nun's sanctity, because this people is peculiarly credulous, and is easily moved to insurrection by prophecies, and in its present disposition is glad to hear any to the king's disadvantage" (*LP*, vol. 6, 1460). The prompt report by the imperial ambassador informing his superiors of the Nun's confession ended with this note: "So that it seems as if he [Henry VIII] had made a total divorce not only from his wife, but from good conscience, humanity, and gentleness, which he used to have" (*LP*, vol. 6, 1460).

examined by the ordinaries In Church law, ordinaries are, besides the Roman Pontiff, diocesan bishops and others who have an immediate ecclesiastical jurisdiction over a particular church or community.

these strange tales no part of our creed Conversing about the discernment of spirits in *A Dialogue of Comfort against Tribulation*, Antony offers his nephew Vincent a list of guiding points, the following one among them: "Or whether he fall into any singularity of opinions, against the scripture of God, or against the common faith of Christ's catholic Church" (*CW*, vol. 12, p. 133). This is characteristic of More's understanding of his faith: there is the creed of the Church and its long-standing traditions, and they should be enough. He accepted change and development from within the common faith and the life of the Church, but he was rather skeptical of any other "belief." Bishop Fisher, his friend and companion in distress, seems to have been more gullible.

I am sure that never one of them all More is thinking of Elizabeth Barton and her group of followers, all under arrest by then, and who might implicate him.

natural liege lord That is, entitled to feudal allegiance and service. More called Henry VIII his "natural prince."

Judas the true apostle . . . Judas the false traitor The reference is to Luke 6:16: "Judas son of James, and Judas Iscariot, who became a traitor." In the Gospels of Matthew and Mark, the first Judas is called Thaddeus. The betrayal of Judas, "an apostle turned traitor," received careful consideration in More's *De Tristitia Christi*. See *CW*, vol. 14, pp. 257-59, 277-81, 373-77, 383-87, 395-413, et passim.

by reason of this disease of mine In a letter to Erasmus dated June 14, 1532 (just one month after his resignation), More had written about his health: "My prayer had been to reach the crowning point of my life healthy and vigorous, no matter how old, or at least without sickness and suffering, as far as one could expect at that age. Perhaps that was a little too bold; in any case, the answer to that prayer is at present in God's hands. For some sort of chest ailment has laid hold of me; and the discomfort and pain it causes do not bother me as much as the worry and fear over the possible consequences. After being troubled with this ailment continually for several months, I consulted the doctors, who said that such a lingering disease could be dangerous; in their view there was no speedy cure possible; healing would be a long, slow process, requiring proper diet, medicines, and rest. They did not predict the length of convalescence, nor did they even give me assurance of a complete cure" (Rogers, *St. Thomas More: Selected Letters*, p. 173; the original Latin text can be found in *Opus Epistolarum Des. Erasmi Roterodami*, ed. P. S. Allen, vol. 10, n. 2659). In a letter to John Cochlaeus dated the same day, More told him that "for the past several months the condition of my health has aroused strong feelings of fear within me, although outwardly I have not appeared very ill" (Rogers, *Selected Letters*, p. 177). In October 1532, in a letter to Quirinus Talesius, Erasmus would comment that if More had stayed in office, he would have given the impression of approving the repudiation of Queen Catherine (Allen, *Opus Epistolarum*, vol. 10, n. 2735). More mentioned this physical condition, "a serious chest ailment," in his own epitaph (Rogers, *Selected Letters*, p. 182).

LETTER 4: TO HENRY VIII

to discharge and disburden me Even as Lord Chancellor, Thomas More seems to have had an understanding with Henry VIII on the question of the marriage. William Roper says that shortly after taking the chancellorship, the King again asked More "to weigh and consider his great matter." According to Roper, the newly appointed Lord Chancellor of England fell on his knees and explained to his sovereign that "he was not able, as he willingly would, with the loss of one of his limbs — for that matter anything to find whereby he could, with his conscience safely, serve his grace's contentation" (p. 224). According to the same account, Henry "was content to accept his service otherwise," and "using the advice of his learned council, whose consciences could well enough agree therewith, would nevertheless continue his gracious favor towards him and never with that matter molest his conscience after" (p. 225).

I never was very greedy More was undoubtedly ambitious, and naturally expected payment for his labor, but as far as we know, he was never greedy, which cannot be said of many other public officials during the Tudor Age. Writing about Cromwell's accumulation of a vast fortune, A. G. Dickens made this telling comment: "It is the misfortune of many Tudor statesmen to be judged by the exceptional criterion of Sir Thomas More" (p. 26). William Roper says that he had heard More say in his later time that "he had never asked the King for himself the value of one penny" (p. 210), while Erasmus described him as "absolutely free from any love of filthy lucre" *(Animus est a sordido lucro alienissimus)* in his famous letter to Ulrich von Hutten (*CWE,* vol. 7, p. 22). More declined a large sum of money (Roper puts it at four or five thousand pounds) collected by bishops and clergy which they thought he deserved for his writing in defense of the Church (see Roper, pp. 222-23, 226-27). More's interest in the virtue of Christian poverty — or better, of detachment as a certain "freedom of the spirit" — was already evident in his *Utopia;* it is also an important theme in *A Dialogue of Comfort against Tribulation* and other works. This does not mean that he was not a rich man. Cf. Brian Byron, "Through a Needle's Eye: Thomas More the Wealthy Saint," pp. 53-69.

the wicked woman of Canterbury While it is quite clear that More wrote "the wykked woman of Canterbery," both Rastell and Harpsfield have instead "the nunne of Canterbury." More was understandably upset and irritated at the fact that some followers of the Nun may have mentioned his own name as if he had been involved with them in some sort of treason or conspiracy. William Roper reminded his readers that although his father-in-law could have talked freely with Elizabeth Barton "at that time without any danger of any law," More had always conducted himself in a way that "deserved not to be blamed, but contrariwise to be commended and praised" (p. 231).

145

such grievous bill . . . against me Here More is referring to the bill of attainder introduced in the House of Lords.

LETTER 5: TO THOMAS CROMWELL

either with the nun or the friars Elizabeth Barton and the two Friars Observant — that is, Father Risby and Father Rich.

my letter written unto the nun See Letter 3 above.

at my coming from beyond the sea From a trip to France in the summer of 1527. (From Calais, More had written to Francis Cranevelt; cf. Rogers, *The Correspondence of Sir Thomas More*, n. 155.) The magnificent embassy was recorded in glorious, triumphant detail by George Cavendish in his *Life and Death of Cardinal Wolsey*, pp. 47-68.

at Hampton Court Cardinal Wolsey's house in Surrey became one of the many royal homes of Henry VIII, who, at his death, possessed more than sixty such magnificent buildings. See Simon Thurley, *The Royal Palaces of Tudor England*.

walking in the gallery The gallery separated public and private areas, the "presence chamber" from the privy chamber, thus becoming "an effective filter between the crush of the Court in one room and the relative tranquility of the privy chamber." These galleries had excellent views and were "places for the King and Queen and carefully invited guests to walk and talk in confidence and comfort" (Thurley, pp. 125, 143). There was also a gallery in the New Building that More had built on his property in Chelsea, along with a chapel and a library. On top of that long gallery More refers to, Henry VIII had built a second one. Years later, in the gallery at Hampton Court, hangs a painting by Girolamo da Treviso the Younger, *The Four Evangelists Stoning the Pope* (c. 1540). Curiously enough, this painting is "the only surviving work of art the location of which can be identified in any of Henry's houses" (Thurley, p. 143).

it could in no wise by the Church be dispensable Dispensation does not mean abrogation but "the relaxation of a merely ecclesiastical law in a particular case" (*Codex iuris canonici*, canon 85). The Roman Pontiff can give dispensation from all purely ecclesiastical (positive) laws. The letter from Pope Julius II to Henry VII on the dispensation is dated July 6, 1504, and can be read in Nicholas Pocock, *Records of the Reformation*, vol. 1, n. 2. In another letter (vol. 1, n. 3), Pope Julius tells Henry VII that a copy of the bull has been sent to Spain at the request of Queen Isabella.

the bull of the dispensation Queen Catherine of Aragon always maintained that her marriage to Prince Arthur had never been consummated. Henry himself admitted this much, although he would later claim that it was in jest (Scarisbrick, *Henry VIII*, pp. 188-89). There was also an official document from the Roman Pontiff with a proper ecclesiastical dispensation so that she could validly marry Arthur's brother in case her previous marriage had indeed been consummated. Scarisbrick offers an exposition of the "great matter" in his masterful biography of Henry VIII (chap. 7, "The Canon Law of the Divorce"). But see also Henry Ansgar Kelly, *The Matrimonial Trials of Henry VIII*. For the figure of the Spanish queen, Garrett Mattingly's biography, *Catherine of Aragon*, is a splendid portrait of a woman defending her honor, her dignity, and her rights.

the Law Levitical and the Law Deuteronomical The first reference is to Leviticus 20:21: "The man who takes to wife the wife of his brother: that is impurity; he has uncovered his brother's nakedness, and they shall die childless." The second reference is to Deuteronomy 25:5: "If brothers live together and one of them dies childless, the dead man's wife must not marry a stranger outside the family. Her husband's brother must come to her and exercising his levirate, make her his wife, and the first son she bears shall assume the dead brother's name; and so his name will not be blotted out." Henry had learned from Robert Wakefield, a humanist and a scholar, that the Hebrew version of Leviticus 20:21 forewarned that such a marriage would be without *sons,* not without *children,* as the Vulgate had it. However, there is no basis in the text for the change. Cf. the introduction by Virginia Murphy to *The Divorce Tracts of Henry VIII*, p. xiii.

the bull should by the law not be sufficient The bull obtained from Pope Julius mentioned the union between Arthur and Catherine as *forsan consummatum* (perhaps consummated). If it was indeed consummated, another impediment (called "affinity" in canon law) arose against the union of Catherine to Henry, and so the bull removed the impediment of affinity and the impediment of public honesty. The document did not enter into the consequences of non-consummation of the union, however, and thus "if the marriage between Catherine and Arthur was *not* consummated then probably the subsequent marriage between Catherine and Henry was rendered invalid by the diriment impediment of public honesty set up by Catherine's contract with Arthur and, by error or misjudgment, apparently not dispensed by the bull" (Scarisbrick, *Henry VIII*, p. 188). But see also Henry Ansgar Kelly, *The Matrimonial Trials of Henry VIII*, chap. 6: "The Attack on the Dispensations."

Master Foxe, now his Grace's Almoner The royal almoner was in charge of distributing alms on behalf of his sovereign. Edward Foxe studied theology in Cambridge, and later became the secretary of Thomas Wolsey. The most important moment in his career was his mission with Stephen Gardiner to Rome in 1528 to ensure that the divorce case of their sovereign be judged in England. They presented Pope Clement VII with a book of materials relevant to the case that seems to have impressed the Roman Pontiff. This is most likely the same book that More refers to in the letter as being still a work in progress (he must have known of a draft; cf. Guy, p. 100). Always laboring on the King's "great matter," Foxe then visited the universities of Cambridge, Oxford, and Paris; he also spoke with Luther and Melanchthon.

a book . . . that then was in making Henry VIII had his first doubts or scruples about his marriage in 1527, and by year's end there were already at least three books that addressed the divorce. The *Censurae academiarum* was published by Thomas Berthelet in April 1530; the English translation (produced by the same publisher) appeared in November of 1531 with the title *Determinations of the most famous and most excellent universities of Italy and France, that it is unlawful for a man to marry his brother's wife, that the pope hath no power to dispense therewith*. The bishop of London, John Stokesley, with Edward Foxe and Nicolas de Burgo, had originally written the book in Latin; subsequently it appeared translated into English. See *The Divorce Tracts of Henry VIII*.

John Stokesley (1475?-1539) had been chaplain, almoner, and member of Henry's council. Erasmus mentions him, along with More and others, as one of the brilliant luminaries in the English royal court. He seems to have been always in favor of the divorce and against papal authority, although he opposed any doctrinal changes. In 1529, Stokesley was sent to France and Italy to gather favorable opinions from the universities. After his return, he was consecrated bishop of London on November 27, 1530 (cf. *DNB*, vol. 18, pp. 1290-91). See Andrew A. Chibi, *Henry VIII's Conservative Scholar* (Bern: Peter Lang, 1997).

After this the suit began "Then was there for the trial and examination of this matrimony procured from Rome a commission, in which Cardinal Campeggio and Cardinal Wolsey were joined commissioners. Who, for the determination thereof, sat at the Blackfriars in London, where a libel was put in for the annulling of the said matrimony, alleging the marriage between the King and Queen to be unlawful. And for proof of the marriage to be lawful was there brought in a dispensation, in which after divers disputations thereon holden, there appeared an imperfection which, by an instrument or brief, upon search found in the Treasury of Spain and sent to the Commissioners into England, was supplied. And so should judgment have been given to the Pope accordingly — had not the King, upon intelligence thereof, before the same judgment, appealed to the next general council. After whose appellation, the Cardinal upon that matter sat no longer" (Roper, p. 217). Roper was wrong about the Treasury of Spain: the bill was found among the papers of the English ambassador (cf. Hitchcock, introduction to Roper, pp. xlvi). For details about the legatine court and related information, see Henry Ansgar Kelly, *The Matrimonial Trials of Henry VIII*, pp. 75-88, and Geoffrey de C. Parmiter, *The King's Great Matter*, chap. 5.

my Lord of London, now of Durham Cuthbert Tunstall (1474-1559) had studied at Oxford and went on to receive doctorates in civil and canon law in Padua. He was ordained a priest in 1511. In his *Utopia* More had written of a trip with Tunstall in an embassy to Flanders, and Tunstall dedicated his own book on arithmetic to More. In 1522 Tunstall was consecrated bishop of London, and in 1528 he gave More the task of defending the Church against English heretics (cf. Rogers, *The Correspondence of Sir Thomas More,* letter n. 160). He was again on a diplomatic mission with More at the signing of the Peace of Cambrai in the summer of 1529 (cf. Rogers, *The Correspondence of Sir Thomas More,* letters n. 170, n. 172). The following year Tunstall became bishop of Durham and was succeeded in London by John Stokesley. In the Northern Convocation of 1531, Tunstall made a clear protestation that there was ambiguity in the declaration on the title of Supreme Head of the Church as claimed by Henry VIII: "For supreme head of the Church carries a complicated and mysterious meaning: for this title may either relate to spirituals or temporals, or both. Now when a proposition is thus comprehensive and big with several meanings, there is no returning a single and categorical answer. And therefore, that 'we may not give scandal to weak brethren,' I conceive this acknowledgment of the king's supreme headship should be so carefully expressed as to point wholly upon civil and secular jurisdiction" (cited in Jeremy Collier, *Ecclesiastical History of Great Britain,* vol. 4 [London: William Straker, 1845], p. 178). Tunstall therefore suggested that the title should be "only and supreme lord, after Christ, in temporal matters" *(unicum et supremum dominum in temporalibus post Christum).* See Charles Sturge, *Cuthbert Tunstal,* p. 192.

the peace . . . at Cambrai The legatine court at Blackfriars examining the King's "great matter" had opened while an international peace conference was being held at Cambrai. Henry felt threatened by the possibility of an understanding between Pope Clement and the Emperor Charles, on one side, and the King of France, Francis I, on the other. This would have excluded and isolated England with, among other results, dire consequences for Henry's plans of divorce and remarriage. The "divorce" was not granted by the Pope, or rather the marriage to Catherine was declared to have been valid. But papal policy on the matter had no negative repercussions on the peace conference. Bishop Tunstall, Thomas More, and John Hacket were the chosen ambassadors, since Cardinal Wolsey could not go. More left on July 1, and the treaty (known as the Ladies' Peace) of Cambrai was signed on August 5, 1529. The royal commission is printed in Rogers, *The Correspondence of Sir Thomas More,* letter n. 169, along with several letters written by Tunstall, More, and Hacket to Henry VIII from Cambrai (nn. 170, 171, 172, and 173). This is William Roper's impression of the trip: "Sir Thomas More so worthily handled himself, procuring in our league far more benefits unto this realm than at that time by the King or his Council was thought possible to be compassed, that for his good service in that voyage, the King, when he after made him Lord Chancellor, caused the Duke of Norfolk openly to declare unto the people (as you shall hear hereafter more at large) how much all England was bound unto him" (p. 217).

his Chancellor of this realm More was back in England by the beginning of September 1529, and the following month he was made Lord Chancellor. William Roper comments on what probably lay behind that appointment: "Now upon the coming home of the Bishop of Durham and Sir Thomas More from Cambrai, the King was as earnest in persuading Sir Thomas More to agree unto the matter of his marriage as before, by many and divers ways provoking him thereunto. For the which cause, as it was thought, he the rather soon after made him Lord Chancellor" (p. 217).

Archbishops of Canterbury and York A reference to Thomas Cranmer (1489-1556), who had been made Archbishop of Canterbury in 1533, and Edward Lee (1482?-1544), Bishop of York since 1531. Cranmer had declared null Henry's marriage to Catherine, and was to become the patron saint of Anglicanism. See Diarmaid MacCulloch, *Thomas Cranmer: A Life*; and Paul Ayris and David Selwyn, *Thomas Cranmer: Churchman and Scholar*. For Cranmer's defense of the divorce, see Nicholas Pocock, *Records of the Reformation*, pp. 334-99.

Doctor Nicholas Nicolas de Burgo was an Italian friar (of the order of Minorites) in the King's employ. See Andrew G. Little, *The Grey Friars in Oxford* (Oxford: Clarendon Press, 1892).

he used in his other business Henry's divorce was the key political question until April 1533. Thomas More spent most of his time campaigning against the dissemination of heretical doctrines arriving from the Continent. In his mind there was no doubt that whatever problems Henry might have in his marriage, he desired to keep the integrity of the Catholic faith in England. See More's preface to *The Confutation of Tyndale's Answer* (*CW*, vol. 8); John Guy, *The Public Career of Sir Thomas More*, pp. 103-12, and the chapter entitled "More, Politics, and Heresy"; and Peter Ackroyd, *The Life of Thomas More*, chaps. 25-26.

the book that Master Abell made Besides bishops Fisher and Standish, Queen Catherine had four theologians as advisers, among them Thomas Abell (c. 1497-1540), who was also her chaplain. Catherine had sent him to Spain to secure a duplicate of the bull of Pope Julius II permitting Henry to marry her. This was a dangerous mission because the King's agents were also after the papal brief, thinking it favored the Queen's case. But Abell successfully obtained a duplicate. Upon his return to London, Abell devoted himself to defending Catherine's interests, and in 1532 he published *a treatise against the royal divorce with the title Invicta veritas (An answer . . . that by no manner of law it may be lawful for King Henry the Eighth to be divorced)*. As a consequence he was incarcerated in the Tower but released at Christmas 1532, only to be sent back again a year leater in connection with the affair of the Nun of Canterbury; for that offense he spent six more years in the Tower. Thomas Abell was executed July 30, 1540, with two other priests — Richard Featherstone and Edward Powell — for denying Henry's new title of "Supreme Head of the Church." He was later beatified (in 1886) by Pope Leo XIII along with other English martyrs. Cf. *DNB*, vol. 1, pp. 34-35.

my Lord of Bath John Clerk (d. 1541) had studied in Cambridge and Bologna, where he obtained a degree in law. He succeeded Wolsey in 1523 as bishop of Bath and Wells, and was one of the counselors of Catherine of Aragon, although he later surrendered and accepted the King's new spiritual supremacy.

and this noble woman really anointed Queen Textual critics point out that the "really" may have been "rially" (that is, "royally") in More's handwriting. Henry VIII and his lover, Anne Boleyn, had been secretly married on January 25, 1533, without the Pope's license. Thomas Cranmer annulled Henry's marriage to Catherine in May, and then pronounced valid the King's union with Anne Boleyn. A spectacular crowning ceremony followed on June 1, 1533, where the absence of Sir Thomas More must have been conspicuous. The phrase "and this noble woman . . ." was edited out by William Rastell in his edition of More's *English Works*. Some of More's friends and family members concentrated their animosity on Anne Boleyn, even to the point of thinking of her as a new Herodias. See E. W. Ives, *Anne Boleyn* (Oxford: Basil Blackwell, 1986).

famous book against . . . Martin Luther The King's book *Assertio septem sacramentorum* had been published by Richard Pynson in July 1521; it was a response to Luther's *Babylonian Captivity*. John Clerk gave a copy to Pope Leo X in October, and that same month the Pope conferred upon Henry VIII the title of *Fidei defensor*, "defender of the faith." Luther's reply to the King's book was one more salvo in the theological paper wars that erupted over the new evangelical ideas; such responses defended or attacked propositions with the weapons of inflated rhetoric, foul language, and personal insults. More, then a counselor to Henry VIII, was asked to answer in kind, and so he did in 1523, but using a pseudonym, William Rosseus, to publish his *Responsio ad Lutherum*.

the holy doctors The phrases "holy doctors" and "old holy doctors" appear frequently in More's works. The humanists of the sixteenth century fostered a rediscovery of the ancient Christian writers, particularly the Fathers and Doctors of the Church. The title of "Doctor" is given by the Popes to some of the Church Fathers and other Christian writers known for their orthodoxy of doctrine, holiness of life, and eminent degree of learning: *Doctor Optime, Ecclesiae sanctae lumen*, "excellent doctor, light of holy church." The four great Eastern Doctors are St. Athanasius, St. Basil of Caesarea, St. Gregory of Nazianzus, and St. John

Chrysostom. And the four Latin Doctors are St. Ambrose, St. Augustine, St. Jerome, and St. Gregory the Great. Three women have been honored as Doctors of the Church: St. Catherine of Siena and St. Teresa of Ávila, both proclaimed by Pope Paul VI in 1970, and St. Thérèse of Lisieux by Pope John Paul II in 1997.

More had told the King that it seemed to him that none of His Majesty's counselors in this matter of his marriage were fitting, since all of them were "your grace's own servants," More himself included. And according to Roper, More elaborated on this point: "But if your Grace mind to understand the truth, such counsellors may you have devised, as neither for respect of their own worldly commodity nor for fear of your princely authority, will be inclined to deceive you." And he proceeded to mention "St. Jerome, St. Augustine, and divers other old holy doctors, both Greeks and Latins" (p. 215).

Saint Ignatius Ignatius, bishop of Antioch, died a martyr in Rome *circa* 110. More may have been thinking here of the famous introductory passage about "the Church of Rome" in the bishop's *Letter to the Romans:* "Ignatius, also called Theophorus, to the Church that has found mercy in the greatness of the Most High Father and in Jesus Christ, His only Son; to the Church beloved and enlightened after the love of Jesus Christ, our God, by the will of Him that has willed everything which is; to the Church also which holds the presidency in the place of the country of the Romans, worthy of God, worthy of honor, worthy of blessing, worthy of praise, worthy of success, worthy of sanctification, and because you hold the presidency of love, named after Christ and named after the Father: her therefore do I salute in the name of Jesus Christ, the Son of the Father. To those who are united in flesh and in spirit by every commandment of His, who are filled with the grace of God without wavering, and who are filtered clear of every foreign stain, I wish an unalloyed joy in Jesus Christ, our God" (Jurgens, *The Faith of the Early Fathers,* p. 21).

holy Saint Gregory Pope Gregory had sent Augustine, then the superior in Gregory's own monastery, on a missionary trip to England in 597. He organized the Church under the Pope and was later canonized as St. Augustine of Canterbury. William Roper says that in the speech at his trial, More spoke these or similar words: "For, as Saint Paul said of the Corinthians, 'I have regenerated you my children in Christ,' so might Saint Gregory, Pope of Rome, of whom by Saint Augustine, his messenger, we first received the Christian faith, of us Englishmen truly say: 'You are my children because I have given you everlasting salvation, a far higher and better inheritance than any carnal father can leave to his child, and by regeneration made you my spiritual children in Christ'" (p. 249).

The English Catholic historian Philip Hughes could not fail to point out the remarkable origins of the Church in England: "It is interesting to notice that the government set up by the pope is the normal system of metropolitan and suffragans. There is no provision for a special vicar of the Apostolic See such as St.

Gregory had recently hoped to establish in France. Nor is any place whatever given to the royal authority. From the very beginning this English Church, the direct creation of the pope, is free of the State" (*A History of the Church*, vol. 2, p. 118).

In this mention of St. Gregory the Great, More may have been thinking more particularly of advice sought by Augustine from the Roman Pontiff about problems the missionary had encountered while laboring toward the new establishment of the Christian faith in England. One of the questions asked, according to the Venerable Bede (673-735), "the father of English history," was this: "To what degree may the faithful marry with their kindred? And is it lawful for a man to marry his stepmother or relative?" After giving the general principle, Pope Gregory answered that it is "a grave sin" to wed one's stepmother, and that "it is also forbidden to marry a sister-in-law, since by a former union she had become one with his own brother" (Bede, Book 1, chap. 27).

And therefore sith all Christendom is one corps "Corps" comes from the Latin *corpus*, meaning "body." The use of the term here obviously means more than just the physical gathering of people doing something together or under the same direction. It would have been difficult for Thomas More to hear the term "corps" in this context without thinking of "corpus," as in the Latin expression *Corpus Christi*, "the Body of Christ," which was also the name given to the feast of the Eucharist. More repeats it in the same paragraph, writing of the "corps of his Catholic Church." Following a long scriptural tradition, he saw the Church as the body of Christ. The expression is also found in *A Dialogue of Comfort against Tribulation*, and More consistently employs it to emphasize the unity and universality of the Church of Christ ("all the corps," "the whole corps"); cf. *CW*, vol. 12, pp. 8, 38, 98. In *De Tristitia Christi*, More defines the Church as "Christ's own mystical body" *(corpore suo mystico)*, and later he writes that God took our nature "to unite with Himself, in the structure of one body [*uelut in unius corporis*] (as it were), all of us whom He regenerated by His saving sacraments and by faith" (*CW*, vol. 14, pp. 99, 345).

As for the general councils Early Christianity had known local, regional, and provincial councils. At Nicea, in 325, all the bishops were present, thus marking the beginning of the general or ecumenical councils. By the time More was writing, there had been eighteen such gatherings; the Fifth General Council of the Lateran had met from 1512 to 1517. See Philip Hughes, *The Church in Crisis*, pp. 11-21.

As for the teaching of the general councils on the primacy of Rome, the second Council of Lyons (1274) declared that "this same holy Roman Church holds the highest and complete primacy and spiritual power over the universal Catholic Church which she truly and humbly recognizes herself to have received with fullness of power from the Lord Himself in Blessed Peter, the chief or head of the Apostles whose successor is the Roman Pontiff. . . . And to her anyone burdened with affairs pertaining to the ecclesiastical world can appeal; and in all cases looking forward to an ecclesiastical examination, recourse can be had to her judgment, and all churches are subject to her; their prelates give obedience and reverence to her" (*Enchiridion Symbolorum,* n. 466). Later the Council of Florence (1438-1445) stated, "We likewise define that the holy Apostolic See, and the Roman Pontiff, hold the primacy throughout the entire world; and that the Roman Pontiff himself is the successor of blessed Peter, the chief of the Apostles, and the true vicar of Christ, and that he is the head of the entire Church [*totiusque Ecclesiae caput*], and the father and teacher of all Christians; and that full power was given him in blessed Peter by our Lord Jesus Christ, to feed, rule, and govern the universal Church; just as is contained in the acts of the ecumenical councils and in the sacred canons" (*Enchiridion Symbolorum,* n. 694). Finally, from the speech of the Legate in the Council of Ephesus in 431 (Third Ecumenical Council): "No one doubts, but rather it has been known to all generations, that the holy and most blessed Peter, chief and head of the Apostles, the pillar of the faith, the foundation stone of the Catholic Church, received the keys of the kingdom from our Lord Jesus Christ the Savior and Redeemer of the human race, and that the power of binding and loosing sins was given to him, who up to this moment and always lives in his successors, and judges" (*Enchiridion Symbolorum,* n. 112). (The English translations that appear here are from Deferrari.) Upon these texts More must have done much thinking.

the corps of his Catholic Church More's ecclesiology has been studied by Brian Gogan in *The Common Corps of Christendom: Ecclesiological Themes in the Writings of Sir Thomas More.* Labels such as "papalist" or "conciliarist" can be easily applied, but they only make it more difficult to see the truth. More's view of the Church and his thought on this particular matter show more complexity than such labels suggest.

the primacy of the See apostolic "Apostolic See" (*Sedes Apostolica*) is one of the early names given to the see of Rome, along with *Sedes Petri Apostoli* (See of the Apostle Peter) and *Apostolicus fons* (apostolic fountain) (cf. *Enchiridion Symbolorum,* nn. 136, 149, 217-18, et passim). It is also known as the Roman See, the Seat of the Universal Roman Catholic Church, or simply Papacy, the office of the Supreme Head of the Church. According to canon law, "The bishop of the Church of Rome, in whom resides the office given in a special way by the Lord to Peter, first of the Apostles and to be transmitted to his successors, is head of the college of bishops, the Vicar of Christ and Pastor of the universal Church on earth; therefore, in virtue of his office he enjoys supreme, full, immediate and universal ordinary power in the Church, which he can always freely exercise" (*Codex iuris canonici,* canon 331).

yet never thought I the Pope above the general council These words were omitted by Thomas Stapleton in his *The Life and Illustrious Martyrdom of Sir Thomas More*

(p. 151). On More and the papacy, see John M. Headley, "Thomas Murner, Thomas More, and the First Expression of More's Ecclesiology," *Studies in the Renaissance* 14 (1967): 73-92, and the introduction to his edition of the *Responsio ad Lutherum.*

my book against the Masker "I shall . . . for lacke of hys other name to call hym mayster Masker" (*CW,* vol. 11, p. 13). More limited himself to quoting the evangelical passage where Simon has his name changed to *Petrus,* "Peter" (meaning "rock"), and then receives the promise that upon this rock the Church shall be built.

my confutation before *The Confutation of Tyndale's Answer* (1532-1533). More had started the book while he was Lord Chancellor. The work contains a number of passages about the institution of the papacy and More's definition of the Church. Cf. *CW,* vol. 8, pp. 131-32, 576-77, etc.

LETTER 6: TO MARGARET ROPER

the Abbot of Westminster William Benson, a Benedictine monk who had studied in Cambridge and was elected abbot, and later dean, of Westminster (cf. *DNB,* vol. 2, pp. 259-60). On April 17, 1534, John Husee wrote to Lord Lisle: "The Bishop of Rochester is in custody of my Lord of Canterbury and Sir Thomas More in the keeping of the Abbot of Westminster and Doctor Wilson in the Tower" (*The Lisle Letters,* vol. 2, p. 127). Muriel St. Clare Byrne, the editor of this amazing epistolary, observes that "Husee's reference is the only other reference in the State Papers to the arrest, nor does he nor any other Englishman, writing in England, even mention More's name in letters in the ensuing months" (p. 127). In a letter of June 28 of the following year, Husee seems to whisper timidly that it seems that Master More will be arraigned at the end of the week.

Tower of London There were several prisons in the city of London. The Tower was used to hold people charged with treason. (More had himself used it to hold heretics.) He had been taken there by boat on April 17, to the Bell Tower, which was "in the large ground floor, lofty-ceilinged and dark," with a narrow window. Naturally, More took care to be as comfortable as his circumstances allowed. When in *A Dialogue of Comfort against Tribulation* Antony tells the anecdote of a woman visiting "of her charity a poor prisoner," More may have given the only description we have of his own room in the Tower. The woman found the prisoner "in a chamber, to say the truth, meetly fair, and at the leastwise it was strong enough. But with mats of straw the prisoner had made it so warm both under the foot and round about the walls that in these things for keeping of his health she was on his behalf glad and very well comforted" (*CW,* vol. 12, p. 77). See also R. J. Minney, *The Tower of London,* p. 128.

Margaret Roper Margaret, More's eldest daughter (1505-1544), was, according to Nicholas Harpsfield, "the chiefest and almost the only worldly comfort Sir Thomas More had," the closest to him "in wit, virtue and learning, as also in merry and pleasant talk" (p. 97). Erasmus, who dedicated one of his books to her, admired her literary talents. She translated into English Erasmus's work on the "Our Father" *(Precatio dominica in septem portiones distributa).* Besides being an accomplished scholar, Margaret was a wife and mother. She was married to William Roper, and the couple had five children.

This first letter from the Tower is best introduced by William Roper's account of the events: "Then Sir Thomas More, as his accustomed manner was always, before he entered into any matter of importance, as when he was first chosen of the King's Privy Council, when he was sent ambassador, appointed Speaker of the Parliament, made Lord Chancellor, or when he took any like mighty matter upon him, to go to church and be confessed, to hear Mass, and be houseled [receive the Eucharist], so did he likewise in the morning early the selfsame day that he was summoned to appear before the lords at Lambeth" (p. 237).

the Lords at Lambeth Sir Thomas Audley, the Lord Chancellor; Thomas Cranmer, Archbishop of Canterbury; Thomas Howard, the Duke of Norfolk; and Charles Brandon, the Duke of Suffolk.

the Vicar of Croydon Rowland Phillips was known as an eloquent preacher. Although he was not expected to swear the oath, he did. He probably did so without suspecting the radical transformations of the Tudor revolution and with complete trust in a sovereign who had merited the title of *defensor fidei* from the Pope himself. But two years later he was imprisoned for his disagreement with new royal policy. From prison in 1533, he asked Cromwell for mercy: "I pray you to have pity on the miserable condition I am in by reason of my restraint. I have many diseases incidental to age and require continual counsel of surgeons, whom I cannot now have. I lack my common diet, — which will shorten my life" (*LP,* vol. 6, 1672). Phillips died about 1538. Cf. Susan Brigden, *London and the Reformation,* pp. 261-63.

Phillips may have been the person More had in mind when writing to Peter Giles — in the letter which serves as the introduction to *Utopia* — about a clergyman who desired to visit the island as a missionary and be appointed its first bishop (Rogers, *The Correspondence of Sir Thomas More,* n. 25, p. 80).

perpetual damnation The oath implicitly denied the spiritual authority of the Pope, as G. R. Elton points out: "What Henry, and Cromwell, wanted was the country's sworn acceptance, not so much of the legitimacy of the issue to be expected from the Boleyn marriage, but rather of the major policy which that marriage symbolized — the political revolution and the religious schism. Unlike other oaths used, that to the succession applied to everyone and in effect worked to commit everyone to the new order. More was quite right in practice: whatever the legal meaning of the oath, those who took it implicitly renounced the papal jurisdiction and supremacy, and they may well have done so the more readily because on the face of it no such drastic statement was required of them" (*Policy and Police*, pp. 226-27).

my Lord Chancellor Thomas Audley (1488-1544), a rather passive tool in the hands of Henry VIII and Cromwell. "Luckily for Audley," wrote Lord Campbell in his *Lives of the Lord Chancellors*, "he has not much attracted the notice of historians" (vol. 2, p. 78). Mere political convenience seems to have been the sum and summit of his moral principles. Audley succeeded More as Chancellor of Lancaster and then, as Speaker of the House of Commons, was the subservient instrument of Henry's desires about his marriage to Anne Boleyn and definitive separation from Rome. In May of 1532, a few days after More's resignation, the King appointed Audley Lord Keeper of the Great Seal, honoring him with the knighthood. In January of the following year he became Lord Chancellor.

According to Campbell, Audley seemed to have been efficient and fair in cases "where the Crown was not concerned," but "as a politician, he is bitterly condemned by all who mention him" (vol. 2, p. 85). Audley presided over the judicial process of Bishop Fisher in June of 1535 and over More's process on July 1 of that same year. Thomas More complained that Audley did not even follow the customary proceedings of the law (Roper, p. 248). Less than a year later, in May 1536, Audley was also the prosecutor and judge in the proceedings against Anne Boleyn, accused of infidelity. (The Queen was executed on May 19.) In addition, he presided over the trials of the Marquess of Exeter and Lord Montague, both executed as traitors. And Thomas Cromwell followed them to the block; he himself was zealously prosecuted by Audley.

"The merit has been ascribed to him [Audley] of favouring the Reformation," Campbell comments, "but, in reality, he had no opinions of his own, and he was now acting merely as an instrument in the hands of the most remarkable adventurer to be met with in England['s] history" (vol. 2, p. 88). Alice Alington's letter does indeed confirm this portrait of a man "merely a tool of the tyrant." In a letter he once sent to Cromwell, Audley asked to receive payment for his services because "I have in this world susteyned great damage and infamie in serving the Kynge's Highness, which this grant shal recompense" (quoted in Campbell, vol. 2, p. 97). Audley did receive the dissolved abbey of Walden and became Baron Audley of Walden, in Essex. Cf. Campbell, vol. 2, pp. 78-113; and *DNB*, vol. 1, pp. 723-26.

because of the heat Richard Marius offers this conjecture: "Perhaps his real reason for not descending was that the garden below swarmed with men who had sworn the oath, and More did not want to be in their company" (pp. 461-62). A year later More would reject an invitation to sit with the members of the Royal commission: "I was offered to sit with them, which in nowise I would" (Letter 20 in this volume).

Master Doctor Latimer Hugh Latimer (c. 1485-1555) was a strong supporter of the divorce and had preached before the King on Wednesdays of the Lenten season in 1534 while he was employed by Thomas Cranmer. He became bishop of Worcester in 1535, and was later charged with heresy and burned at the stake under Queen Mary. Cf. *DNB,* vol. 11, pp. 612-20; Germain Marc'hadour, "Hugh Latimer and Thomas More"; and G. R. Elton, *Policy and Police,* pp. 112-20.

my Lord of Canterbury Thomas Cranmer, the Archbishop of Canterbury, suggested that More and Bishop Fisher be asked to take only the oath to the Succession, but Henry VIII rejected the idea.

Master Doctor Wilson See the note for Letter 13.

my Lord of Rochester John Fisher (1469-1535), bishop of Rochester, at the time the smallest and poorest diocese in England, has been rightly called "the life and soul of the resistance" to Henry's revolution and despotism (Scarisbrick, *Henry VIII,* p. 330) and was literally true to the old Christian saying, *Episcopus ergo martyr* ("Bishop, therefore martyr"). Fisher's vindication as a humanist is only now beginning to take place, as two important scholarly works show, both published by the press of Cambridge University, an institution that was very close to the holy bishop: see Richard Rex, *The Theology of John Fisher,* and Brendan Bradshaw and Eamon Duffy, *Humanism, Reform, and the Reformation: The Career of Bishop John Fisher.* "The relative lack of scholarly attention given to his career in the past reflects at least to some extent the success of the 'non-personing' of Fisher by the Henrician regime," writes Richard Rex in his excellent book (p. 12).

The bishop was the only member of the English hierarchy who remained faithful to the Roman Pontiff. By 1533 he had probably been arrested twice already. Fisher had sent messages to Chapuys, the imperial ambassador, which would have made him guilty of high treason. The prelate was an example of priestly virtue, chancellor of Cambridge University, confessor to Queen Catherine, and as friendly to the Renaissance as he was hostile to the ideas of what would later be called the Protestant Reformation. The references to Fisher in More's works are clear proof of the respect and admiration he had for the bishop. The two men exchanged a number of letters: "He [More] had written divers scrolls or letters to Dr. Fisher, and received others from him, containing for the most part nothing but comfortable words and thanks for meat and drink sent by one to the other. But about a quarter a year after his coming to the Tower he wrote to Fisher, saying he had refused the oath of succession, and never intended to tell the council why; and Fisher made him answer, showing how he had not refused to swear to the succession. No other letters passed between them touching the king's affairs, till the council came to examine this deponent upon the Act of Supreme Head; but after his examination he received a letter of Fisher desiring to know his answer. Replied by another letter, stating that he meant not to meddle, but to fix his mind on the Passion of Christ, or that his answer was to that effect. He afterwards received another letter from Fisher, stating that he was informed the word maliciously was used in the statute, and suggesting that therefore a man who spoke nothing of malice did not offend the statute. He replied that he agreed with Fisher, but feared that it would not be so interpreted" (*LP,* vol. 7, 867).

According to T. E. Bridgett, it is reasonable to assume that each man wrote a total of four letters to the other (*The Life of Blessed John Fisher,* p. 348). While in the Tower, More sent his fellow prisoner an image of St. John as well as apples and oranges; and on New Year's Day of 1535, More sent him a piece of paper on which he had written "2000 pounds of gold."

Pope Paul III made Bishop Fisher a cardinal of the Catholic Church on May 20, 1535. Scarcely a month later, on June 22, the old bishop was beheaded. He was canonized four hundred years later, in 1935, along with Thomas More. Cf. Bridgett, *Blessed John Fisher*; E. L. Surtz, *The Works and Days of John Fisher*; and Jean Rouschausse, *John Fisher.* The Catholic Church celebrates them together as martyrs and saints on June 22.

quod ille notus erat pontifici From the Vulgate version of John 18:15: ". . . the disciple who was known to the high priest." Cf. J. Duncan M. Derrett, "Two Dicta of More's and a Correction."

valde familiariter Very familiarly, intimately, on friendly terms.

My Lord of Canterbury Archbishop Thomas Cranmer.

whither side he list soileth all the doubts That is, "whichever side he is pleased upon solves all doubts." Both irony, one of More's favorite literary devices, and contempt are evident in these words. R. W. Chambers comments, "For the argument is that in all matters wherein we are not prepared to condemn the consciences of others, we are bound, for ourselves, to accept the orders of the state. Such an argument would mark the end of religious freedom, of academic freedom, of all freedom. More was staggered that it should be put forward by the Primate of England, the successor of Warham and Becket, of Anselm and Dunstan, of Lawrence and Augustine" (p. 303). If before Henry there was room for digression or doubt, "one result of the work of the Reformation Parliament," writes G. R. Elton, "was to end such doubts: divinely inspired or not, the Parliament's statutes now stood omnicompetently sovereign" (*Reform and Renewal,* p. 67).

my Lord of Westminster William Benson. See note above.

Master Secretary Thomas Cromwell.

his own only son Cromwell's wife was Elizabeth Wykys; their son, Gregory, had been born in 1513. Two daughters, Anne and Grace, their names mentioned (and then crossed out) in Cromwell's will, may have died young. R. B. Merriman comments, "If the tone of Gregory's letters to his father be taken as a criterion of the boy's character, he must indeed have been stupid and slow beyond belief" (vol. 1, p. 53). Merriman describes the young man as "entirely without ambition" (p. 145). Ever busy with his own incipient public career, Cromwell seems not to have been much concerned with his son's problems at school. But Gregory was his only son, and Cromwell wished him to reach a permanent place among the English nobility by having at least the benefit of an education, as is clear in Cromwell's will of 1529 (cf. Merriman, pp. 56-63). In 1533 Gregory left Cambridge University and, through his father's influence, married Elizabeth Seymour (a widow and the sister of Jane Seymour). He became a member of Parliament in 1539. The following year Henry VIII made him Lord Cromwell. Cf. also Helen Miller, *Henry VIII and the English Nobility*, p. 32, and *DNB*, vol. 5, p. 195.

but leave every man to his own conscience In his commentary on Psalm 5, Augustine had written, "'In thy sight,' he says, 'direct my way:' that is, where no man sees; who are not to be trusted in their praise or blame. For they can in no wise judge of another man's conscience, wherein the way toward God is traversed. . . . To whose judgment of course then there is no trusting, and therefore must we fly within to conscience, and the sight of God" (*Expositions on the Book of Psalms,* vol. 8 of *The Nicene and Post-Nicene Fathers* [Grand Rapids: Eerdmans, 1974], 5.11.14).

should leave me to mine More's use of the term *conscience,* so conspicuous in his letters from the Tower, is far from modern individualism or moral relativism. The English humanist understood conscience in the long tradition of classic and Christian moral thought. "All that is not from conscience is sin," wrote St. Paul (Rom. 14:23); he also admonished Christians to have "a good conscience" (1 Tim. 1:19). Thomas More believed the authority of conscience to be anchored in objective reality and in the community of faith, in what Thomas Aquinas and other medieval theologians had called *veritas rerum,* "the truth of things." For More, therefore, conscience was not a vague feeling (or a strong feeling, for that matter) about something; on the contrary, it depended upon right reason and a well-disposed will. In the case of the Christian believer, the life and teachings of Christ, as transmitted by the Church, shape the Christian conscience, and thus the Christian's inner voice is Christ himself. Here More is not denying what was a principle for the inhabitants of his famous island: "Actually, they count this principle among their most ancient institutions, that *no one should suffer for his religion*" (*CW*, vol. 4: *Utopia*, p. 133; emphasis added).

LETTER 7: TO MARGARET ROPER

written with a coal A piece of charcoal More had to use for writing when pen or ink was wanting. He seems to have had writing materials during most of his time in prison.

in good quiet of mind "Sometimes the principal emotion of the person arrested is relief and even happiness!" writes a veteran prisoner in the Gulag, Aleksandr Solzhenitsyn. William Roper had been repeatedly impressed by More's serenity and even joy after the events that shattered his good fortune in life and sent him to his death. "Wilt thou know, Son Roper, why I was so merry?" asked More after coming home from his meeting with the Bishop of Canterbury, the Lord Chancellor, the Duke of Norfolk, and Thomas Cromwell. Roper supposed that everything had gone well and that his father-in-law was discharged and out of danger. "'In good faith, I rejoiced, Son,' quoth he, 'that I had given the devil a foul fall; and that with those Lords I had gone so far as, without great shame, I could never go back again.'" These perhaps were the last words Roper heard from More: "Son Roper, I thank our Lord the field is won!" Years later, Roper simply acknowledged that he had not understood these words then, "but as I conjectured afterwards, it was for that the love he had to God wrought in him so effectually, that it conquered all his carnal affections utterly" (*The Lyfe of Sir Thomas Moore, Knighte,* ed. James Mason Cline, pp. 61, 63-64).

of worldly things I no more desire than I have In one of the prayers he composed in the Tower, More asked for the grace "to set the world at nought." And he continued, "Of worldly substance, friends, liberty, life and all, to set the loss at right nought, for the winning of Christ." See *The Tower Works: Devotional Writings,* ed. Garry E. Haupt (New Haven: Yale University Press, 1980), p. 302.

your shrewd Will William Roper. See the note to Letter 3 in this volume. Roper had accompanied his father-in-law from Chelsea to Lambeth; there is no evidence that the two men ever saw each other again.

mine other sons More had three daughters and one son: Margaret, Elizabeth, Cecily, and John. His "other sons" are his sons-in-law, the husbands of Elizabeth and Cecily: William Daunce and Giles Heron. (Both marriages took place in 1525.) Daunce once told More that he had thought that his father-in-law, having been named Lord Chancellor of England, would nicely profit by it, yet he soon "found it nothing profitable." More listed the ways in which he could be of help, and then told him this: "Howbeit this one thing, son, I assure thee on my faith, that if the parties will at my hands call for justice, then all were it my father stood on the one side and the devil on the other, his cause being good, the devil should have right" (Roper, p. 220).

John Harris More's secretary and the tutor of his children. In a letter written during 1534, More calls him "gentle John Harris" (Rogers, *St. Thomas More: Selected Letters,* p. 88). One of his assignments had been to keep Simon Grynaeus company during his visit to England, and the Greek scholar would later describe Harris as "a young man of considerable literary attainments" (Rogers, *The Correspondence of Sir Thomas More,* n. 196, p. 479). On Good Fridays, Harris would read "the whole of our Lord's Passion" to the family gathered together (Stapleton, p. 89). He married Dorothy Colly, who is mentioned in More's last letter. Harris died, exiled in Namur, in 1565.

my shrewd wife above all More's first wife, Joanna Colt, died in 1511 after six years of marriage, leaving her husband with four little children. Within a month, More married Alice, widow of John Middleton, a wealthy merchant of London. This is Erasmus's description of More's second wife in his famous letter to Ulrich von Hutten: "A few months after his wife's death, he married a widow, more to have someone to look after his household than for his own pleasure, for she was neither beautiful nor in her first youth, as he used to remark in jest, but a capable and watchful housewife, though they lived on as close and affectionate terms as if she had been a girl of the most winning appearance" (*CWE,* vol. 7, p. 21). If More sent any letters to Alice from the Tower, they were lost. But the one we have, written five years earlier, in September 1529, on the occasion of a fire at Chelsea when More was away on a trip, suggests affection, respect, and trust between the spouses (cf. Rogers, *The Correspondence of Sir Thomas More,* n. 174). In the Latin epitaph for his first wife, More expressed his love for and gratitude to both women, Joanna and Alice. The text deserves to be quoted in full, here in translation: "Here lies Joanna, the beloved wife of Thomas More, who intend that this same tomb shall be Alice's and mine, too. One of them, my wife in the years of our vigorous youth, has made me father of a son and three daughters; the other has been as devoted to her stepchildren (a rare and splendid attainment in a stepmother) as very few mothers are to their own children. The one lived out her life with me, and the other still lives with me on such terms that I cannot decide whether I did love the one or do love the other more. O, how happily we could have lived all three together if fate and religion permitted. But the grave will unite us, and I pray that heaven will unite us too. Thus death will give what life could not" (*CW,* vol. 3, part 2, pp. 271-73).

LETTER 8: TO MARGARET ROPER

your lamentable letter Margaret's letter is lost, but the phrase brings to memory by contrast the many occasions on which More took so much joy and delight in reading his daughter's letters. *Epistola tua, dulcissima filia, qua me voluptate perfuderit, supersedebo dicere:* "I need not express the extreme pleasure your letter gave me, my darling daughter," reads one of them (Rogers, *The Correspondence of Sir Thomas More*, n. 108, p. 257; Rogers, *St. Thomas More: Selected Letters*, p. 151). And another: *Explicare calamo non possum, vix etiam cogitatione complecti, quanta me voluptate perfuderunt elegantissimae literae tuae, Margareta charissima:* "I cannot put down on paper, indeed I can hardly express my own mind, the deep pleasure that I received from your most charming letter, my dearest Margaret" (Rogers, *Correspondence*, n. 128, p. 301; Rogers, *Selected Letters*, p. 154). And in a letter to all his children, he offered this praise: *Itaque nulla fuit epistolarum vestrarum quae mihi non perplacuerit:* "There has not been one of your letters that did not please me extremely" (Rogers, *Correspondence*, n. 107, p. 256; Rogers, *Selected Letters*, p. 150). In the same letter "to his dearest children," More told them that he expected "from each one of you a letter almost every day."

Nam in manu Dei . . . impellit illud Proverbs 21:1 : "Like flowing water is the heart of the king in the hand of God, who turns it where he pleases." The same quotation appears three more times in More's prison letters: to Nicholas Wilson (n. 14), to Margaret Roper (n. 16), and to Master Leder (n. 19). In *Utopia* More had written that "from the monarch, as from a never-failing spring, flows a stream of all that is good or evil over the whole nation" (*CW*, vol. 4, p. 57).

the remembrance of that bitter agony The passion and death of Christ had become the very center of More's reflection and contemplation during his imprisonment. In such meditation he sought strength to deal with his own fear and anxiety. His *Dialogue of Comfort against Tribulation* reaches a crescendo in the image of the suffering Jesus; and his last work, written also in prison, *De Tristitia Christi*, is a commentary on the agony of Christ in Gethsemane.

LETTER 9: FROM MARGARET ROPER

and fast knit only in the love of God In *The Scale of Perfection* (*Scala Perfectionis*), a favorite book among the English laity and one that More himself recommended in the preface to *The Confutation of Tyndale's Answer*, Walter Hilton had written that "Jesus is knitted and fastened to a person's soul by a good will and a great desire for him, to have him alone and to see him in his spiritual glory. The greater this desire, the more firmly is Jesus knitted to the soul; the less the desire, the more loosely is he joined. Then whatever spirit or feeling it is that lessens this desire and wants to draw it down from its natural ascent toward Jesus in order to set it upon itself, this spirit will unknit and undo Jesus from the soul; and therefore it is not from God but from the working of the Enemy. Nevertheless, if a spirit, a feeling or a revelation by an angel increases this desire, knits firmer the knot of love and devotion to Jesus, opens the sight of your soul more clearly to spiritual knowledge, and makes it humbler in itself, this spirit is from God" (Book 1, chap. 12). Hilton's writings were being copied at the Charterhouse of London while young More lived there (cf. Chambers, "Continuity of English Prose," in Harpsfield, p. 130), and both father and daughter were familiar with this book, which was most influential in the development of More's own spirituality.

ut sit mens sana in corpore sano "Orandum est ut sit mens sana in corpore sano," wrote Juvenal (*Satyra X,* v. 356): "Pray for a sound mind in a sound body." What follows in the context of this proverbial phrase is worth quoting here because it illuminates the text of Margaret's letter. She may well have thought of the satire's theme, "on the vanity of human wishes." This is the full text (from *The Satires of Juvenal,* p. 134):

> Pray for a healthy mind in a healthy body, a spirit
> Unafraid of death, but reconciled to it, and able
> To bear up, to endure whatever troubles afflict it,
> Free from hate and desire, preferring Hercules' labors
> To the cushions and loves and feasts of Sardanapallus.
> I show you what you can give to yourself: only through virtue
> Lies the certain road to a life that is blessed and tranquil.
> If men had any sense, Fortune would not be a goddess.
> We are the ones who make her so, and give her a place in the heavens.

Years before, More had given his own understanding of the phrase in a letter to Margaret: "Though I earnestly hope that you will devote the rest of your life to medical science and sacred literature, so that you may be well furnished for the whole scope of human life *(nempe vt sit mens sana in corpore sano),* and I know that you have already laid the foundations of these studies, and there will be always opportunity to continue the building, yet I am of the opinion that you may with great advantage give some years of your yet flourishing youth to humane letters and so-called liberal arts" (Rogers, *St. Thomas More: Selected Letters,* p. 149; Rogers, *The Correspondence of Sir Thomas More,* n. 106, p. 255).

your life past and godly conversation William Roper was a witness to this kind of talk in More's home: "In the time somewhat before his trouble, he would talk with his wife and children of the joys of heaven and the pains of hell, the lives of holy martyrs, of their grievous martyrdoms, of their marvellous patience, and of their passions and deaths that they suffered rather than they would offend God. And what an happy and blessed thing it was, for the love of God, to suffer loss of

164

goods, imprisonment, loss of lands, and life also. He would further say unto them that, upon his faith, if he might perceive his wife and children would encourage him to die in a good cause, it should so comfort him that, for very joy thereof, it would make him merrily run to death" (pp. 227-28).

has bought us with his precious blood "Knowing that you were not redeemed with corruptible things, as gold or silver, from your vain conversation of the tradition of your fathers: but with the precious blood of Christ, as of a lamb unspotted and undefiled" (1 Pet. 1:18-19).

in John Wood's stead John à Wood remained More's servant during his fourteen months of imprisonment in the Tower. Wood had to swear that "if he should hear or see him [More] at any time speak or write any manner of thing against the King, the council, or the state of the realm, he should open it to the Lieutenant" (Roper, p. 239).

LETTER 10: TO ALL HIS FRIENDS

to all his friends Erasmus described More to Ulrich von Hutten as a man born for friendship: *Ad amicitiam natus factusque videtur, cuius et syncerissimus est cultor et longe tenacissimus est:* "Friendship he seems born and designed for; no one is more openhearted in making friends or more tenacious in keeping them, nor has he any fear of that plethora of friendships again which Hesiod warns us" (*CWE,* vol. 7, p. 18). This note is probably one that More gave to Margaret during one of her visits so that she could show it to her father's close friends.

LETTER 11: ALICE ALINGTON TO MARGARET ROPER

Alice Alington The daughter of More's second wife, Alice, and of John Middleton. She was two or three years older than Margaret Roper and had grown up and been educated as one of More's own children. Alice married Thomas Elrington in 1516. After he died, she married Sir Giles Alington in 1524; the couple had nine children.

at my coming home Halesworth, in Suffolk, one of the homes of the Alingtons.

Sir Thomas Barmeston Head of a family in Suffolk.

the matter of the nun A reference to Elizabeth Barton, the holy Nun of Kent. See Letters 2 and 3 in this volume.

save only the blind Bishop John Fisher, bishop of Rochester. "Blind" is Audley's epithet quoted by More.

LETTER 12: MARGARET ROPER TO ALICE ALINGTON

But whether this answer . . . More This long letter is a dialogue between father and daughter. R. W. Chambers writes that "the Margaret speeches in the dialogue are pure Margaret, the More speeches pure More. When William Rastell published the letter, long years after the death of both, their nearest and dearest could not say which had written it" (p. 308). Rogers has "hym self" instead of "her selfe" (*The Correspondence of Sir Thomas More*, p. 514), and Rastell wrote, "But whether thys aunswer wer writen by syr Thomas More in his daughter Ropers name, or by her selfe, it is not certaynelye knowen" (*English Works*, sig. YY, v). Louis Martz comments, "One can imagine the father and daughter planning it together and speaking much of it aloud in More's Tower room. But its art seems to be all the father's" (pp. 58-59). But it is quite clear that it was written by Thomas More.

of his diseases See the note to Letter 3 in this volume. In the account of the trial known as the *Paris News Letter*, More appears even more debilitated — to the point that he could barely stand and a chair had to be brought for him. The same document quotes him as saying, "Concerning now the matters you charge and challenge me withall, the articles are so prolix and long that I fear, what for my long imprisonment, what for my long lingring disease, what for my present weakness and debilitie, that neither my wit, nor my memorie, nor yet my voice, will serve to make so full, so effectual and sufficient answer as the weight and importance of these matters doth crave" (quoted in Harpsfield, p. 184; in the French text it is quoted on pp. 258-59). A cervical disc lesion would explain the pains More felt in prison: see Salvador Hernández Conesa, "Did Thomas More Have a Cervical Disc Lesion?" *Moreana* 83-84 (1984): 27-31. Another thesis, proposed by K. M. Flegel, is that More suffered from angina: see "Thomas More: Was a Sick Man Beheaded?"

seven psalms and the litany The seven penitential psalms — traditionally psalms 6, 31, 37 (38), 50 (51), 101 (102), 129 (130), and 142 (143) — were usually followed by the litany of the saints, a prayer of responsive petition that begins with invocations to the holy Trinity, and then to the Virgin Mary and the saints. This devotion was part of More's prayer life at home, as William Roper points out: "As Sir Thomas More's custom was daily, if he were at home, besides his private prayers, with his children to say the Seven Psalms, Litany and Suffrages following, so was his guise [custom] nightly before he went to bed, with his wife, children and household, to go to his chapel and there upon his knees ordinarily to say certain psalms and collects with them" (pp. 210-11). The litany is still recited in public services as well as in private devotions.

What, mistress Eve Margaret does not abandon her efforts to persuade her father to take the oath, but at the same time she develops increasing respect and admiration for her father's loyalty to Christian principles and his "clear conscience." And More seems almost delighted at being thus challenged and admired by the daughter who was so close to his heart. "For Eve will be Eve though Adam would say nay." More can jokingly call his own daughter "mistress Eve," perhaps aware that her great love for him was helping him to conquer temptation and remain steadfast in his determination. In the *Enchiridion militis Christiani,* Erasmus had written, "By 'woman' we mean, of course, the carnal or sensual part of man. For this is our Eve, through whom the crafty serpent entices and lures our minds to deadly pleasures" (I, 1). The first English version of this book was published in London in November 1533 with the title *The Manuel of the Christian Knight.* St. Augustine, More's favorite Church Father, wrote in his commentary of Genesis, "After the woman had been seduced and had eaten of the forbidden fruit and had given Adam some to eat with her, he did not wish to make her unhappy, fearing she would waste away without his support, alienated from his affections, and that this dissension would be her death. He was not overcome by the concupiscence of the flesh, which he had not yet experienced in the law of the members at war with the law of his mind, but by the sort of attachment and affection by which it often happens that we offend God while we try to keep the friendship of men" (*The Literal Meaning of Genesis,* vol. 2, Book 11, chap. 42, p. 59).

God hath given me to the straight "Straight" = "strait," meaning "strict, narrow, a difficult passage," the "strait gate" of Luke 13:24 (KJV).

one of the greatest estates That is, a person of high rank, a statesman or dignitary — in this instance, Thomas Audley, the Lord Chancellor, who had already helped More in the affair of Elizabeth Barton, the Nun of Kent.

and one other man The bishop of Rochester, John Fisher.

mine other good son her first A reference to Alice's first husband, Thomas Elrington.

my lord's Aesop fables See *Aesopica,* vol. 1, pp. 644-45.

my Lord Cardinal From the moment Thomas Wolsey became Lord Chancellor, his was the guiding voice in English affairs.

the Emperor and the French King Unlike his father, Henry VIII began and ended his reign at war. France and England had been enemies for almost two hundred years, and not since Henry V had an English king been so eager to invade French territory. In 1519 the three great powers in Europe were France, England,

and the Empire. The neutrality of England guaranteed continental peace: she was potentially friend and foe of both Charles V and Francis I. For three years Henry VIII kept a policy of peace and then of mediation between the emperor and the French king. Then, in the summer of 1523, England went to war against France with an army of ten thousand led by the Duke of Suffolk. The invasion was Henry's second major war. Cf. J. J. Scarisbrick, *Henry VIII,* pp. 127-32. The early military campaign is examined by Charles Cruickshank in *Henry VIII and the Invasion of France.* The best comprehensive study of the reign of Francis I is R. J. Knecht, *Renaissance Warrior and Patron.*

to spend many a fair penny Between 1509 and 1520 the English crown spent about 1.7 million pounds, of which one million was spent on troops and military equipment (Guy, *Tudor England,* p. 99). In the spring of 1522 a survey was conducted to assess the military capabilities of the country. Cardinal Wolsey was a genius at raising taxes and was able to obtain "the fantastic sum of 260,000 pounds from taxpayers in 1522 and 1523" (Guy, *Tudor England,* p. 78). Henry was ready to invade France again in the spring of 1525, and therefore more taxes had to be levied (the so-called amicable grant) when the "loans" of 1522 had not been paid back. See also Richard Hoyle, "War and Public Finance," chap. 4 in *The Reign of Henry VIII,* ed. Diarmaid MacCulloch; and S. J. Gunn, *Early Tudor Government, 1485-1558,* chap. 3.

his Grace is gone Cardinal Wolsey had died a natural death at Leicester Abbey on November 29, 1530, while on his way back to London.

Non sum Œdipus, sed Morus "Davus sum, non Œdipus" (Terence, *Andria,* Act I, scene ii, l. 23). Davus is a stock character in Roman comedy. Horace describes another Davus as a "slave-confidential-and-clerk" (*Satires,* trans. Smith Palmer Bowie [Chicago, 1959], p. 79). This theatrical character, servant or slave, says, "I am a homely man and do not understand hints and riddles like Oedipus."

as my name is in Greek More was fond of playing with his name, which means "fool" in Greek. Erasmus dedicated his celebrated and controversial *Encomium moriae (The Praise of Folly)* to More, mentioning his friend's name in the origin of the book's theme: "First of all, there was your family name of More, which is as close to the Greek word for folly as you are far from the meaning of the word." Cf. the article by Germain Marc'hadour, "A Name for All Seasons." In the following quatrain in Latin, More plays with the meaning of his own name; he wrote it three years before his death:

> *Moraris, si sit spes hic tibi longa morandi:*
> *Hoc te vel morus, More, monere potest.*

Desine morari, et caelo meditare morari:
Hoc te vel morus, More, monere potest.

You are playing the fool if you expect to stay long here below.
Even a fool, More, can tell you that.
Stop playing the fool and contemplate staying in heaven.
Even a fool, More, can tell you that.

Latin Poems (*CW*, vol. 3, part 2, pp. 302-3)

The distich that follows the quatrain is printed at the end of More's letters in this edition.

truly number and reckon me "[More] was obviously nettled at the suggestion that his obstinacy was due to a desire to rule. He was equally nettled by the suggestion that his obstinacy was due to Fisher's example" (Chambers, p. 309). In several of his works — *Utopia, The History of King Richard III, A Dialogue of Comfort against Tribulation* — More had dealt with the same theme and was ever consistent throughout his life. His *Richard III* is a narrative about the human presumption of those in public office and the frail subsistence of all things temporal. More used the story to offer a critique of tyranny and the abuse of power. More's political career has been studied at length by John Guy; see *The Public Career of Sir Thomas More.*

in which as Boethius saith More is thinking of *The Consolation of Philosophy*, the classical work of prison literature by Boethius (480-524) and one of More's favorite books (Liber II, vi, ed. Raffaello Del Re [Rome, 1968]). This is an English translation of the passage: "However, let us examine this much lauded and much sought after power of yours. You creatures of earth, don't you stop to consider the people over whom you think you exercise authority? You would laugh if you saw a community of mice and one mouse arrogating to himself power and jurisdiction over the others. Again, think of the human body: could you discover anything more feeble than man, when often even a tiny fly can kill him either by its bite or by creeping into some inward part of him? The only way one man can exercise power over another is over his body and what is inferior to it, his possessions. You cannot impose anything on a free mind, and you cannot move from its state of inner tranquility a mind at peace with itself and firmly founded on reason" (trans. V. E. Watts [New York: Penguin Books, 1969]).

the five foolish virgins Cf. Matthew 25:1-13. In the parable, the virgins fell asleep because the bridegroom or spouse was delayed in his coming. In *De Tristitia Christi* More noticed how we "try to escape our awareness of sadness by looking for consolation in sleep" (*CW*, vol. 14, p. 287) when the proper conduct is to stay "awake and praying." The sleepiness of the three Apostles — Peter, James, and John — while Jesus was in his agony gave More occasion to lament the general stupor of the members of the Church, especially the bishops: "Does not this contrast between the traitor and the apostles present to us a clear and sharp mirror image (as it were), a sad and terrible view of what has happened through the ages from those times even to our own? Why do not bishops contemplate in this scene their own somnolence? Since they have succeeded in the place of the apostles, would that they would reproduce their virtues just as eagerly as they embrace their authority and as faithfully as they display their sloth and sleepiness" (*CW*, vol. 14, pp. 259-61).

The second fable, Marget, seemeth not to be Aesop's More seems to have liked the fable; he wrote an expanded version of it for *A Dialogue of Comfort against Tribulation*, in which Antony tells Vincent that when he was a little boy, Mother Maud, "a good old woman," told them that "the ass and the wolf came upon a time to confession to the Fox." The confessor, Father Fox, has been quickly and amusingly transformed by More into a sort of Protestant minister, discreet in his rejection of the Lenten fast as "an invention of man" (*CW*, vol. 12, pp. 114-18).

my Lord of Rochester say the same That More had written to Fisher, a known traitor, while in prison, upholding the bishop's opinions, was part of the indictment against him. During his trial, More said that he had written Fisher about eight letters in all, and that all he had admitted in them was the simple fact that he would be silent on the grave matter of the King, advising Fisher to follow common sense. Cf. J. Duncan M. Derrett, "The Trial of Sir Thomas More," pp. 64-65. For More's relationship with Fisher, see E. L. Surtz, "More's Friendship with Fisher," pp. 169-79.

if they say one thing and think the while the contrary In *A Dialogue of Comfort against Tribulation*, Antony discusses with Vincent a sort of case or perhaps a "thought-experiment" that Christians will find difficult to avoid: In case of religious persecution, what would I do? Would I accept torture and even death for Christ? "But now is all the peril," Antony responds, "if the man answer himself, that he would in such case rather forsake the faith of Christ with his mouth, and keep it still in his heart than for the confessing of it, to endure a painful death; for by this mind he falleth in deadly sin, while he never cometh in the case indeed if he never had put himself the case he never had fallen in. But in good faith methinketh that he which upon that case put unto himself by himself, will make himself that answer hath the habit of faith so faint and so cold, that to the better knowledge of himself and of his necessity, to pray for more strength of grace he had need to have the question put him either by himself or some other man" (*CW*, vol. 12, p. 197).

as a woman reasoned once More's biographers seem to be expected at least to ask whether this woman was Dame Alice More.

pie Sir William Pounder . . . at Bartholomew fair From the French *pied poudré*, "piepowder," *pede-pulverosus*, "dusty-footed," an itinerant merchant. According to the *Oxford English Dictionary*, the Court of Piepowders, a court of wayfarers, was "a summary court formerly held at fairs and markets to administer justice among itinerant dealers." The Bartholomew Fair was held annually from 1133 to 1855 at West Smithfield. As Justice Overdo, in Ben Jonson's *Bartholomew Fair*, says, "Many are the yearly enormities of this Fair, in whose courts of Pie-powders I have had the honor during the three days sometimes to sit as judge" (Act II, scene i).

an escheator of London An escheator, "an officer appointed by the Lord Treasurer to take notice of the escheats [return of lands if there was no heir] in the country to which he is appointed, and to certify them into the Exchequer" *(OED)*.

the name of his bare office alone The "escheator" is a "cheater," which is actually the term used by Shakespeare for the job.

quoth one of the northern men More is imitating the language of Northern people: "Where wonnes thou? Be not aleuen here, and you but ene la alone, and we all agreed?"

that by another law they may need to be reformed There is in More a certain acknowledgment of a growth in awareness of the Christian truth, what later will be known as development of doctrine. See his *Confutation of Tyndale's Answer* (CW, vol. 8, p. 249).

plain promises in Scripture "All authority in heaven and on earth has been given to me. Go, therefore, make disciples of all nations; baptize them in the name of the Father and of the Son and of the Holy Spirit, and teach them to observe all the commands I gave you. And know that I am with you always; yes, to the end of time" (Matt. 28:18-20); "But when the Spirit of truth comes he will lead you to the complete truth" (John 16:13). More frequently uses these two texts in his polemical works to assert the truth of the Catholic Church.

the feast of her conception The "feast of the Conception of St. Mary" had been established in some English monasteries by Anglo-Saxon monks, but was later taken out of the Canterbury calendar by Lanfranc. From the sixteenth century on, the feast became widespread in the Catholic world.

yet was holy Saint Bernard against that part of her praise St. Bernard of Clairvaux (1090-1153) protested this new title for the mother of Christ. The letter mentioned by More was addressed to the canons of the cathedral of Lyons, and it was a call to prudence in the midst of the controversy surrounding the Virgin's conception, reproving them for not consulting with the Holy See (*Epistola clxxiv:*

Ad canonicos lugdunenses, de conceptione S. Mariae, PL 182, 332-36). As in many a controversy, the opposition to the title was partly due to a different understanding of the word "conception," and to the difficulty of reconciling it with the doctrine of Christ's universal redemption from sin. Cf. "The Medieval Controversy over the Immaculate Conception up to the Death of Scotus," in *The Dogma of the Immaculate Conception: History and Significance,* ed. Edward D. O'Connor (Notre Dame: University of Notre Dame Press, 1958), pp. 161-212.

the blessed holy bishop, Saint Anselm St. Anselm of Canterbury (1033-1109), the father of Scholasticism and a Doctor of the Church, did not actually defend this marian title. Richard Southern thinks that Anselm would not have approved of the title on theological grounds because "he held that no one, not even the Virgin Mary, could be exempt from Original Sin without destroying the strict necessity for the Incarnation" (p. 435, and pp. 432-36). More here follows a common attribution to Anselm of a treatise about the conception of Mary that was written by Eadmer, his disciple and biographer: *De Conceptione Sanctae Marie editum ab Eadmero monacho magno peccatore.* To give a theological ground to the title, Eadmer applied the argument from congruity developed by Anselm in his *Cur Deus Homo?* Another Anselm, a nephew of the bishop of Canterbury, was one of the early advocates of the feast.

nor for any provincial council either An Oxford Carmelite in the fourteenth century referred to the doctrine of the Immaculate Conception as a "fantastic kind of heresy." But the book by Eadmer attributed to St. Anselm gave a new impetus to the feast, and a provincial council in London in 1328 re-established the feast as a local celebration. In 1438 the Council of Basel decreed the obligatory observance of the feast. The doctrine was not solemnly defined until 1854, when Pope Pius IX proclaimed in the bull *Ineffabilis Deus* that the Immaculate Conception is to be believed as a truth of the Catholic faith (*Enchiridion Symbolorum,* n. 2803).

this conscience is very damnable In *The Scale of Perfection,* Walter Hilton distinguishes bodily pride and spiritual pride, the latter a trademark of hypocrites and heretics. The text deserves to be quoted at length because it captures More's mind: "A heretic sins mortally in pride, because he chooses his resting place and his delight in his own opinion and in what he says, and he supposes it to be true. That opinion and word is against God and holy church; and therefore he sins mortally in pride, for he loves himself and his own will and wit so much that he will not leave it even though it is plainly against the ordinance of holy church; but he wants to rest in it, as if in the truth, and thus he makes it his god. But he deceives himself, for God and holy church are so united and agreed together that whoever acts against the one is acting against both. Therefore, anyone who says he loves God and keeps his commandments, and yet despises holy church and cares nothing for its laws and ordinances (made by its sovereign head for the government of all Christian people) — he lies. . . . Those others who commit mortal sins of the flesh and lie in them commonly have misgivings every now and then and feel remorse in their conscience that they are not going the right way, but a heretic supposes he is doing well and teaching well, and nobody as well as he, and so he thinks his way is the right way. Therefore he feels no remorse of conscience or humility in his heart, and unless God in his mercy sends him meekness, he certainly goes to hell in the end. And nevertheless he still supposes himself to have done well, and to be getting himself the bliss of heaven for his teaching" (Book 1, chap. 58).

and that are I trust in heaven Ignominious though the martyr's death seems, it is otherwise for God and the company of saints in heaven, or so More believed. Thus Antony tells Vincent at the end of their conversation in More's *Dialogue of Comfort against Tribulation:* "Then Cousin, can there no man that hath faith, accompt [reckon] himself shamed here, by any manner death that he suffereth for the faith of Christ, while how vile and how shameful so ever it seem in the sight here of a few worldly wretches, it is allowed and approved for very precious and honourable in the sight of God and of all the glorious company of heaven which as perfectly stand and behold it as those pevish [foolish] people do and are in number mo than an hundreth to one" (*CW*, vol. 12, p. 290).

Dulcarnon, even at my wit's end "But whether that ye dwelle or for hym go, I am, til God me bettre mynde sende, at Dulcarnon, right at my wittes ende" (*Troilus and Criseyde*, III, ll. 929-31). The term *Dulcarnon*, of Arabic origins, is literally translated as "possessor of two horns" and means "perplexity, dilemma." "At Dulcarnon" means "at one's wit end."

Master Harry Patenson More's jester, a feeble-minded person. He appears in the family portrait by Hans Holbein. In 1521, Harry Patenson accompanied More on one of his diplomatic trips to the Continent, where his behavior was not very diplomatic. More told the story in *The Confutation of Tyndale's Answer* (*CW*, vol. 8, pp. 900-901). See also Peter Ackroyd, *The Life of Thomas More*, pp. 260-62.

for I have sworn myself A marginal gloss in More's *English Works* notes that Margaret took the oath "as far as would stand with the law of God."

a man may leese his head and have no harm "No man can take harm but of himself," wrote More to John Frith (Rogers, *The Correspondence of Sir Thomas More*, n. 190; also nn. 542, 557). In *A Dialogue of Comfort against Tribulation*, Antony says, "Or if they prevail, yet if we take the way that I have told you we shall by their persecution take little harm, or rather none harm at all, but that that shall seem harm shall indeed be to us none harm at all but good. For if God make us and keep us good men as he hath promised to do, if we pray well therefore, then saith holy scripture, *Bonis omnia cooperantur in bonum,* unto good folk, all things turn them to good" (*CW*, vol. 12, p. 248). And again: "For surely if a man may (as indeed he may) have great comfort in the clearness of his conscience, that hath a false crime put upon him, and by false witness proved upon him, and he falsely punished and put to worldly shame and pain therefore, an hundred times more comfort may he have in his heart who, where white is called black and right is called wrong, abideth by the truth and is persecuted for justice" (*CW*, vol. 12, p. 33). There is a sermon by St. John Chrysostom on the same theme that was translated into English by one of More's friends, Thomas Lupset (*A Sermon of Chrysostom, that, No man is hurte but of hym selfe*). And Erasmus had written in his *Enchiridion militis Christiani* that "no one is harmed except by himself" (sixth rule). The idea, of course, had already been well understood and taught by Socrates. Peter the Apostle or one of his disciples may have learned it from another master: "No one can hurt you if you are determined to do only what is right; if you do have to suffer for being good, you will count it a blessing" (1 Pet. 3:13-14).

the counsel of Christ in the Gospel Luke 14:28-30: "And indeed, which of you here intending to build a tower, would not first sit down and work out the cost to see if he had enough to complete it? Otherwise, if he laid the foundation and then found himself unable to finish the work, the onlookers would all start making fun of him and saying: Here is a man who started to build and was unable to finish." At the beginning of the third book of *A Dialogue of Comfort against Tribulation*, Antony discusses with Vincent "whither a man should cast in his mind and appoint in his heart before, that if he were taken with the Turks, he would rather die than forsake the faith." Antony believes that "very few men can escape" the thought of this possibility, that Christians are bound to have that intention "actually some time, and ever more habitually." Finally, convinced that this readiness to martyrdom should be a disposition in "every Christian man and woman," Antony goes on to propose that "every curat should often counsel all his parishons, and every man and woman their servants and their children, even beginning in their tender youth, to know this point and think thereon, and little and little fro their very childhed, to accustom them dulcely and pleasantly in the meditation thereof" (*CW*, vol. 12, p. 198). I have provided a brief commentary in "Martyrdom and Christian Morals."

my prisonment even the very chief The physical deprivations of life in prison seemed to reaffirm a realization that More had come to years before: that life in this world is also a sort of prison. The idea was more than a prisoner's consolation: it was a way of expressing what for him was an important existential truth — namely, that the human being is a creature, and human freedom a created freedom, and therefore not an absolute power. In *The Four Last Things*, More had written, "I shall put [give] thee a more earnest image of our condition and that not a feigned similitude, but a very true fashion and figure of our worshipful estate. Mark this well, for of this thing we be very sure, that old and young, man and woman, rich and poor, prince and page, all the while we live in this world we be but prisoners, and be within a sure prison, out of which there can no man escape" (p. 42). More may have been thinking of Psalm 139:7: "Whither shall I go from thy spirit, and whither shall I flee from thy face?" The same striking image receives extensive treatment in the last part of *A Dialogue of Comfort against Tribulation,* where More writes of an "everlasting liberty" for those who die in the truth of Christ (*CW,* vol. 12, p. 254).

release of my pain in purgatory In *A Dialogue of Comfort against Tribulation,* Antony reaffirms his Church's teaching on purgatory as the state of souls still in need of purification after death (*CW,* vol. 12, pp. 33, 36-38). Accordingly, there is a temporary pain of loss (that is, the privation of *lumen gloriae,* of the vision of God) and physical pain, though the Catholic Church has never explicitly defined the latter. The existence of purgatory was denied by Protestants as a diabolic invention. Only a few years before, in 1529, in his work *A Supplication of Souls,* More wrote extensively about purgatory, defending its existence and arguing its biblical foundation against a pamphlet called *A Supplication for the Beggars,* authored by Simon Fish. In another passage in *A Dialogue of Comfort* that illuminates More's expression in this letter, Antony recognizes the purifying value of suffering and death when accepted for Christ, since a martyr's death cleanses all sins and pays all debts: "The bare pacient taking of his death, should have served for the satisfaction of his sin through the merit of Christ's passion, I mean, without help of which no pain of our own could be satisfactory. But now shall Christ for his forsaking of his own life in the honour of his faith, forgive the pain of all his sins of his mere liberality and accept all the pain of his death for merit of reward in heaven and shall assign no part thereof to the payment of his debt in purgatory but shall take it all as an offering, and requite it all with glory. And this man among christen men, all [although] had he been before a Devil, nothing would I after doubt to take him for a martyr" (*CW,* vol. 12, pp. 32-33).

call upon Christ and pray him to help "Then Peter got out of the boat and started walking towards towards Jesus across the water, but as soon as he felt the force of the wind, he took fright and began to sink. 'Lord! save me!' he cried. Jesus put out his hand at once and held him. 'Man of little faith,' he said, 'why did you doubt?'" (Matt. 14:29-31).

if he suffer me to play Saint Peter further The Apostle Peter denied any knowledge of or friendship with Christ three times, an account given by the Four Evangelists: Matthew 26:69-75; Mark 14:66-72; Luke 22:56-62; and John 18:17, 25-27. The character of Simon Peter seems to have been ever present in More's meditation in the last years of his life. The possibility of breaking down and failing in his resolution was never a distant thought for More, and this fragility of goodness became also a path toward further humility and penance. In *A Dialogue of Comfort* *against Tribulation,* he wrote, "And here must he be put in remembrance of Mary Magdalene, of the prophet David, and specially of Saint Peter whose high bold courage took a foul fall and yet because he despaired not of God's mercy, but wept and called upon it, how highly God took him into his favour again, in his holy Scripture is well testified, and well through Christendom known" (*CW,* vol. 12, p. 146). Later on in the same work, More used the same expression referring to those who "peradventure of right good courage too would play Saint Peter if they were brought to the point" (*CW,* vol. 12, p. 246). He explained that Peter fell by denying his Master in "a sudden fear," but then "he confessed his master again, and soon after that he was imprisoned therefore, and not ceasing so was thereupon sore scourged for the confession of his faith and yet after that imprisoned again afresh and being from thence delivered, stintid [ceased] not to preach on still until that after manyfold labours, travails and troubles he was at Rome crucified and with cruel torment slain" (*CW,* vol. 12, p. 300).

Erasmus contemplated a rather different course of action when writing to Richard Pace (1482?-1536), fried and diplomat, on July 5, 1521: "[Mine] was never the spirit to risk my life for the truth. Not everyone has the strength needed for martyrdom. I fear that, if strife were to break out, I shall behave like Peter. When popes and emperors make the right decisions I follow, which is Godly; if they decide wrongly I tolerate them, which is safe. I believe that even for men of goodwill this is legitimate, if there is no hope of better things" (*CWE,* vol. 8, p. 259).

shall I then serve for a praise of his justice Medieval theologians relished both divine justice and even mercy toward those condemned to everlasting punishment. Hell, therefore, was not a useless state, but served as "a praise of his justice." Of course, the very words of Thomas More imply the highest abandonment in the mercy of God, and thus the hope for salvation. His paradoxical comment is reminiscent of those by other saints that they would rather be lost forever than displease God.

it shall indeed be the best lines quoted in the catechism of the Catholic Church (Rome, 1994, n. 313).

LETTER 13: TO DOCTOR NICHOLAS WILSON

Nicholas Wilson As chaplain and confessor of Henry VIII, Nicholas Wilson (d. 1548), a doctor in divinity, had been asked to study in detail the matter of the King's marriage. In 1533, Wilson sided with the minority position defending the power of the Roman Pontiff to concede dispensations from marriage impediments and therefore to declare on the question of the validity of Henry's marriage to Catherine. Wilson had been imprisoned in the Tower a week before More — April 10, 1534 — and this letter and the one following it reflect the priest's mental anguish and agony. In 1537 Wilson accepted the oath and was released from the Tower; two years later he surrendered to the Tudor authorities, declaring his intention to abide by whatever the King and the bishops of the Anglican Church declared on doctrinal and disciplinary matters. There is a letter from Thomas Cromwell to Michael Throcmorton (the loyal secretary of Reginald Pole) suggesting that Wilson would be the perfect man to deal with Cardinal Pole, and instructions on how to proceed in such a mission, but it never took place. In 1540 Wilson was sent to the Tower again, suspected of secret communications with Rome. He was released by the King the following year. Cf. *DNB*, vol. 21, pp. 590-91.

LETTER 14: TO DOCTOR NICHOLAS WILSON

places of Scripture and of the old holy Doctors Thomas More had already explained himself on many of the points dealt with here in his letter to Cromwell of March 5, 1534. See the notes to Letter 5 in this volume.

that you had written his Highness a book The book seems to have immediately vanished. Apparently it was sent to Paris, to a Spanish theologian, either Pedro de Garay or Alvaro de Moscoso. See *LP,* vol. 8, 335, 859, and Guy Bedouelle and Patrick Le Gal, *Le "divorce" du Roi Henry VIII,* p. 436.

De ciuitate Dei In *The City of God* St. Augustine did not contemplate the case in question — that is, of a man marrying his brother's wife — but he insisted on the principle of binding together the largest number of people by family affection, which seems to discourage that practice, along with marriage among blood relations. Augustine wrote about the propagation of "the two cities," the earthly and the heavenly, and of marriage between blood-related people. The present laws and customs could not bind earliest ages, when men took their sisters for wives, "an act which was as certainly dictated by necessity in these ancient days as afterwards it was condemned by the prohibitions of religion." Although some people have allowed a brother to marry his sister, "a finer morality" did not condone it, insisted Augustine. "For custom has very great power either to attract or to shock human feeling. And in this matter, while it restrains concupiscence within due bounds, the man who neglects and disobeys it is justly branded as abominable. For if it is iniquitous to plough beyond our own boundaries through greed of gain, is it not much more iniquitous to transgress the recognized boundaries of morals through sexual lust?" (Book 15, chap. 16, pp. 500-502). St. Augustine thought that marriage between cousins was not prohibited by divine law nor by human law, yet, he wrote, "people shrank from it."

the epistle of Saint Ambrose The addressee, Aemilius Florus Paternus, Proconsul of Africa and holder of an important position at the imperial court, had asked the bishop of Milan to obtain a rescript from the emperor so that his son could marry his daughter's daughter. Ambrose refused to secure the petition, expressing his dislike for such marital unions "not forbidden by the law which was promulgated through Moses, yet forbidden by the voice of nature" (*Letters,* n. 86, p. 483). In another letter (n. 59), the longest in the bishop's correspondence, written for the church at Vercelli, there is a strong statement against second nuptials and in praise of widowhood. Cf. Neil B. McLynn, *Ambrose of Milan,* p. 259, and F. H. Dudden, *The Life and Times of St. Ambrose,* vol. 1, pp. 136-37.

The text about the Paternus case appeared in the third chapter of *Censurae academiarum (The Determinations of the most famous...).* Cf. *The Divorce Tracts of Henry VIII,* pp. 96-100.

If More was familiar with other letters from the Ambrosean correspondence, he must have been surprised by the timeliness of a few of them. In one letter, Ambrose writes that "many have betrayed the faith when lured by women's charms" (*Letters,* n. 35, p. 176). And in the one to the Christian community in Vercelli, Ambrose talks of great heroes like Daniel, Ananiah, Azariah, and Mishael, whom More must have remembered because, as the bishop of Milan puts it, "[they] were reared in a royal palace, were fed with fasting, as though in the desert, with coarse food and ordinary drink. Rightly did these royal slaves prevail over kingdoms, despise captivity.... They were found most strong when they were esteemed most weak; they fled not from the mocking of men, for they hoped for heavenly rewards; they did not dread the darkness of prison, for on them shone the beauty of eternal life" (*Letters,* n. 59, p. 346).

the epistle of Saint Basil In a letter to Diodorus (dated 373 or 374), St. Basil of Caesarea expressed his disgust at the fact that when a certain person was asked "if it was allowable for him to marry the sister of his dead wife, he did not shudder in horror at the question, but even listened calmly, and very nobly and gloriously supported the wanton desire." Here again, the principle at work in the moral case was the force of "instinctive conviction" rather than any positive law, and it was expressed in the behavior of decent Christian people. "The custom is as follows: If anyone being overcome at any time by the vice of impurity falls into an unlawful union with two sisters, this is neither considered marriage, nor, in short, are they admitted to the membership of the Church before they have separated from each other" (*Letters,* vol. 1, n. 160, pp. 314-15).

the writing of Saint Gregory Is More thinking of the *Dialogues?* In Book 4, Gregory tells the story of Galla, a noble girl who married at a very early age and a year later lost her husband: "Her age and wealth invited her to a second marriage in a world glowing with opportunity, but she preferred a spiritual marriage with the Lord. Marriages of this kind usually begin with sorrow and suffering, but in the end lead to the eternal joys of heaven, whereas an earthly marriage always begins with joy but ends in sorrow." Then he says that the girl refused second nuptials in spite of the fact that her doctors told her that "if she did not marry again, she would grow a beard even though she was a woman." See *Dialogues,* trans. Odo John Zimmerman, pp. 205-6.

in Leviticus and in the Deuteronomy Leviticus 20:21 and Deuteronomy 25:5. See the note to Letter 5 in this volume.

in the Gospel Texts on the indissolubility of marriage are Matthew 5:31-32; 19:3-9; Mark 10:2-12; and Luke 16:18. "Back in the house the disciples questioned him again about this, and he said to them, 'The man who divorces his wife and marries another is guilty of adultery against her. And if a woman divorces her husband and marries another she is guilty of adultery too'" (Mark 10:11-12).

in Saint Paul's epistles "A married woman, for instance, has legal obligations towards her husband while he is alive, but all these obligations come to an end if the husband dies" (Rom. 7:2). More may have been thinking also of Paul's informal treatise on marriage and virginity in 1 Corinthians 7: "There is something I want to add for the sake of widows and those who are not married; it is a good thing for them to stay as they are, like me, but if they cannot control the sexual urges, they should get married, since it is better to be married than to be tortured" (7:8-9). And More would certainly have remembered this passage: "I think it is best for young widows to marry again and have children and a home to look after, and not give the enemy any chance to raise a scandal about them" (1 Tim. 5:14).

in that other place of Saint Augustine . . . other places of his In the *Censurae academiarum* there is mention of Augustine and a text from his *Contra Faustum Manichaeum* (lib. xxii, 8-10); cf. *The Divorce Tracts of Henry VIII,* p. 100. St. Augustine also wrote about the institution of marriage in his *De bono coniugali* (*PL,* vol. 40, pp. 373-96) and *De nuptiis et concupiscentia ad Valerium comitem* (*PL,* vol. 44, pp. 413-74). More was well-acquainted with Augustine's thought and must have known his definition of Christian marriage as a "sacrament" in view of its indissolubility. For the bishop of Hippo, such an indissoluble bond between a man and a woman was a *sacramentum* — that is, a sign of the union of Christ with his Church, which is Christ's body. One passage from his book *On Marriage and Concupiscence* will suffice: "Certainly it is not fecundity only, the fruit of which is in offspring, not chastity only, the bond of which is in fidelity, but a certain sacramental bond of marriage that is recommended to the faithful who are married, when the Apostle says: 'Men, love your wives, as also Christ loved the Church.' Undoubtedly the substance of the Sacrament [*sacramenti res*] is of this bond, so that when man and woman have been joined in marriage they must continue inseparable as long as they live, nor is it allowed for one spouse to be separated from the other except for cause of fornication. For this is preserved in the case of Christ and the Church, so that, as a living one with a living one, there is no divorce, no separation forever. So

perfect is the observance of this bond . . . in the Church of Christ by all married be-
lievers, who are undoubtedly members of Christ, that, although women marry
and men take wives for the purpose of procreating children, one is never permitted to put away even an unfruitful wife for the purpose of getting another to bear
children" (*De nuptiis et concupiscentia,* I, 10, 11).

the words of Saint Jerome The text from Jerome that appears in *Censurae
academiarum* is taken from his *De perpetua virginitate B. Mariae, adversus Helvidium*
(lib. I, sec. 15); cf. *The Divorce Tracts of Henry VIII,* p. 100. His famous defense of
chastity and virginity was so exalted that it carried the good ascetical Church doctor into diminishing the religious excellence of the married state, which is practi-
cally seen in his writings as a lesser evil. St. Jerome was, of course, against second
marriages. His long polemical pamphlet "Against Jovinian" *(Adversus Iovinianum)*
is typical. Several of Jerome's letters also dealt with individual cases related to this
matter: Carterius, a Spanish bishop in his second nuptials (letter 79); Fabiola, a
divorced woman who had remarried, and with whom Jerome would be unusually
understanding (letters 64 and 77); another woman, Salvina, whom he admonished not to marry after her husband's death (letter 79); and Geruchia, a widow in
Gaul, to whom Jerome explained that the collapse of civilization should be reason
enough not to bother to seek second nuptials (letter 123). See J. N. D. Kelly,
Jerome, pp. 182-86, 210-11, 216, 297.

Saint Chrysostom More might be referring to a text that Thomas Aquinas had
quoted in the *Summa theologiae:* "As Chrysostom says *(Hom. XLVIII. super Matth.),*
because death was an unmitigated evil for the Jews, who did everything with a
view to the present life, it was ordained that children should be born to the dead
man through his brother: thus affording a certain mitigation of his death" (I-II, q.
105, a. 4 ad 7). Chrysostom was hostile to remarriage, writing on the pitiful as-
pects of second nuptials in his book *On Virginity and against Remarriage* (xxxvii, 3).
In another book against remarriage, *De non iterando conjugio,* he wrote that a second marriage bespeaks "of a soul weak and carnal, one tied to the earth and inca-
pable of ever displaying anything great and lofty." See *On Virginity and against Remarriage,* pp. 129-45 (quotation on 132).

by the canon laws of the Church For an excellent exposition of this matter, cf.
J. J. Scarisbrick, *Henry VIII,* chap. 7: "The Canon Law of the Divorce."

faults found in the bull of dispensation See the corresponding explanatory
notes to Letter 5 in this volume.

by a general council More was confident that whenever it was time for change
and development in the Church, the Holy Spirit would accomplish this by con-
vening a general council. Yet the council did not diminish the Pope's authority.

The relationship between Pope and council had been written about in the Fifth Lateran Council (1512-1517). The Bull "Pastor aeternus gregem" (Session XI, December 19, 1516) says, "It is clearly established that the Roman Pontiff alone [*solum Romanum Pontificem*], possessing as it were authority over all Councils [*tamquam auctoritatem super omnia concilia habentem*], has full right and power of proclaiming Councils, or transferring and dissolving them" (*Enchiridion Symbolorum,* n. 740). The Council of Trent would be convened under the authority of Pope Paul III in 1545 and would close its sessions in 1563.

Sicut diuisiones aquarum . . . inclinabit illud "Like flowing water is the heart of the king in the hand of God, who turns it where he pleases" (Prov. 21:1). See the note to Letter 8 in this volume.

Spes non confundit "Hope is not deceptive" (Rom. 5:5). This is its context: "But that is not all that we can boast about; we can boast about our sufferings. These sufferings bring patience, as we know, and patience brings perseverance, and perseverance brings hope, and this hope is not deceptive, because the love of God has been poured into our hearts by the Holy Spirit which has been given us" (vv. 3-5).

Quia quanquam . . . nolim rescire "Although there is nothing evil in it, yet I would not want to be discovered because of the servant." More wanted to keep the letter in order to be able to show that there was nothing in it that could be used against him.

LETTER 15: FROM MARGARET ROPER

the pure temple of the Holy Spirit of God 1 Corinthians 3:16: "Didn't you realize that you were God's temple and that the Spirit of God was living among you?" Also 2 Corinthians 6:16: "The temple of God has no common ground with idols, and that is what we are — the temple of the living God."

restraining you from the Church In the Tower there were two chapels, St. John and St. Peter ad Vincula. The first, in the White Tower, was reserved for the royal family; the other one was open to the garrison and nearby residents. Prisoners were not generally brought to church for Sunday Mass, unless a privilege was granted them. It seems that More had enjoyed this kind of liberty during part of his imprisonment and then, suddenly, it was taken away from him. His house in Chelsea was very close to the parish church; in addition, he had a chapel at home and also had built a little chapel on his property, in the New Building.

LETTER 16: TO MARGARET ROPER

your daughterly loving letters The word "daughterly" is one that More contributed to the English language.

The cause of my close keeping Nicholas Harpsfield offers three reasons for the prisoner's more strict confinement: "the sooner to draw him and cause him to incline to the king's pleasure; or for such very plain words that he used to the Commissioners; or that they intended to deal with him and others more sharply and to make sharper laws, as they did indeed the Parliament next following" (p. 174).

searches . . . in every house of ours Besides his own properties, like the old home in London on Bucklersbury Street, which he had leased since moving to Chelsea, More was probably thinking of the properties of his daughters' husbands: William Roper, William Daunce, and Giles Heron.

the clearness of my conscience . . . for joy In *The Scale of Perfection*, Walter Hilton writes, "This is how the soul feels then, with humble assurance and great gladness of spirit, and through making of this accord it conceives a great confidence in salvation, for it hears in its conscience the hidden testimony of the Holy Spirit. . . . This testimony of the conscience truly felt through grace is the real joy of the soul, as the Apostle says: *Gloria mea est testimonium conscientiae meae.* That is, My joy is the testimony of my conscience, and that is when it bears witness to peace and accord, true love and friendship between Jesus and a soul, and when it is in this peace it is in highness of thought" (Book 2, chap. 40, p. 282).

the hearts of kings in his hand Cf. Proverbs 21:1. More quotes this text four times in these letters. See the note to Letter 8 in this volume.

and reason with help of faith "Finally . . . it isn't a matter of reason; finally it's a matter of love," reads a very fine line that Robert Bolt gave Thomas More in his play *A Man for All Seasons*. Nevertheless, More was always intent on respecting reason and its rights, and we should expect no less from a humanist and the author of *Utopia,* a book that is both an homage to reason and a warning about its abuses. Even at the end of his life, during his imprisonment, when everything was lost, More did not despise a good rational argument, for he saw the Christian faith as going certainly beyond reason but not against reason. If the act of faith is a reasonable act, so likewise must be the living of the faith even in temptation — particularly in this case, as More would have added.

   This is well-proven throughout the Tower Works. Reason has a place in the design and structure of *A Dialogue of Comfort against Tribulation.* Discussing temptation, Antony affirms, "Resist must a man for his own part with reason, considering what a folly it were to fall where he need not while he is not driven to it in avoiding of any other pain, or in hope of winning any manner of pleasure but contrariwise, should by that pain lose everlasting life and fall into everlasting pain" (*CW*, vol. 12, p. 154). More seems to have conquered as a reasonable man "the fear of his own fantasy" and "his own foolish Imagination" (*CW*, vol. 12, p. 154). And at the end, when the conversation comes to the suffering of painful death, Antony insists on the power of reason to help decide for faithfulness: "Now if reason alone be sufficient to move a man to take pain for the gaining of some worldly rest or pleasure, and for the avoiding of another pain though peradventure more yet endurable but for a short season, why should not reason grounded upon the sure foundation of faith, and holpen also forward with aid of God's grace . . . why should not then reason, I say, thus furthered with faith and grace, be much more able, first to engender in us such an affection and after by long and deep meditation thereof, so to continue that affection, that it shall turn into an habitual fast and deep rooted purpose of patient suffering the painful death of this body here in earth, for the gaining of everlasting wealthy life in heaven, and avoiding of everlasting painful death in hell? (*CW*, vol. 12, pp. 293-94).

Finally, in his commentary on the agony of Christ, composed in the Tower, More saw another figure for reason in Malchus, the high priest's servant whose ear was cut off during Jesus' arrest (John 18:10): *Malchus igitur quum in hebrea lingua significet quod in latina rex/rationem nobis non absurde figurat.* "For in man," he wrote, "reason ought to reign like a king, and it does truly reign when it makes itself loyally subject to faith and serves God. For to serve Him is to reign" (*Ratio enim tamquam rex regnare debet in homine / regnatque uere / quum in obsequium fidei se captiuans deo seruit cui seruire regnare est*) (*CW*, vol. 14, p. 509). The high priest, More adds, "used piety as a pretext to oppose piety and sought eagerly to eliminate the founder of true religion. . . . And so whenever the rational mind rebels against the true faith of Christ and devotes itself to heresies, it becomes a fugitive from Christ [*fugitiuus christi Heresiarchae seruus*] and a servant of the heresiarch whom it follows" (*CW*, vol. 14, p. 509).

which I would after wish that I had died More makes this point through Antony in *A Dialogue of Comfort against Tribulation*: "For as God did more for poor Lazarus, in helping him patiently to die for hunger at the rich man's door than if he had brought him to the door all the rich glutton's dinner so though he be gracious to a man whom he delivereth out of painful trouble yet doth he much more for a man if through right painful death, he deliver him from this wretched world into eternal bliss. From which whosoever shrink away with forsaking his faith, and falleth in the peril of everlasting fire: he shall be very sure to repent it ere it be long after. For I ween that whensoever he falleth sick next, he will wish that he had been killed for Christ's sake before. What folly is it than for fear to fly from that death which thou seest thou shalt shortly after wish thou hadest died? Yea, I ween almost every good Christian man would very fain this day that he had been for Christ's faith cruelly killed yesterday, even for the desire of heaven, though there were none hell" (*CW*, vol. 12, p. 319). Antony has argued before that what men call "natural" death is indeed a "violent" death (*CW*, vol. 12, pp. 301-2).

he forsook and forsware our Savior Cf. Matthew 26:69-75; Mark 14:66-72; Luke 22:56-62; and John 18:17, 25-27.

for any desire of or pleasure of my house According to William Roper, Dame Alice More, during her first visit to her husband in the Tower, reminded him of the comforts and pleasures at home in Chelsea: "I marvel that you that have been always hitherto taken for so wise a man will now so play the fool to lie here in this close, filthy prison and be content thus to be shut up among mice and rats when you might be abroad at your liberty and with the favor and good will of the King and his council, if you would but do as all the bishops and best learned of this realm have done. And seeing that you have at Chelsea a right fair house, your library, your books, your gallery, your garden, your orchard, and all other necessaries so handsome about you, where you might in the company of me your wife, your children, and household, be merry, I muse what, a God's name, you mean here still thus fondly to tarry." And her husband answered: "Is not this house as nigh heaven as my own?" (p. 243). More's house seems to have been rather unlike the Utopian homes in their stark austerity; it was filled with all kinds of things and living creatures whose contemplation gave his owner much delight and pleasure. Erasmus wrote in 1519 that if More "sees anything outlandish or otherwise remarkable, he buys it greedily, and has his house stocked with such things from all sources, so that everywhere you may see something to attract the eyes of the visitor; and when he sees other people pleased, his own pleasure begins anew" (*CWE*, vol. 7, 19). By contrast, his room in the Tower must have seemed sad and empty. On the loss of lands, possessions, and goods of fortune, there is ample discussion in the third and last book of *A Dialogue of Comfort against Tribulation*.

I commit all wholly to his goodness In *A Dialogue of Comfort against Tribulation*, Antony says that "for the salvation of our soul may we boldly pray," as well as for grace, faith, hope, charity, and all other virtues. "But as for all other things before remembered in which is contained the matter of every kind of tribulation, we may never well make prayer so precisely, but that we must express or imply a condition therein, that is to wit, that if God see the contrary better for us, we refer it whole to his will" (*CW*, vol. 12, p. 21).

LETTER 17: TO MARGARET ROPER

Mihi viuere . . . et esse cum Christo "For to me to live is Christ, and to die is gain. . . . I desire to depart and to be with Christ" (Phil. 1:21, 23). In *A Dialogue of Comfort against Tribulation*, Antony says, "The case, I fear me, Cousin, falleth not very often, but yet some time it doth as where there is any man of that good mind that Saint Paul was, which for the longing that he had to be with God, would fain have been dead, but for the profit of other folk, was content to live here in pain, and defer and forbear for the while his inestimable bliss in heaven. *Cupio dissolui et esse cum Christo: bonum autem mihi manere propter vos*" (*CW*, vol. 12, p. 284). Cf. Germain Marc'hadour, *The Bible in the Works of Thomas More*, vol. 2, p. 114.

funiculo triplici . . . difficile rumpitur "A threefold cord," as Scripture says, "is not quickly broken" (Eccl. 4:12).

Sufficit tibi gratia mea "My grace is sufficient for thee" (2 Cor. 12:9). In *A Dialogue of Comfort against Tribulation*, Antony says that God's strengthening St. Paul in his tribulation was "far better for him than to take the tribulation from him" (*CW*, vol. 12, p. 22).

Virtus in infirmitate perficitur "For my strength is made perfect in weakness" (2 Cor. 12:9).

Omnia possum in eo qui me confortat "I can do all things with the help of the One who gives me strength" (Phil. 4:13).

while my wife had weened I had slept In *A Dialogue of Comfort against Tribulation*, More wrote, "Some man that in worldly prosperity is very full of wealth, and hath deep stepped into many a sore sin which sins, when he did them, he counted for part of his pleasure, God willing of his goodness to call the man to grace, casteth a remorse into his mind among after his first sleep and maketh him lie a little while and bethink him. Then beginneth he to remember his life and and from that he falleth to think upon his death, and how he must leave all this worldly wealth within a while behind here in this world, and walk hence alone he wotteth not where, nor how soon he shall take his journey thither, nor can tell what company he shall meet there. And then beginneth he to think that it were good to make sure and to be merry so that we be wise therewith lest there hap to be such black bugs indeed as folk call devils whose torments he was wont to take for poets' tales.

"These thoughts if they sink deep, are a sore tribulation and surely if he take hold of the grace that God therein offereth him, his tribulation is wholesome and shall be full comfortable to remember that God by this tribulation calleth him and biddeth him come home out of the country of sin that he was bred and brought up so long in, and come into the land of byhest [promised land] that floweth milk and honey" (*CW*, vol. 12, pp. 59-60).

LETTER 18: LADY MORE TO HENRY VIII

by reason of a new act or twain In November 1534 Parliament passed the Act of Supremacy, which declared the King the Supreme Head of the Church of England, but without the qualification "so far as the law of Christ allows" (as in the Convocation of Canterbury on February 11, 1531). The Act of Treason came into force after February 1, 1535. It said in effect that words *maliciously* spoken against the new royal title constituted high treason, the penalty for which was death by disembowelment. Parliament also passed acts of attainder against Bishop Fisher and More.

The key word was *maliciously* in more ways than one. The goal was the imposition of a new order of things by brutally enforced obedience and the rewriting of English history. According to Richard Rex, "Obedience was the central theme of the propaganda for the royal supremacy and indeed of the entire Henrician reformation. To some extent this betrayed the insecurity of the regime" (*Henry VIII and the English Reformation*, pp. 25-26).

This letter by Lady Alice is full of the extreme anxiety and perplexity such revolution produced.

all spent in your Grace's service "And whereas you have heard before, he was by the King from a very worshipful living taken into his grace's service, with whom in all the great and weighty causes that concerned his highness or the realm, he consumed and spent with painful cares, travails, and troubles as well beyond the seas as within the realm, in effect the whole substance of his life, yet with all the gain he got thereby, being never wasteful spender thereof, was he not able after the resignation of his office of the Lord Chancellor, for the maintenance of himself and such as necessarily belonged unto him, sufficiently to find meat, drink, fuel, apparel, and such other necessary charges" (Roper, p. 227). Of course, Lady Alice had an inheritance from her first husband and was a rather wealthy woman in her own right (Ackroyd, pp. 379-80).

There can be no doubt that Dame Alice is exaggerating about her financial distress; yet it is not difficult to understand her situation after her husband's arrest. His salary as royal councillor stopped, and the children with their families left More's home; all had changed and over the whole household hung the threat of even greater material loss. Her new situation must have seemed to her one of total destitution. See also her letter to Thomas Cromwell, where she says that she has been forced to sell her own things to pay for her husband's expenses in the Tower.

LETTER 19: TO MASTER LEDER

Master Leder Stephen Leder, vicar of Ware, was associated to the Carthusians at Sheen. He had been licensed to preach in the diocese in 1533. Apparently this priest had heard rumors of More's capitulation and wrote to him a letter of congratulation on having thus escaped from certain death. More wrote back to set the record straight: by taking the oath, he would certainly save his life, but "I should sweare deadly against mine own conscience." Father Leder died on February 6, 1535. See Seymour B. House, "Sir Thomas More and Holy Orders: More's Views of the English Clergy, Both Secular and Regular" (Ph.D. diss., University of St. Andrews, 1987), p. 227. I owe this information to the kindness of Seymour House.

Fidelis Deus . . . vt possitis sustinere "But God is faithful, who will not suffer you to be tempted above what you are able, but will with the temptation also make a way to escape that you may be able to bear it" (1 Cor. 10:13). This was another favorite biblical quotation of More. Cf. Germain Marc'hadour, *The Bible in the Works of Thomas More*, III, pp. 67-68.

In cuius manu corda regum sunt "In whose hand the hearts of the kings are" (Prov. 21:1). See the note to Letter 8 in this volume.

LETTER 20: TO MARGARET ROPER

these fathers of the Charterhouse The Order of the Carthusians, founded by St. Bruno in 1084, was highly praised among the religious orders in England because of its fidelity and spiritual zeal. These monks were strictly contemplative, vowed to silence, and in their daily routine were totally absorbed by work and prayer. Thomas More had much respect for the Charterhouse of London, "religiously living there without vow about four years" while he was a student (Roper, p. 198). In *A Dialogue of Comfort against Tribulation*, Antony mentions with much admiration several cloistered religious orders: the Carthusians, the Bridgettines (founded by St. Bridget of Sweden in 1370), and the Poor Clares (founded by St. Clare, a friend of St. Francis of Assisi, in 1212). The "fathers" mentioned in this letter are John Houghton, prior or superior in London; Robert Lawrence, superior in Beauvale; and Augustine Webster, superior in Axholme. The last two had come to London to seek advice from Houghton, and during this time the "visitation" by government agents took place. They were executed along with several others on May 4, 1535, in Tyburn. According to William Roper, More and his daughter Margaret saw them leaving the prison: "Lo, dost thou not see, Meg, that these blessed fathers be now as cheerfully going to their deaths as bridegrooms to their marriage" (p. 242). Another three monks were executed later: Humphrey Middlemore, William Exmew, and Sebastian Newdigate. These Carthusians were canonized in a group of forty English martyrs by Pope Paul VI in 1970. On the Charterhouse of London, see David Knowles, *The Religious Orders in England*, vol. 3: *The Tudor Age*, pp. 224-26; on Houghton, see Thompson, *The Carthusian Order in England*, pp. 371-485.

Master Reynolds Richard Reynolds was the prior of Syon Abbey, the only house of the Order of St. Bridget in England. He had studied in Cambridge, was an excellent theologian, and a man of vast erudition. Little is known about the details of his arrest. In April 1535 he was accused of having affirmed a year earlier that Catherine of Aragon was the true Queen. He was taken to the Tower, processed with the other priests in Westminster on April 28, and executed on May 4. See *DNB*, vol. 16, pp. 953-54.

Master Lieutenant Sir Edmund Walsingham (c. 1490-1550) had been named the Tower's lieutenant after 1525. He took personal charge of eminent state prisoners during Henry's reign; torture was inflicted under his supervision. As reward for his work, his fortune was abundantly increased before his retirement (in 1539, Sir Edmund received nine homes in London). William Roper says that going up to the scaffold, More was so weak and ready to fall that he said merrily to Walsingham, "I pray you, Master Lieutenant, see me safe up and for my coming down, let me shift for myself" (p. 254). Cf. *DNB*, vol. 20, pp. 685-86.

Master Attorney Sir Christopher Hales (d. 1541) had been appointed Attorney General in 1529, and took part in the investigation of Elizabeth Barton. In 1535 Hales directed the judicial proceedings against Sir Thomas More, Bishop Fisher, and later Queen Anne Boleyn. He largely profited from the dissolution of monasteries, obtaining many grants of land that had belonged to religious communities in Kent. Hales died in 1541. See *DNB*, vol. 8, pp. 910-11.

Master Solicitor Sir Richard Rich (c. 1496-1567), one of the most ignominious figures of the Tudor regime, saw in the new order of things an expeditious way to fulfill his own ambitions. As Solicitor General he played a leading role in the prosecutions of those who would not accept the oath to the Succession and Supremacy. Rich went to the Tower to confiscate More's books and spoke with him (Roper, pp. 244-45). He was the only witness needed to condemn More. Later he became Lord Chancellor. See *DNB*, vol. 15, pp. 1009-12; and John Campbell, *Lives of the Lord Chancellors*, vol. 2, pp. 143-59.

Master Bedill One of the clerks in the Privy Council, Thomas Bedill (d. 1537) had studied at Oxford, then served as secretary to the Archbishop of Canterbury, William Warham. When the latter died, he moved on to the service of Henry VIII. Bedill was involved in obtaining oaths to the Royal Supremacy from members of religious houses and assessing their ecclesiastical possessions. See *DNB*, vol. 2, pp. 120-21.

Doctor Tregonwell Sir John Tregonwell (d. 1565) also took part in the proceedings against the Carthusian monks and Anne Boleyn. He showed much diligence in the dissolution of the monasteries and, though he died rich, complained of having received small reward for his services. See *DNB*, vol. 19, pp. 1099-1100.

I was offered to sit with them, which in no wise I would William Roper tells of another similar instance, before More's detention in the Tower, when he appeared before Cromwell, Thomas Audley, Cranmer, and Thomas Howard: "And at his coming before them, according to their appointment, they entertained him very friendly, willing him to sit down with them, which in no wise he would" (p. 233). Without making explicit his contempt for the authorities and new laws of the land, More showed his disgust at the situation and the travesty of justice. Simply put, an honest citizen declined the invitation to sit down in the company of thieves. Perhaps More remembered the splendid thought from Augustine: "Justice being taken away, then, what are kingdoms but great robberies? For what are robberies themselves, but little kingdoms?" (*The City of God*, IV, 4).

Head of the Church The Act of Royal Supremacy says, "Albeit the King's Majesty justly and rightfully is and oweth to be the supreme head of the Church of England, and so is recognized by the clergy of this realm in their Convocations; yet nevertheless for corroboration and confirmation thereof, and for an increase of virtue in Christ's religion within this realm of England, and to repress and extirp all errors, heresies and other enormities and abuses heretofore used in the same, be it enacted by authority of this present Parliament that the King our sovereign lord, his heirs and successors kings of this realm, shall be taken, accepted and reputed the only supreme head in earth of the Church of England called *Anglicana Ecclesia,* and shall have and enjoy annexed and united to the imperial crown of this realm as well the title and style thereof, as all honours, dignities, preeminences, jurisdictions, privileges, authorities, immunities, profits and commodities, to the said dignity of supreme head of the same Church belonging and appertaining" (from *An Act concerning the King's Highness to be Supreme Head of the Church of England,* 1534: 26 Henry VIII, chap. 1). In 1536, an act was given "extinguishing the authority of the bishop of Rome": "the extirpation, abolition and extinguishment, out of this realm and other his Grace's dominions, seignories and countries, of the pretended power and usurped authority of the bishop of Rome, by some called the Pope" (28 Henry VIII, c. 10).

LETTER 21: LADY MORE TO THOMAS CROMWELL

to sell part of mine apparel At the beginning of May, Dame Alice More had sold to John Lane a flock of lambs for 36 pounds and 8 pennies, but still could not pay for her husband's imprisonment and so was forced to sell her own clothes.

extreme age Dame Alice had been born in 1471, so she was sixty-four years old, considered an advanced age at that time.

LETTER 22: TO MARGARET ROPER

Here sat ... and Master Secretary Thomas Cranmer, Thomas Audley, Charles Brandon, Thomas Boleyn, and Thomas Cromwell. The Earl of Wiltshire, Thomas Boleyn (1477-1539), had been present at the meeting of the Emperor Charles V and Henry VIII at Gravelines in 1520, but his rising importance at the English court was due to the King's infatuation with his daughter, Anne Boleyn. In January 1530, Sir Thomas Boleyn, together with John Stokeley and Edward Lee, was commissioned to go to the Emperor and explain the King's plan to divorce Queen Catherine; the three met with the Emperor and the Pope in Bologna. On their return, they visited the University of Paris with the idea of gaining academic support for the divorce. See *DNB*, vol. 2, pp. 783-85.

in the Star Chamber The court of the Star Chamber. Its name came from the room in Westminster where the Lord Chancellor, the justices, and other members of the Royal Council sat and exercised their jurisdiction. Apparently, the original roof was painted with stars.

suo domino stat et cadit To the Romans St. Paul wrote, "It is not for you to condemn someone else's servant: whether he stands or falls it is his own master's business [in the Vulgate: *domino suo stat aut cadit*]; he will stand, you may be sure, because the Lord has power to make him stand" (Rom. 14:4). And to the Corinthians: "The man who thinks he is safe, must be careful that he does not fall [*qui se existimat stare videat ne cadat*]" (1 Cor. 10:12). More used the text as a cautionary statement in *A Dialogue of Comfort against Tribulation* (*CW*, vol. 12, p. 162). Some fifteen years earlier, in 1519, More had written to a monk that "there was nothing more dangerous in religious life" than arrogance and the self-assurance of one's holiness: "You should make it your habit instead to look up even to inferior attainments in others and not only to think more modestly of your own attainments but also to hold them all suspect, and live not without hope but yet always in fear, not just of falling hereafter (for which there is the saying, 'He who stands, let him take heed of falling'), but of having fallen long before now, in particular when you yourself thought that you were ascending most rapidly, namely when you entered the religious life" (*CW*, vol. 15, p. 301).

LETTER 23: TO ANTONIO BONVISI

Antonio (Anthony) Bonvisi Born in Lucca, Italy, Antonio Bonvisi (1487-1558) belonged to a family that had business concerns in England. Bonvisi was a banker and a good friend of the London humanists. Maybe he is the "Italian merchant" of More's anecdote in his letter to Dorp (Rogers, *St. Thomas More: Selected Letters*, p. 30). Until he was forbidden to do so, Bonvisi often sent clothes, food, wine, and other goods to More and Bishop Fisher while they were in the Tower. He was exiled as a "papist" in 1548 and died in Louvain. There is another note of More to Bonvisi by which we know that his friend had read with pleasure *Utopia* (cf. Rogers, *The Correspondence of Sir Thomas More*, n. 34). Cf. Elizabeth McCutcheon, "'The Apple of My Eye': Thomas More to Antonio Bonvisi: A Reading and a Translation," pp. 37-56; and *Dizionario Biografico degli Italiani*, vol. 15, pp. 295-99.

LETTER 24: TO MARGARET ROPER

and sent it to her Along with this letter and the objects More mentioned, Margaret received her father's hair shirt, an instrument of penance used by religious. For him, wearing it had been a way of keeping humble and temperate in the affairs of public life. In his biography William Roper notes, "The day before he suffered, he sent his shirt of hair — not willing to have it seen — to my wife, his dearly beloved daughter, and a letter written with a coal" (p. 252). It is the last piece of writing by the hand of Thomas More.

Cecily More's youngest daughter, born in 1507, had married Giles Heron on September 29, 1525. She had gotten to know her husband in an interesting way. When his father, Sir John Heron, treasurer of the Chamber for Henry VIII, died, his son Giles had become a ward entrusted to Sir Thomas More. Giles Heron would become Treasurer of the Chamber for Henry VIII and the foreman of the Middlesex grand jury in the original indictment of Anne Boleyn. He was himself under suspicion (for allegedly "plotting" with Thomas More) and finally accused of high treason. He was drawn and quartered at Tyburn on August 4, 1540. See William Roper, *The Lyfe of Sir Thomas Moore, knighte*, pp. 117-22.

I send her an handkercher "The sending of a handkerchief to his daughter Cecily is reminiscent of those handkerchiefs people took away from Paul at Ephesus so they could touch the sick with them — one of the great proof texts for the validity of relics. Perhaps Cecily had asked him for such a token, and he sent it to her" (Marius, p. 512).

Daunce More's second daughter Elizabeth married William Daunce in 1525, the same day her younger sister Cecily married Giles Heron, in the oratory of Giles Alington, the second husband of Alice Alington (see Letters 11 and 12). William's father, Sir John Daunce, was a member of the King's council.

my Lady Conyers Most likely married to one of the descendants of Sir John Conyers, whose son, of the same name and title, died in Edgecote, and whose grandson, William, was born in 1468.

Dorothy Colly Or Colley, Margaret Roper's maid. While Thomas More was in the Tower, Margaret would often send Dorothy there with food and gifts for her father. Dorothy married John Harris, More's secretary. Later, the couple had to leave England and went to the Low Countries, saving More's papers and letters. Thomas Stapleton says that "the two Margarets [More's daughter and his ward Margaret] and Dorothy most reverently buried the body" of Thomas More (p. 192).

Joan Aleyn Another maid who likely grew up with Margaret and her sisters and attended the school that More ran at home in Chelsea.

Saint Thomas' Even and the Vtas of Saint Peter The eve of St. Thomas Becket (c. 1118-1170) and the octave of St. Peter the Apostle. The feast of the translation of Becket's relics was celebrated on July 7. The feast of St. Peter falls on June 29. More's trial had taken place on July 1, and his love and loyalty for the universal (catholic) Church as well as for the Church in his country are reflected in this co-incidence of the liturgical calendar: the remembrance of the apostle martyred in Rome, and the remembrance of the martyr of Canterbury whose execution had been ordered by another king, Henry II. In 1538 St. Thomas Becket was publicly denounced a traitor, and his relics were to have a sad ending, as Harpsfield made sure to tell his audience: "Albeit we have of late (God illuminate our beetle blind hearts to see and repent our folly and impiety) unshrined him, and burned his holy bones; and not only unshrined him and unsancted him, but have made him also, after so many hundred years, a traitor to the King that honored him, as we have said, as a blessed martyr" (p. 215).

In this letter, Thomas More gladly notices the coincidence, perhaps reaf-firming in a simple manner his profound belief in God's eternal providence. For More there was always an order beyond human scheming. The names of Peter and Thomas take his mind to the one he believes is Lord of history, Christ. Later, this gracious and modest expansion of More's heart was blown out of proportion by Harpsfield, who compared More to both Peter and Becket, making his biographi-cal subject even more deserving of the martyr's bloody crown and glory. But the similarities between Thomas Becket and Thomas More make only more poignant the different outcome of their deaths.

when you kissed me last Margaret's husband explains this last encounter in de-tail: "As soon as she saw him — after his blessing on her knees reverently received — she hasting towards him and, without consideration or care of herself, pressing in among the midst of the throng and company of the guard, that with halberds and bills went round about him, hastily ran to him and there openly, in the sight of them all, embraced him, took him about the neck, and kissed him. Who, well liking her most natural and dear daughterly affection towards him, gave her his fatherly blessing and many goodly words of comfort besides.

192

"From whom after she was departed she, not satisfied with the former sight of him and like one that had forgotten herself, being all-ravished with the entire love of her dear father, having respect neither to herself nor to the press of people and multitude that were there about him, suddenly turned back again, ran to him as before, took him about the neck, and divers times together most lovingly kissed him — and at last, with a full heavy heart, was fain to depart from him. The beholding whereof was to many of them that were present thereat so lamentable that it made them for very sorrow thereof to mourn and weep" (Roper, pp. 251-52).

Clement Margaret (Giggs) Clement, born in 1505, had been More's ward and had grown up with his daughters. She was skilled in Greek and Latin as well as in medicine, and could very likely be the protagonist of one of the anecdotes told in *A Dialogue of Comfort against Tribulation,* about "a young girl here in this town whom a kinsman of hers had begun to teach physic. . . . For she is very wise and well learned and very virtuous too" (*CW*, vol. 12, pp. 88-90). Referring to Margaret's childhood, Thomas Stapleton says that she "used to relate how sometimes she would deliberately commit some fault that she might enjoy More's sweet and loving reproof" (p. 89). In 1526 Margaret married John Clement, himself a member of More's household; he is mentioned as being present with More at Peter Giles's house in Antwerp while More was thinking about *Utopia.* For a while John Clement lectured in rhetoric at Oxford, but later he went into medicine, becoming a royal physician. The Clements lived in More's house on Bucklersbury Street. Their daughter Winifred (probably the oldest of eleven) married William Rastell, editor of several books by More (see Letter 1 in this volume). It was while paying a visit to the Clements in London one Sunday — April 12, 1534 — that Sir Thomas More was served with the warrant to appear before the Commissioners at Lambeth. Margaret Clement was the only person of the family present at More's execution and took care of burying his body in the chapel of St. Peter ad Vincula in the Tower. To escape from religious persecution, the Clements moved their family to Louvain, and returned to England just before Mary came to the throne. They left their country for good under Queen Elizabeth. Margaret Clement died on July 6, 1570. See William Roper, *The Lyfe of Sir Thomas Moore, knighte,* pp. 127-28; R. W. Chambers, *Thomas More,* pp. 347-50; and *Contemporaries of Erasmus,* vol. 1, pp. 311-12.

algorism stone A slate or a counter (counting board) that More used as a board or tablet for writing. When these tools became obsolete, the boards used in stores and banks were still called "counters." Cf. *The World of Mathematics,* ed. James R. Newman (New York: Simon & Schuster, 1956), vol. 1, pp. 458-63.

John More Thomas More's only son and, since 1529, husband of Anne Cresacre, another ward of Thomas More. He says that John should be grateful to his wife because she had inherited her father's property of Barnbrough, in Yorkshire. The couple had seven sons (two of them, Thomas and Austin, are mentioned in this letter) and one daughter. John More died in 1547.

if the land of mine come to his hand William Roper comments on More's last will and his attempt to transfer his property to his wife and children. Roper says that after his resignation of the Chancellorship, More transferred all of his lands to his family "to the intent he might from thenceforth the more quietly settle himself to the service of God." But he may have already foreseen the possibility of royal confiscation. In any case, More's plans were frustrated after his attainder. "And so were all his lands," Roper continues, "that he had to his wife and children by the said conveyance in such sort assured, contrary to the order of law, taken away from them, and brought into the king's hands, saving that portion which he had appointed to my wife and me" (p. 241).

Thomas and Austin Two of the eight children John More and Anne Cresacre were to have, and the only ones born before their grandfather's execution. Thomas was born at Chelsea in 1531 and Austin in 1533. Antonio Bonvisi was Austin's godfather.

Glossary

abashed confounded
abjected cast off, rejected
acquieting quieting, coming to rest
adventure to venture, hazard; **at adventure** by chance
advertise to inform, notify
advertisement instruction, advice, admonition
advised considered
advisedly deliberately
affection disposition, inclination, emotional attachment
aileth hinders
al although, even if
allies kin
appellation act of appeal
as lief willingly
assoil to absolve, pardon
away to take away

beadsman, beadswoman one who prays for another
bill formal petition
black dark
blaming condemning
blind obstinate
book oath oath sworn on the Bible
bounden bound by more than legal obligation
break *to break with* to disclose

but if unless
byhest *land of byhest* promised land
by her of her
by me of me
by and by at once, immediately
by that since
by time at once

cast convict
chance happen
charge responsibility
clear innocent, pure
close *close prison* strict confinement
color pretext, appearance
comfort strength, courage, and consolation
commodities advantages, benefits
common, commune to communicate, converse, discuss
communication conversation
concluded legally bound
conferred compared, collated
construction interpretation
contended contented
convenient appropriate, suitable
correction *under correction* subject to correction
cost expenditure of time and labor
cousin relative
credence credibility, confidence
cumber trouble, distress
cunning learned
curat parish priest

declare to explain, clarify
declaration explanation
decline to concede, give in
defoiled defiled
demeaned conducted
desire to express a wish, request
devise to imagine, contrive
devise to deliberate, meditate
discharge exoneration, acquittal

discharge to clear, exonerate
dispicions disputations
disposeth ordains
do by me act towards me
dread revered
drift design, scheme
dulcely sweetly

eftsoon, eftsoons again, a second time
embassiate embassy
escheator see note to Letter 12
estates persons of high rank, dignitaries
estimation appreciation
even eve

fain gladly, eagerly
fantasy caprice, delusion
fashion demeanor, behavior
feigned since invented after
fillip flick of finger
fond foolish
forceth matters
forgat forgot
frame shape, build; plan in advance
fro from
fruit spiritual fruit

game fun
gear matter
geast guess
ghostly spiritually, pertaining to the soul
ghostly father spiritual father, confessor
ghostly mind devout
godly spiritual
groat silver coin
grudge to trouble, vex
grudge scruple, murmur of conscience, uneasiness

had taken
halberds and bills combination of pike and battle-axe with a long handle

happly, haply by chance, perhaps
heading beheading
heavy sad
homely familiar
houseled *to be houseled* to receive the Eucharist
howbeit although
hugeness huge burden, enormity
huswife hussy

indifferent impartial
insectation calumny, calumniation

knot binding condition
knowledged acknowledged

laid unto imputed
late lately, recently
left *hath left* stopped
lest least
let to refrain
let to prevent
leifer, lever rather
lewd ignorant
lewdness wickedness
light (people) irresponsible
lightly probably
lightness levity
like to please
like alike
list to please
looked expected
loving labor personal exertion

manner kind(s) of
marked considered
Marry!, Mary an exclamation derived from Mary the Virgin
meddle to take part, interest oneself in
meet suitable, fit
meetly suitably, fairly
mere pure

mind intention
minded intended
minish to diminish
misaffectionate disordered
mishap, mishapped unfortunately happened
misliketh displeases
mo more
mote must
move influence

natural thoroughly legitimate
noble notable
noddies fools
note to denote, mean
not though even though

occasion v. take occasion, take advantage
oft often
or before
oratrix petitioner, supplicant
order providence; condition
of truth indeed, in truth

pain *temporal pain* penalty, punishment

panged anguished
parishons parishioners
parts sides in dispute
part taker partisan
part *to take in good part* take without offense
persuasion argument
piece part
plain straightforward
pleasure will, desire
pretty clever, astute
process account, narrative
procure to cause
protest to assert, declare formally
put have

quest jury

reason *of reason* with good reason
recomfort to comfort
recommend to commend
relation account, narrative
rehearsal repetition, relating; **made rehearsal**: gave an account
rehearse repeat
reins kidneys
repair to visit
require to ask
resort to have access, visit
room position, office
ruffle disturbance
rustical lacking in social graces or polish

sample example
scruple doubt
season *in the mean season* meanwhile
self itself
shrewd clever
simple uneducated, ordinary
singularly exceptionally
sinister misleading
silly naive, helpless
sith since
slenderly slightly
soileth resolves, solves
sore severely, grievously
sore troubled
sore deeply, harshly
sorry distressed
sowning tending
sped to obtain, succeed
speed success, outcome
spiritual law church law
spiritualty clergy
sprite spirit
stack persisted
stay sustain, support

stick to hesitate
sticking hesitation
stiff obstinate, stubborn
straightly at once, immediately; rigorously, strictly
strength strengthen
suage assuage, ease
sudden instant
sued pleaded
suit petition
surmise allegation, suspicion

temporal temporal men, lay men
temporalty lay people
tender to attend to; to appreciate
terminate definitive
that what
them themselves
tolling taking
took gave
toward favorable
train trick, entrapment
translate to transfer
treating *a treating* to be studied
treat entreat
troth truth
troth loyalty
trow to believe
truth *by my truth* upon my honor
turn ponder

ungodly wickedly
unpossible impossible
unrequired unasked

very actual, true, authentic

wanton frivolous
warrant assurance, guarantee
warning summons
wayed weighed, considered

ween to think, suppose; **went** thought
well minded disposed
willers wishers
wis to think
wit intelligence, mind
wit to know; **wist** knew
wittingly knowingly
worship distinction, dignity, fame
worshipful distinguished (title)
wot, wotteth to know, knows

Bibliography

Works of Thomas More

The Complete Works of St. Thomas More. 15 vols. New Haven: Yale University Press, 1963-1997. References to these works are cited as *CW* followed by volume and page.

Volume 1 *English Poems; Life of Pico; The Last Things;* ed. Anthony S. G. Edwards, Katherine Gardiner Rodgers, and Clarence Miller (1997)

Volume 2 *The History of King Richard III,* ed. Richard S. Sylvester (1963)

Volume 3 Part I: *Translations of Lucian,* ed. Craig R. Thompson (1974)

Volume 3 Part II: *Latin Poems,* ed. Clarence H. Miller, Leicester Bradner, Charles A. Lynch, and Revilo P. Oliver (1984)

Volume 4 *Utopia,* ed. Edward Surtz and J. H. Hexter (1965; rpt., 1979)

Volume 5 *Responsio ad Lutherum,* ed. John M. Headley, trans. Sister Scholastica Mandeville (1969)

Volume 6 *A Dialogue Concerning Heresies,* ed. Thomas M. C. Lawler, Germain Marc'hadour, and Richard Marius (1981)

Volume 7 *Letter to Bugenhagen, Supplication of Souls, Letter against Frith,* ed. Frank Manley, Germain Marc'hadour, Richard Marius, and Clarence H. Miller (1990)

Volume 8 *The Confutation of Tyndale's Answer,* ed. Louis L. Martz, Richard C. Marius, James P. Lusardi, and Richard J. Schoeck (1973)

Volume 9 *The Apology,* ed. J. B. Trapp (1979)

Volume 10 *The Debellation of Salem and Bizance,* ed. John Guy, Ralph Keen, Clarence H. Miller, and Ruth McGugan (1987)

Volume 11 *The Answer to a Poisoned Book,* ed. Stephen Merriam Foley and Clarence H. Miller (1985)

Volume 12 *A Dialogue of Comfort against Tribulation,* ed. Louis L. Martz and F. Manley (1976)

Volume 13 *Treatise on the Passion, Treatise on the Blessed Body, Instructions and Prayers,* ed. G. E. Haupt (1976)

Volume 14 *De Tristitia Christi,* ed. and trans. Clarence H. Miller (1976)

Volume 15 *In Defense of Humanism: Letter to Martin Dorp, Letter to the University of Oxford, Letter to Edward Lee, Letter to a Monk,* ed. Daniel Kinney (1986)

Campbell, W. E., ed. *The English Works of Sir Thomas More.* First published by Willam Rastell. London: Eyre and Spottiswoode, 1931.

Martz, Louis L., and Richard S. Sylvester, eds. *Thomas More's Prayer Book: A Facsimile Reproduction of the Annotated Pages.* 1969; reprint, New Haven: Yale University Press, 1976.

O'Connor, D., ed. *The Four Last Things.* London, 1935.

Rogers, Elizabeth F., ed. *The Correspondence of Sir Thomas More.* Princeton: Princeton University Press, 1947.

————. *St. Thomas More: Selected Letters.* New Haven: Yale University Press, 1961.

Sixteenth-Century Biographies

Harpsfield, Nicholas. *The Life and death of Sir Thomas Moore, Knight, sometymes Lord High Chancellor of England* (1557). Ed. Elsie Vaughan Hitchcock. London: Oxford University Press, 1932.

Roper, William. *The Lyfe of Sir Thomas Moore, knighte* (1557). Ed. Elsie Vaughan Hitchcock. London: Oxford University Press, 1935. In 1950, Swallow Press brought out an edition edited by James Mason Cline. A modernized version was published in *Two Early Tudor Lives,* ed. Richard S. Sylvester and Davis P. Harding (New Haven: Yale University Press, 1962).

Stapleton, Thomas. *The Life and Illustrious Martyrdom of Sir Thomas More* (1588). Trans. Philip E. Hallett. London: Burns & Oates, 1928. This was later revised by E. E. Reynolds (London: Burns & Oates, 1966).

Other Works and Articles

Ackroyd, Peter. *The Life of Thomas More.* New York: Doubleday, 1998.

Aesopica. A Series of texts relating to Aesop or ascribed to him or closely connected with the literary tradition that bears his name. Ed. Ben Edwin Perry. Urbana: University of Illinois Press, 1952.

Ambrose, St. *Letters*. Trans. Mary Melchior Beyenka. New York, 1954.

Augustine, St. *The City of God*. Trans. Marcus Dodd. New York, 1950.

———. *The Literal Meaning of Genesis*. 2 vols. Trans. John Hammond Taylor. New York: Newman Press, 1982.

Ayris, Paul, and David Selwyn, eds. *Thomas Cranmer: Churchman and Scholar*. New York: Boydell Press, 1993.

Basil, St. *Letters*. Trans. Agnes Clare Way. New York: Father of the Church, Inc., 1951.

Bede. *A History of the English Church and People*. Trans. Leo Sherley-Price. New York: Dorset Press, 1985.

Bedouelle, Guy, and Patrick Le Gal. *Le "divorce" du Roi Henry VIII. Etudes et documents*. Geneva: Droz, 1987.

Bell, Philip Ingress. "Lady Alice the Unknown." *Moreana* 15, no. 59 (1978): 9-12.

Bradshaw, Brendan. "The Controversial Thomas More." *The Journal of Ecclesiastical History* 36 (1985): 535-69.

———, and Eamon Duffy, eds. *Humanism, Reform, and the Reformation: The Career of Bishop John Fisher*. Cambridge: Cambridge University Press, 1989.

Bridgett, Thomas Edward. *The Life and Writings of Sir Thomas More: Lord Chancellor of England and Martyr under Henry VIII*. London: Burns & Oates, 1891.

———. *The Life of Blessed John Fisher*. London: Burns & Oates, 1888.

Brigden, Susan. *London and the Reformation*. Oxford: Oxford University Press, 1989.

Byron, Brian. "The Fourth Count of the Indictment of St. Thomas More." *Moreana* 3, no. 10 (1966): 33-46.

———. *Loyalty in the Spirituality of Thomas More*. Nieuwkoop: De Graaf, 1972.

———. "Through a Needle's Eye: Thomas More the Wealthy Saint," in *Thomas More: Essays on the Icon*. Ed. Damian Grace and Brian Byron. Pp. 53-69. Melbourne: Dove Communications, 1980.

Campbell, John. *Lives of the Lord Chancellors and Keepers of the Great Seal of England, from the earliest times till the reign of George IV*. 5th ed. 10 vols. London: J. Murray, 1868.

Cavendish, George. *The Life and Death of Cardinal Wolsey*. In *Two Early Tudor Lives*, ed. Richard S. Sylvester and Davis P. Harding. New Haven: Yale University Press, 1962.

Chambers, Raymond Wilson. *Thomas More*. London: Jonathan Cape, 1935.

Chrysostom, St. John. *On Virginity and against Remarriage*. Trans. Sally Rieger Shore. Lewiston, N.Y.: Edwin Mellen Press, 1983.

Codex iuris canonici. Rome: Libreria Editrice Vaticana, 1983.

Collier, Jeremy. *Ecclesiastical History of Great Britain*, 9 vols. London: William Straker, 1845-46.

Collected Works of Erasmus. Toronto: University of Toronto Press, 1974-. Cited as *CWE*.

Contemporaries of Erasmus: A Biographical Register of the Renaissance and Reformation. 3 vols. Ed. Peter G. Bietenholz et al. Toronto: University of Toronto Press, 1985-87.

Cruickshank, Charles. *Henry VIII and the Invasion of France.* New York: St. Martin's Press, 1991.

de C. Parmiter, Geoffrey. *The King's Great Matter: A Study of Anglo-Papal Relations, 1527-1534.* London: Longmans, 1967.

Deferrari, Roy J., ed. *The Sources of Catholic Dogma.* St. Louis: Herder, 1955.

Derrett, J. Duncan M. "More's Attainder and Dame Alice's Predicament." *Moreana* 2, no. 6 (1965): 7-26.

———. "More's Convergence of His Lands and the Law of Fraud." *Moreana* 2, no. 5 (1965): 19-26.

———. "Sir Thomas More and the Nun of Kent." *Moreana* 4, no. 15 (1967): 267-84.

———. "The Trial of Sir Thomas More." In *Essential Articles for the Study of Thomas More.* Ed. Richard S. Sylvester and Germain P. Marc'hadour. Pp. 55-78. Hamden, Conn.: Archon, 1977.

———. "Two Dicta of More's and a Correction." *Moreana* 2, no. 8 (1965): 67-72.

Dickens, A. G. *Thomas Cromwell and the English Reformation.* New York: Macmillan, 1959.

Dictionary of National Biography. 63 vols. London: Oxford University Press, 1885-1900. Cited as *DNB.*

Dictionnaire de théologie catholique. 15 vols. Paris: Letouzey et Ané, 1908-1950.

The Divorce Tracts of Henry VIII. Ed. Edward Surtz and Virginia Murphy. Angers: Moreana, 1988.

Documents Illustrative of English Church History. Ed. Henry Gee and W. J. Hardy. 1896; reprint, London: Macmillan, 1972.

Dudden, F. H. *The Life and Times of St. Ambrose.* Oxford: Clarendon Press, 1935.

Elton, G. R. *Policy and Police: The Enforcement of the Reformation in the Age of Thomas Cromwell.* Cambridge: Cambridge University Press, 1972.

———. *Reform and Renewal: Thomas Cromwell and the Common Weal.* Cambridge: Cambridge University Press, 1973.

———. "Sir Thomas More and the Opposition to Henry VIII." *Bulletin of the Institute of Historical Research* 41 (1968): 19-34; reprinted in *Essential Articles for the Study of Thomas More.* Ed. Richard S. Sylvester and Germain P. Marc'hadour. Pp. 79-91. Hamden, Conn.: Archon, 1977.

———, ed. *The Tudor Constitution: Documents and Commentary.* Cambridge: Cambridge University Press, 1978.

Enchiridion Symbolorum definitionum et declarationum de rebus fidei et morum. Ed. Henricus Denzinger and Adolfus Schönmetzer. 33rd edition. Barcinone: Herder, 1965.

Erasmus, Desiderius. *Enchiridion militis Christiani*. Ed. Anne M. O'Donnell. Oxford: Oxford University Press, 1981.

Essential Articles for the Study of Thomas More. Ed. Richard S. Sylvester and Germain P. Marc'hadour. Hamden, Conn.: Archon, 1977.

Flegel, Kenneth M. "Was a Sick Man Beheaded?" *Moreana* 13, no. 49 (1976): 15-27.

Giles, Edward, ed. *Documents Illustrating Papal Authority: A.D. 96-454*. London: S.P.C.K., 1952.

Gogan, Brian. *The Common Corps of Christendom: Ecclesiological Themes in the Writings of Sir Thomas More*. Leiden: E. J. Brill, 1982.

Gordon, Walter M. "Tragic Perspective in Thomas More's Dialogue with Margaret in the Tower." *Cithara* 2 (1978): 3-12.

Greenblatt, Stephen. *Renaissance Self-fashioning: From More to Shakespeare*. Chicago: University of Chicago Press, 1980.

Gregory, St. *Dialogues*. Trans. Odo John Zimmerman. New York: Fathers of the Church, Inc., 1959.

Gunn, Steve J. *Early Tudor Government, 1485-1558*. New York: St. Martin's Press, 1995.

Guy, John. *The Public Career of Sir Thomas More*. New Haven: Yale University Press, 1980.

———. *Tudor England*. Oxford: Oxford University Press, 1988.

Gwyn, Peter. *The King's Cardinal: The Rise and Fall of Thomas Wolsey*. London: Barrie & Jenkins, 1990.

Hale, John. *The Civilization of Europe in the Renaissance*. New York: Atheneum, 1994.

Harris, Barbara J. *Edward Stafford, Third Duke of Buckingham, 1478-1521*. Stanford: Stanford University Press, 1986.

Headley, John M. "Thomas Murner, Thomas More, and the First Expression of More's Ecclesiology." *Studies in the Renaissance* 14 (1967): 73-92.

Hilton, Walter. *The Scale of Perfection*. Ed. John P. Clark and Rosemary Dorward. New York: Paulist Press, 1991.

Hughes, Philip. *The Church in Crisis: A History of the General Councils, 325-1870*. New York: Doubleday, 1961.

———. *A History of the Church: An Introductory Study*. New York: Sheed & Ward, 1935.

Ives, E. W. *Anne Boleyn*. Cambridge, Mass.: Basil Blackwell, 1986.

Jurgens, W. A., ed. *The Faith of the Early Fathers*. Collegeville, Minn.: Liturgical Press, 1970.

Juvenal. *The Satires of Juvenal*. Trans. Rolfe Humphries. Bloomington: Indiana University Press, 1958.

Kelly, Henry Ansgar. *The Matrimonial Trials of Henry VIII*. Stanford: Stanford University Press, 1976.

Kelly, J. N. D. *Jerome: His Life, Writings, and Controversies*. London: Duckworth, 1975.

Knecht, R. J. *Renaissance Warrior and Patron: The Reign of Francis I*. Cambridge: Cambridge University Press, 1994.

Knowles, David. *The Religious Orders in England*, vol. 3: *The Tudor Age*. Cambridge: Cambridge University Press, 1959.

Lehmberg, Stanford. *The Reformation Parliament (1529-1536)*. Cambridge: Cambridge University Press, 1970.

Letters and Papers, Foreign and Domestic, of the Reign of Henry VIII. 23 vols. Ed. J. S. Brewer, J. Gairdner, and R. H. Brodie. London, 1862-1932. Reprint, London: Longman, Green, Longman, & Roberts, 1965. Cited as *LP*.

The Letters of King Henry VIII. Ed. Muriel St. Clare Byrne. 1936; reprint, New York: Funk & Wagnalls, 1968.

The Lisle Letters. 6 vols. Ed. Muriel St. Clare Byrne. Chicago: Chicago University Press, 1981.

MacCulloch, Diarmaid, ed. *The Reign of Henry VIII: Politics, Policy, and Piety*. New York: St. Martin's Press, 1995.

———. *Thomas Cranmer: A Life*. New Haven: Yale University Press, 1996.

McCutcheon, Elizabeth. "'The Apple of My Eye': Thomas More to Antonio Bonvisi: A Reading and a Translation." *Moreana* 18, nos. 71-72 (1981): 37-56.

McLynn, Neil B. *Ambrose of Milan: Church and Court in a Christian Capital*. Berkeley and Los Angeles: University of California Press, 1994.

Marc'hadour, Germain. *The Bible in the Works of Thomas More*. 5 vols. Nieuwkoop: B. de Graaf, 1969-1972.

———. "Hugh Latimer and Thomas More." *Moreana* 5, no. 18 (1968): 29-48.

———. "A Name for All Seasons." In *Essential Articles for the Study of Thomas More*. Ed. Richard S. Sylvester and Germain P. Marc'hadour. Pp. 539-62. Hamden, Conn.: Archon, 1977.

———. "Supplique de Dame Alice More au Chancelier Audley (1538?)." *Moreana* 4 (1964): 69-75.

———. *L'Univers de Thomas More: Chronologie critique de More, Erasme et leur époque, 1477-1536*. Paris: J. Vrin, 1963.

Marius, Richard. *Thomas More: A Biography*. New York: Alfred A. Knopf, 1984.

Martz, Louis. *Thomas More: The Search for the Inner Man*. New Haven: Yale University Press, 1990.

Mattingly, Garrett. *Catherine of Aragon*. Boston: Little, Brown, 1941.

Merriman, R. B. *Life and Letters of Thomas Cromwell*. 2 vols. Oxford: Clarendon Press, 1902.

Miller, Helen. *Henry VIII and the English Nobility*. New York: Blackwell, 1986.

Minney, R. J. *The Tower of London*. London: Cassell, 1970.

Neame, Allan. *The Holy Maid of Kent: The Life of Elizabeth Barton, 1506-1534*. London: Hodder & Stoughton, 1971.

O'Connor, E. D. *The Dogma of the Immaculate Conception: History and Significance.* Notre Dame: University of Notre Dame Press, 1958.

Pineas, R. "George Joye's Controversy with Thomas More." *Moreana* 38 (1973): 27-36.

Pocock, Nicholas, ed. *Records of the Reformation: The Divorce (1527-1533).* 2 vols. Oxford: Clarendon Press, 1870.

Pollard, A. F. *Wolsey: Church and State in Sixteenth-Century England.* New York: Longmans, Green, 1929.

Prévost, André. *Thomas More et la crise de la pensée européenne.* Paris: Mame, 1969.

Reed, A. W. "William Rastel and More's English Works." In *Essential Articles for the Sutyd of Thomas More.* Ed. Richard S. Sylvester and Germain P. Marc'hadour

————. *Early Tudor Drama: Medwall, the Rastells, Heywood, and the More Circle.* London: Methuen, 1926.

Rex, Richard. "The Execution of the Holy Maid of Kent." *Historical Research* 64 (1991): 216-20.

————. *Henry VIII and the English Reformation.* New York: St. Martin's Press, 1993.

————. *The Theology of John Fisher.* Cambridge: Cambridge University Press, 1991.

Reynolds, E. E. The Field Is Won: The LIfe and Death of St. Thomas More. London: Burns & Oates, 1968.

————. *Margaret Roper, Eldest Daughter of St. Thomas More.* London: Burns & Oates, 1960.

————. "More's Cell in the Tower." *Moreana* 5, no. 19 (1968): 27-28.

Rouschausse, Jean. *John Fisher: sa vie et son œuvre. Humaniste, évêque, réformateur, martyr: 1469-1535.* Angers: Moreana, 1972.

Scarisbrick, J. J. *Henry VIII.* Berkeley and Los Angeles: University of California Press, 1968.

————. *The Reformation and the English People.* New York: Blackwell, 1984.

Schoeck, Richard J. "On the Letters of Thomas More." *Moreana* 15 (1967): 193-203.

Silva, Alvaro de. "Martyrdom and Christian Morals." *Communio: International Catholic Review* 21 (1994): 286-97.

Skeat, Walter W. *A Glossary of Tudor and Stuart Words.* Ed. with additions by A. L. Mayhew. Oxford: Clarendon Press, 1914.

Southern, Richard W. *Saint Anselm: A Portrait in a Landscape.* Cambridge: Cambridge University Press, 1990.

Sturge, Charles. *Cuthbert Tunstal: Churchman, Scholar, Statesman, Administrator.* London: Longmans, 1938.

Surtz, E. L. "More's Friendship with Fisher." In *Essential Articles for the Study of*

Thomas More. Ed. Richard S. Sylvester and Germain P. Marc'hadour. Pp. 169-79. Hamden, Conn.: Archon, 1977.

————. *The Works and Days of John Fisher*. Cambridge, Mass.: Harvard University Press, 1967.

Thompson, E. M. *The Carthusian Order in England*. New York: Macmillan, 1930.

Thurley, Simon. *The Royal Palaces of Tudor England: Architecture and Court Life, 1460-1547*. New Haven: Yale University Press, 1993.

Tudor Royal Proclamations. 3 vols. Ed. Paul L. Hughes and James F. Larkin. New Haven: Yale University Press, 1964-69.

Valadier, Paul. *Eloge de la conscience*. Paris: Seuil, 1994.

Von Balthasar, Hans Urs. *The Office of Peter and the Structure of the Church*. Trans. Andrée Emery. San Francisco: Ignatius, 1986.

Whatmore, L. E., ed. "The Sermon against the Holy Maid of Kent and Her Adherents." *The English Historical Review* 58 (1943): 463-75.

Williams, C. H., ed. *English Historical Documents, 1485-1558,* vol. 5. New York: Oxford University Press, 1967.

Wright, Thomas, ed. *Three Chapters of Letters Relating to the Suppression of Monasteries*. London: Camden Society, 1843.

Index

Note: The numbers in **boldface** type below correspond to the numbers of letters in the text.